EDWARD LUCIE-SMITH was born in Jamaica and
Merton College, Oxford, where he read History
a poet, novelist, biographer, as well as a writer
on art, he is the author of numerous books – an
*in Western Art, Symbolist Art, Latin American Art of the Twentieth
Century* and *The Thames and Hudson Dictionary of Art Terms* –
all published in the World of Art series.

Thames & Hudson world of art

This famous series provides the widest available
range of illustrated books on art in all its aspects.

If you would like to receive a complete list
of titles in print please write to:

THAMES & HUDSON
181A High Holborn
London WC1V 7QX

In the United States please write to:

THAMES & HUDSON INC.
500 Fifth Avenue
New York, New York 10110

Printed in Singapore

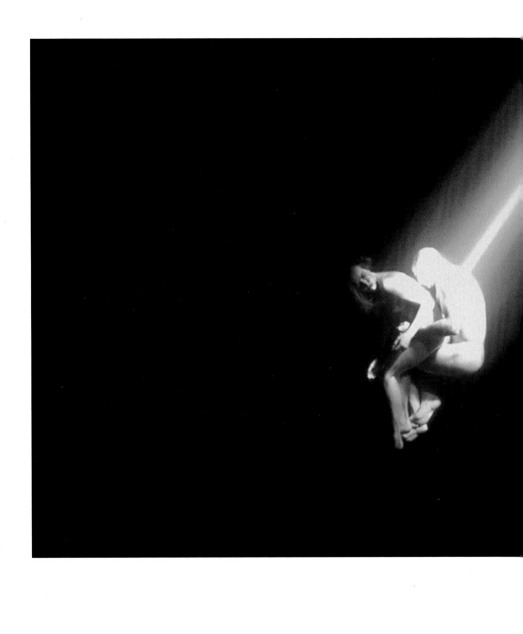

Edward Lucie-Smith

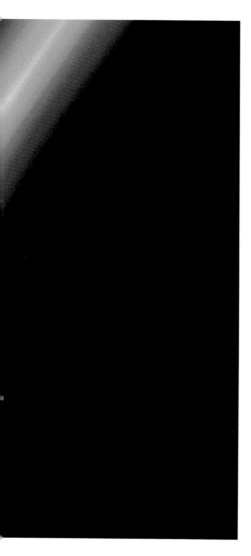

WITHDRAWN

Movements in
Art since 1945

New edition

288 illustrations, 90 in color

 Thames & Hudson world of art

For Agatha Sadler

Any copy of this book issued by the publisher as a paperback is sold subject to the condition that it shall not by way of trade or otherwise be lent, resold, hired out or otherwise circulated without the publisher's prior consent in any form of binding or cover other than that in which it is published and without a similar condition including these words being imposed on a subsequent purchaser.

© 1969, 1975, 1984, 1995 and 2001
Thames & Hudson Ltd, London

Published in paperback in the United States of America in 1995 by Thames & Hudson Inc., 500 Fifth Avenue, New York, New York 10110

thamesandhudsonusa.com

Revised 1975, 1984, 1995
New edition 2001

Library of Congress Catalog Card Number 00-109243

ISBN 0-500-20344-X

The first two editions of this book were published under the title
Late Modern: The Visual Arts Since 1945

1. **Chris Cunningham**, *flex,* 2000

Printed and bound in Singapore by C. S. Graphics

Contents

7   **Introduction**

15   **Chapter 1**
Abstract Expressionism

40   **Chapter 2**
The European scene

75   **Chapter 3**
Post-painterly abstraction

97   **Chapter 4**
Pop, Environments and Happenings

136   **Chapter 5**
Abstract sculpture, Minimal art, Conceptual art

162   **Chapter 6**
An age of pluralism

176   **Chapter 7**
Neo-Expressionist tendencies

190   **Chapter 8**
The USA – 1970s to 1990s

206   **Chapter 9**
Issue-based art and globalization

236   **Chapter 10
The rise of video**

247   **Chapter 11
The photographic medium**

259   **Chapter 12
Post-Pop blues**

273   **Chapter 13
New classicism**

287   Text References
288   Select Bibliography
291   Chronology
295   List of Illustrations
300   Index

Introduction: This book has already enjoyed a long life. This is in fact the fifth version of the text to have appeared since it was first published in 1969. All of these editions have been responses to the changes which have taken place in the world of contemporary art during three tumultuous decades. During this time, opinions about the nature and role of art have varied widely. One common factor, however, has been the steady advance of contemporary art towards the very centre of our culture. The audience for art at the beginning of the twenty-first century is both very different from and much wider than the one that existed three decades ago. The growth of contemporary art and its increasing centrality in our culture is one of the factors that has encouraged a great rush of museum-building. Some of these museums, notably James Stirling's and Michael Wilford's New State Gallery in Stuttgart, Frank Gehry's Guggenheim Museum in Bilbao, and Herzog and de Meuron's adaptation of London's Bankside power station as the Tate Modern, have immediately been recognized as architectural masterpieces – they are clearly the buildings that best sum up and express the sensibility of our time.

2

On the other hand, the creation of these new museums, and the immense financial investment they represent, serve to stress another, more problematic element in the development of contemporary art, which is that it has become more and more obviously an aspect of official culture and high commerce. The art of the first half of the twentieth century was rooted in a rebellion against social norms, and this rebellion has become part of the myth that the artists of succeeding decades inherited from these predecessors. It is something that artists, critics and curators alike now find it extremely difficult to give up. In their eyes, contemporary art, in order to retain its claim to authenticity, must continue to stress its adversarial attitude towards many aspects of contemporary society. Nevertheless, what has been called 'the culture of spectacle' has resulted in a pact between these attitudes and consumer values.

One important factor has been the swing back, particularly noticeable during the 1980s, from an art which existed in isolation from political, social and commercial issues – as, for example, the Minimal art of the 1970s tended to do – to one which seemed obsessed with them. It was not, however, widely acknowledged that this development represented a reversion to attitudes which had first expressed themselves forcefully in the art of the immediately pre-Modern epoch. For example, many of the artists who featured in the Paris Salons at the end of the nineteenth century, in the Summer Exhibitions at the Royal Academy of Arts in London and in similar large officially-sponsored exhibitions elsewhere, devoted themselves to work that illustrated the social problems of the day. The examples that now most immediately come to mind are Gustave Courbet and Camille Pissarro, but many artists now dismissed as stylistically conservative followed the same direction, and, indeed, were much more specific in the social criticism they offered. A number of the leading Salon painters in France are known to have been Socialists. One name worth mentioning is that of the now largely forgotten Jules Adler (b. 1865–1952), who painted powerful images of militant workers. In Britain, works that anticipate Soviet Socialist Realism were painted by artists such as Luke Fildes (b. 1844–1927) and Frank Holl (1845–88). In the late Victorian epoch, stylistic conservatism did not necessarily go hand in hand with conservative political beliefs.

The equivalence between the art of today and that of the late Victorian age has been masked by several factors. When the Victorians aimed to shock, their target was the moral and social conscience of their time. The strict conventions that then prevailed regarding sexual content or sexual representation meant that the audience was intensely aware of any allusion of this nature, therefore such references were usually very heavily coded, on the practical grounds that deliberate breaches of decorum might frustrate efforts to bring about reform. Today the situation is apparently quite different. Sexual representations and allusions of all kinds are the common currency of much contemporary art, and artists often seem to strain to outdo one another in the overt use of imagery of this type. This springs, first from the inherited Modernist desire to excite controversy, and second from the intense interest in sexuality shown throughout the last hundred years. A third reason is the fact that sexuality, in an age when most organized systems of belief are in disarray, is one of the few areas where artists know they occupy common ground with their audience.

In addition, there is a radical difference in the media employed by artists. From the birth of the Modern Movement artists showed a fascination with new technology. This technology has gradually come to dominate current definitions of avant-garde activity, to the point where many curators dismiss traditional forms, such as painting and sculpture, as inherently 'non-contemporary'. Currently most attention is devoted to the photographic media – straight photography, digitized images, video and film. These, in turn, are often linked to various forms of installation and environmental art. Today theoreticians talk about what Rosalind Krauss has called the 'post-medium' condition of the visual arts. By this they mean that not only are there no specially privileged art media, but it is of absolutely no importance which media are used.

A number of comments need to be made about this. One is that the alliance between the visual arts and what one may call the 'entertainment arts' is not new, but can be traced very far back in the story of Western culture. In the mid-eighteenth century, for example, the works of artists like Greuze and Hogarth were discussed chiefly in terms of their dramatic content – that is, they were treated like frozen moments from plays. This approach to narrative painting remained customary almost throughout the nineteenth century.

There are much closer parallels than this. The tournaments and feasts of the late Middle Ages, the so-called 'triumphs' staged in Renaissance Florence, the ephemeral pageants and stage-like settings contrived by Baroque artists – all these involved the participation of the leading artists of the day, and all attracted a great deal of attention from the commentators of the period. The reason why they do not play a large part in later histories of art is the lack of adequate surviving visual evidence. Despite the much greater resources now available to us for recording and storing visual images, it is clear that the same problems may affect the survival of many now much admired manifestations of contemporary visual creativity. Most environmental artworks, for example, survive, if at all, only in photographs. Where video is concerned, the medium is threatened as well as driven forward by the rapid technological development of all the electronic arts. Artists' videos made in the 1970s often seem laughably crude from a technical point of view when viewed some twenty-five years later, and there is no guarantee that the machines which deliver images to the spectator will not have changed out of all recognition within the next decade. Contemporary art has in fact embraced the ephemeral.

The swing towards photography, video and environmental artworks as the most highly-publicized transmitters of a contemporary sensibility is linked to the growth of museums, which offer facilities for the display of works of this sort. Museums provide the arena where a constantly renewed, but never fully graspable, spectacle takes place, and where, in theory at least, it is offered democratically to a mass public rather than to an elite. These phenomena, in turn, are linked to the notion that art is not essentially a possession – a transferable vessel, containing financial as well as cultural value, which is the role it has traditionally played in Western capitalist culture – but is instead simply a catalyst for physical and emotional experience: a way of facilitating some form of catharsis. Despite the way in which the art market has survived the best efforts of artists to frustrate its operations, the pendulum has now swung so far from the purely material aspect of art-making that it now sometimes seems as if the most important product of certain artistic careers is the artist's own personality. The prime example of this development, and also one of the earliest, is that offered by the career and personality of the German artist Joseph Beuys (1921–86), who sometimes presented himself as a kind of shaman, attempting to operate in a modern industrial society.

Emphasis on new media, allied to the strong emphasis on content, has led critics to suggest that the most recent art is essentially indifferent to stylistic considerations. It is said that the procession of styles which seemed to define the progression of Modernism came to an end with the radical simplifications of Minimal art, and that a new era began with a kind of art which was primarily concerned with content. This art often served propaganda or political functions, and promoted the interests of particular groups, self-defined in terms of culture, race or sexual orientation – African-Americans, feminists or gays, etc. At the beginning of a new century, however, it is rapidly becoming apparent that this view is much too simplistic. Thrust out of one door, stylistic considerations enter by another.

One of the most striking aspects of the art of the last twenty years has been its ever-increasing geographical scope. Although from its beginnings Modernist art had pretensions to being universal, it was nevertheless in real terms chiefly a manifestation of Western European culture, which afterwards took root in the United States. In the final decades of the twentieth century what was now called simply 'contemporary art' became genuinely universal. Universality did not, however, mean uniformity. Each culture which began to produce art that could be described as contemporary tended to blend its own local elements with others learned from Modernism and Post-Modernism. Often these borrowed elements were recycled with an element of conscious or even unconscious parody. The most sustained example of this

2. Tate Modern, London, interior showing the turbine hall and Louise Bourgeois's work *Maman*, 1999

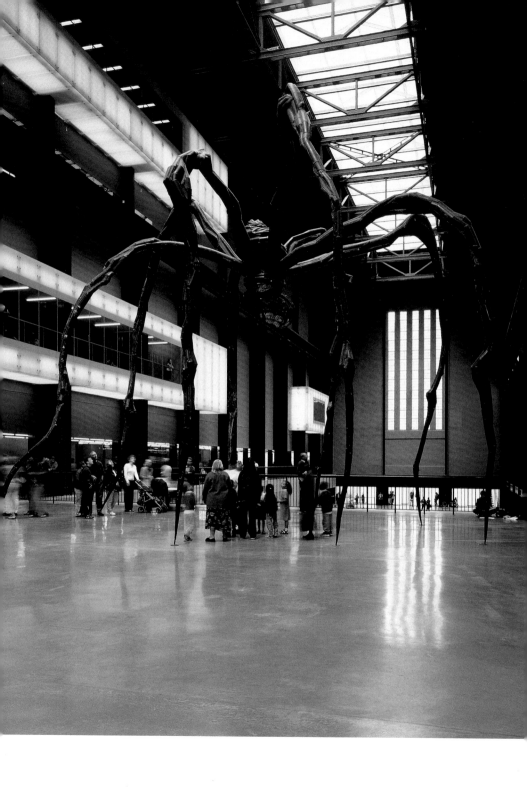

evolution is the art of Latin America, but striking recent examples can also be found in the recent artistic production of China and Japan.

Sometimes art of this type was shaped by local political circumstances. For instance, the *perestroika* era in Russia and the subsequent collapse of the Soviet regime produced a kind of art which relied for its energy on analysing the complex codings of the Soviet state. No one wholly unfamiliar with either the regime's symbolisms or the real conditions of life in Communist Russia could fully understand it, though its exotic and often arcane symbolisms appealed to a Western audience. To deny that this art represented a coherent stylistic episode is to fly in the face of common sense.

The overall effect of the appearance of new centres for contemporary art, each propagating ideas linked to local conditions, produced the breakdown of a situation which had prevailed since the birth of Modernism. The accepted myth was that contemporary art must have a physical centre, a city that generated the ideas that fertilized the imaginations of artists everywhere. Up to the start of World War II, that city was Paris – briefly challenged in the 1920s by the Berlin of the Weimar Republic. From the 1940s to the 1970s, it was New York. Now the world of contemporary art simply became too big for such an arrangement. Information about new ideas passed from region to region at ever-increasing speed, as the available means of communication became ever more sophisticated. Illustrated art books and magazines did some of the work, but their influence was supplemented not only by an increasing number of international exhibitions – regular Biennales in Venice and São Paulo; the Documenta exhibitions in Kassel – but by television reportage and, more recently, by the Internet.

The interesting thing was that this plethora of means of communication seemed to promote diversity rather than uniformity. In some respects this was a good and healthy situation, in others it was less productive. Minimal art offered critics their last opportunity to approach the productions of contemporary artists through the analysis of formal relationships, even if the philosophy of Minimalism reduced these to their most rudimentary condition. It is impossible to apply techniques of this kind to conceptual or environmental work, or with much profit to video. Judgments of the most recent contemporary art are thus more than ever subjective, or, at the very least, respond only to the prevailing consensus.

Looking for ways into the complexities of the present situation, the following elements seem important. First, that it is not technology in a general sense that is of primary importance, but specifically technologies related to the photographic image. Though photography was invented in the first half of the nineteenth century, it still exercises a profound influence over contemporary art-making. Wherever image-making is involved, it stands at the centre of the process. Photography claimed at one stage to be a separate but equal form; now there are no barriers between it and other forms of art-making. The digital manipulation of photographs, possible thanks to increasingly powerful and sophisticated computers, blurs the boundaries still further. Yet one notes that digitization is often used simply as a way of achieving things which the Victorians did more crudely and laboriously by hand – for example, in creating elaborate compositions through the use of multiple negatives.

On the other hand, photography, despite the ease with which photographic images can now be manipulated, is also used to certify authenticity. The work of Nan Goldin (b. 1953) in the United 263 States and Richard Billingham (b. 1970) in Britain, for example, seems to offer unmediated access to lives very different from those lived by members of the vast majority of their audience. The pursuit of this kind of authenticity is a central theme in the work of the group of artists who perhaps garnered the greatest share of attention in the course of the 1990s – the so-called YBAs, or Young British Artists, who transformed the London art scene during the decade. At least part of the publicity garnered by the group was due to fascination, not with their work, but with their personal lives.

This was a tendency which began in New York's short-lived East Village galleries in the 1980s but which has now been continued in Britain, a country which, ever since the advent of Punk Rock in the mid-1970s, has shown an affinity with grunge culture. Fascination with a bohemian mode of existence is nothing new in art – it is already fully recorded in nineteenth-century books like Henri Murger's *La Vie de Bohème* and in Puccini's opera which derives from it. The work of YBAs like Tracey Emin (b. 1963) can therefore be seen as yet another episode in the continuing history of Romanticism.

This tendency has recently been opposed by another – a return to classical themes and values which has manifested itself most strongly in Italy and in Russia. In both cases the 'local' factors I have already described come into play. The centre of activity in Russia is St Petersburg rather than Moscow. In Italy it is Rome rather than Milan. Both cities look back with nostalgia to a classical past, though it is a very different sort of classicism. In each case, however, there is also a strong theoretical basis.

The Neo-Classical movement of the late eighteenth century was perhaps the first art movement in which general intellectual concerns preceded actual artistic practice. In this sense, Neo-Classicism was the true ancestor of twentieth-century Conceptual art. This fact is acknowledged by many of the Italian artists who belong to the groups know as Pittura Colta or La Nuova Maniera Italiana. Many of these artists in fact began by making Conceptual artworks and installations and by doing performances. The best known of them internationally, Carlo Maria Mariani (b. 1948), remains insistent that he is essentially a Conceptual artist.

282

There are, of course, differences between the Italian and Russian situations. The artists of the Novia Akademia in St Petersburg have a much greater interest in photography and make frequent use of digitized images. Their Italian counterparts often show the influence of Giorgio de Chirico, who died in 1978, on the eve of the emergence of the Pittura Colta movement. De Chirico (1888–1978) and his contemporary Francis Picabia (1879–1953) are now often described as the forerunners of Post-Modernism.

What the Italian and Russian groups have in common is their exploration of ideas about Beauty and the Ideal which essentially have not been much heard of since the demise of the Symbolist Movement. Rather than stressing the squalor of contemporary urban life, they have gone in search of an alternative universe. Often, however, this search leads them into areas which are also explored in a different fashion by their rivals. They too – though this is truer of the Russians than it is of the Italians – are sometimes heavily influenced by contemporary advertising, which used to follow in the footsteps of fine art, but now seems to offer a lead to its development. In addition, the new Neo-Classicism often walks a fine line between, on the one hand, an ironic acknowledgment of the link between commercial idealization and kitsch, and, on the other, a determined refusal to recognize how powerful this alliance has become.

Chapter 1:   Abstract Expressionism

Abstract Expressionism, the first of the great post-war art movements, had its roots in Surrealism, the most important movement
of the period immediately before the war. Surrealism had routed
Dada in Paris in the early 1920s. It is perhaps most satisfactorily
defined by its leading figure, André Breton, in the First Surrealist
Manifesto of 1924.

*Surrealism, n. Pure psychic automatism, by which an attempt is
made to express, either verbally or in writing, or in any other
manner, the true functioning of thought. . . . Surrealism rests on
the belief in the higher reality of certain neglected forms of
association, in the omnipotence of dream, in the disinterested play
of thought. It tends to destroy the other psychic mechanisms and
to substitute itself for them in the solution of life's principal problems.*[1]

Since 1924 its history, under the leadership of the volcanic
Breton, had been one of schisms and scandals. In particular, the
Surrealists had become increasingly preoccupied with their relationship with Communism. The question was: could artistic
radicalism be reconciled with the political variety? So much time
and energy was wasted in controversy, that, by the time the war
came, the movement was visibly in decline. Maurice Nadeau, in
his authoritative history of the movement, remarks: 'The adherence to the political revolution required the adherence of all the
surrealist forces, and consequently the abandonment of the
particular philosophy which had constituted the movement's
very being at its origin.'[2]

By the time the war came, it looked as if this, the most vigorous and important of the art movements of the period between
the wars, had exhausted its impetus. But the 'particular philosophy' of which Nadeau speaks was still very much alive when the
Surrealist movement arrived, almost *en bloc*, in New York shortly
after the outbreak of war. The exiles included not only Breton
himself but also some of the most famous Surrealist painters:
Max Ernst (1891–1976), Roberto Matta (b. 1911), Salvador Dalí
(1904–89), and André Masson (1896–1987). Peggy Guggenheim, then married to Ernst, supplied the group with a centre for

their activities by opening the Art of This Century Gallery in 1942. Many of the most important American painters of the 1940s were later to show there.

The situation of the Surrealist exiles was governed by several factors. For example, in the midst of the conflict, the old, rending political arguments were no longer relevant. New York provided a fresh and challenging territory for their activities, and they began to make converts among American artists.

As previously said, the United States had long been hospitable to the avant-garde art of Europeans. New York had a tradition of intermittent avant-gardism which stretched back to the Armory Show of 1913, and, beyond that, to the pre-World War I activities of Alfred Stieglitz, who presented a series of exhibitions by artists such as Rodin, Matisse, Picasso, Brancusi, Henri Rousseau, and Picabia in a small gallery at 291 Fifth Avenue. During World War I there had been an active group of Dadaists in the city, among them Marcel Duchamp (1887–1968), Picabia, and Man Ray (1890–1976). But the Depression years of the 1930s turned American art in upon itself. American critics, such as Barbara Rose in her classic book *American Art since 1900*, stress the fact that this period of introspection and withdrawal was crucial for American artists. They point to the effect, in particular, of the Federal Art Project (or WPA), the measure by which the American government sought to give relief to artists suffering from the prevailing economic conditions. Rose contends that 'by making no formal distinction between abstract and representational art',[3] the Project helped to make abstract art respectable, and that the *esprit de corps* which the scheme created among artists carried over into the 1940s. Nevertheless, in 1939 American art counted for little where the European avant-garde was concerned, though a few distinguished *émigrés*, such as Josef Albers (1888–1976) and Hans Hofmann (1880–1966), were already preparing the ground through their teaching for the change that was to come. Albers taught at Black Mountain College in North Carolina, Hofmann at the Art Students' League in New York and at his own schools on 8th Street and in Provincetown, Massachusetts.

Yet it was not these, but the more-recently arrived Surrealists who provided the decisive stimulus. Without their presence in New York, Abstract Expressionism would probably never have been born.

The transitional figure, the most important link between European Surrealism and what was to follow, was Arshile Gorky

(1904–48). Gorky was born in Armenia in 1904, and did not arrive in America until 1920. His early work (undertaken in conditions of the bitterest poverty) shows a steady progression through the basic Modernist styles, typical of an artist in a provincial environment who is conscious of his own isolation. He absorbed the lesson of Cézanne, then of Cubism. In the 1930s, under the spell of Picasso, he was already veering towards Surrealism. Then came the war, and he started to explore more boldly. Basically, the Surrealist tradition seemed to offer the convert two choices. One was the meticulously detailed style of Magritte (1898–1967), whose *Exhibition of Painting* is but one example; or Salvador Dalí, as in his dazzling perspectival depiction of *Christ of St John of the Cross*. Even in those of Dalí's pictures where the distortions are most violent, objects to some extent retain their identity. The other choice was the biomorphic style of artists such as Miró (1893–1983) or Tanguy (1900–55), where the forms merely hint at a resemblance to real objects, usually parts of the human body – breasts, buttocks, the sexual organs, as Tanguy's *The Rapidity of Sleep* demonstrates. Gorky adopted this method, and used it with increasing boldness. Harold Rosenberg speaks of the characteristic imagery of Gorky's developed styles as:

3. **Salvador Dalí**, *Christ of St John of the Cross*, 1951

4. **René Magritte**, *Exhibition of Painting*, 1965

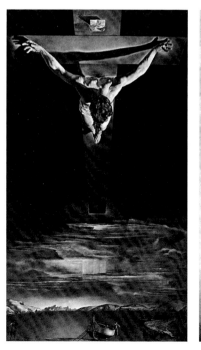

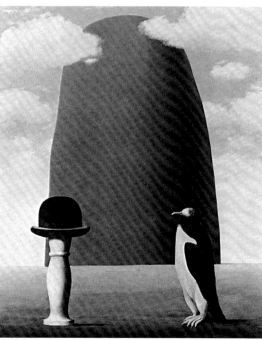

... overgrown with metaphor and association. Amid strange, soft organisms and insidious slits and smudges, petals hint of claws in a jungle of limp bodily parts, intestinal fists, pudenda, multiple limb folds.[4]

The painter himself, in a statement written in 1942, declared:

I like the heat the tenderness the edible the lusciousness the song of a single person the bathtub full of water to bathe myself beneath the water. . . . I like the wheatfields the plough the apricots those flirts of the sun. But bread above all.[5]

Gorky was especially influenced by the Chilean-born painter Roberto Matta, which can be seen by comparing his *Being With* with the former's *The Betrothal II*, and his work is often close to that which was being done by the veteran French Surrealist André Masson, as in *Landscape with Precipices*, during the years the latter spent in America. He did not finally come into contact with Breton until 1944, and this completed his liberation as an artist. By 1947 he had begun to outstrip his masters, and the way in which he outstripped them was through the freedom with which he used his materials. The boldness of his technique can be seen in the second version of *The Betrothal*, which dates from 1947. The philosophy of art which Gorky put forward in an interview with a journalist the same year had important implications for the future of American painting:

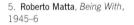

5. **Roberto Matta**, *Being With*, 1945–6

6. **Arshile Gorky**, *The Betrothal II*, 1947

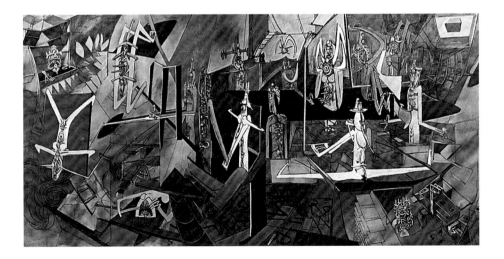

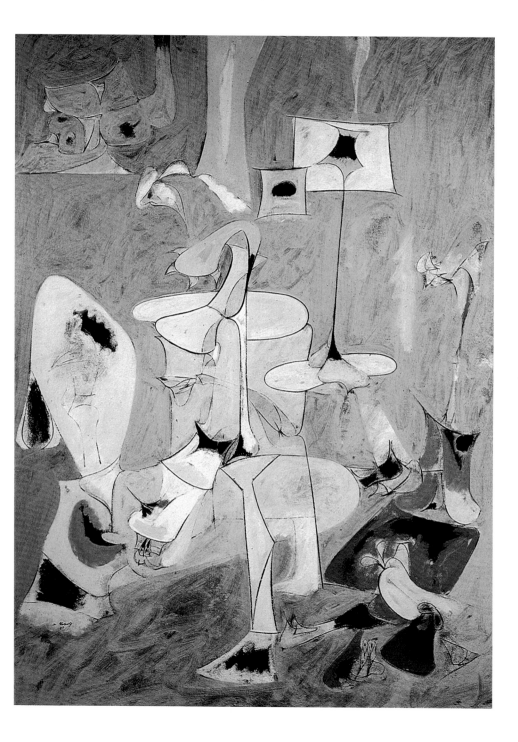

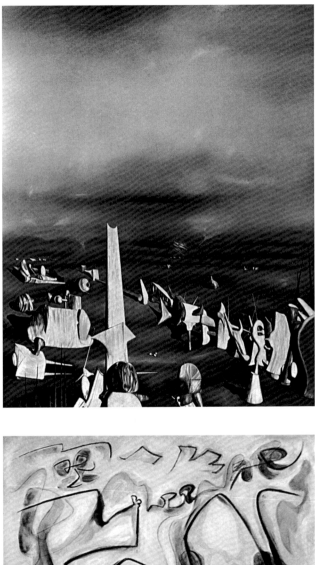

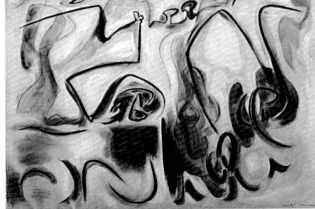

When something is finished, that means it's dead, doesn't it? I believe in everlastingness. I never finish a painting – I just stop working on it for a while. I like painting because it's something I never come to the end of. Sometimes I paint a picture, then I paint it all out. Sometimes I'm working on fifteen or twenty pictures at the same time. I do that because I want to – because I like to change my mind so often. The thing to do is always to keep starting to paint, never finishing painting.[6]

This idea of a 'continuous dynamic' was to play an important part in Abstract Expressionism, and especially in the work of Jackson Pollock (1912–56). Gorky himself was unable to press it further. After a long series of misfortunes, he committed suicide in 1948. He was perhaps the most distinguished Surrealist that America has produced.

Far less 'European' was the work of Jackson Pollock, though it was Pollock who became the star of the Art of This Century Gallery. Like Gorky, Pollock developed very slowly. He spent his youth in the West, in Arizona, northern California, and (later) southern California. In 1929 Pollock left Los Angeles and came to New York to study under Thomas Hart Benton (1889–1975), a 'regionalist' painter. During the 1930s, like many American artists of his generation, he fell under the influence of the contemporary Mexicans. Diego Rivera's (1886–1957) enthusiasm for a public art 'belonging to the populace' may well have helped to develop Pollock's sense of scale. Later, like Gorky, he fell under the Surrealists' influence, and Peggy Guggenheim put him under contract for her gallery. By 1947, Pollock had broken through to the style for which he is now best known: free, informal abstraction, based on a technique of dripping and smearing paint on to the canvas, a spectacular example of which is his *Number 2*.

Here is Pollock's own description of what took place when he worked on such pictures:

My painting does not come from the easel. I hardly ever stretch my canvas before painting. I prefer to tack the unstretched canvas on the hard wall or floor. I need the resistance of a hard surface. On the floor I feel more at ease. I feel nearer, more part of the painting, since this way I can walk around it, work from the four sides and literally be in the painting. This is akin to the Indian sand painters of the West. I continue to get further away from the usual painter's tools such as easel, palette, brushes, etc. I prefer sticks, trowels, knives and dripping fluid paint or a heavy impasto with sand, broken glass or other foreign matter added.

7. **Yves Tanguy**, *The Rapidity of Sleep*, 1945

8. **André Masson**, *Landscape with Precipices*, 1948

9

10

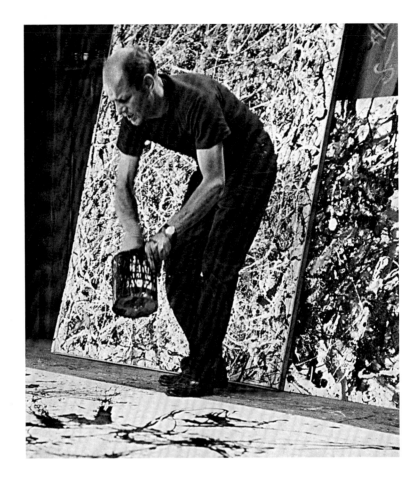

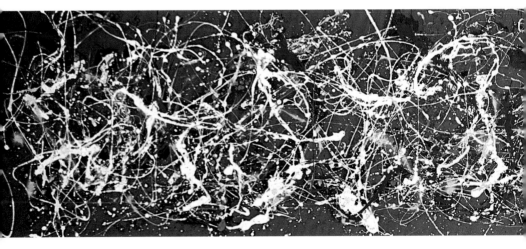

When I am in the painting I'm not aware of what I'm doing. It is only after a sort of 'get acquainted' period that I see what I have been about. I have no fears about making changes, destroying the image, etc., because the painting has a life of its own. I try to let it come through. It is only when I lose contact with the painting that the result is a mess. Otherwise there is pure harmony, an easy give and take, and the painting comes out well.[7]

Compare this to Breton's instructions as to how to produce a Surrealist text, as given in the manifesto of 1924:

Have someone bring you writing materials after getting settled in a place as favourable as possible to your mind's concentration on itself. Put yourself in the most passive, or receptive, state you can. Forget about your genius, your talents, and those of everyone else. Tell yourself that literature is the saddest path that leads to everything. Write quickly, without a preconceived subject, fast enough not to remember and not to be tempted to read over what you have written.[8]

I think it is clear that in many ways Pollock's and Breton's attitudes correspond. It is important, for example, to remember that even in so-called 'gestural' or 'action' painting there is a large element of passivity.

One of the more radical consequences of Pollock's method of working, so far as the spectator was concerned, was the fact that it completely changed the treatment of space. Pollock does not ignore spatial problems; his paintings are not flat. Instead, he creates a space which is ambiguous. We are aware of the surface

9. Jackson Pollock at work, 1949

10. **Jackson Pollock**, *Number 2*, 1949

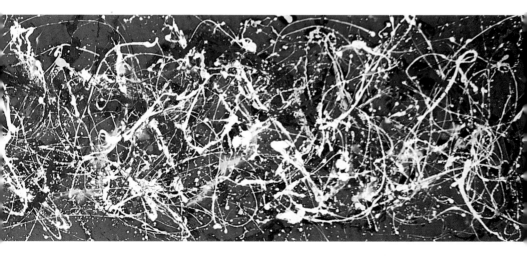

of the picture, but also of the fact that most of the calligraphy seems to hover a little way behind this surface, in space which has been deliberately compressed and robbed of perspective. Pollock is thus linked not only to the Surrealists, but to Cézanne. Indeed, when we think of the illusionist perspective used by Dalí in *Christ of St John of the Cross* and even by Tanguy in *The Rapidity of Sleep*, it will be clear that this is one of the points where Pollock differs most strikingly from his mentors. The shuttling rhythms that Pollock uses tend to suggest a spatial progression across the canvas, rather than directly into it, but this movement is always checked, and in the end returns towards the centre, where the main weight of the picture lies. As will be seen from his own description, these characteristics reflect Pollock's method of work. The fact that the image was created before the actual boundary of the canvas was settled (it was trimmed afterwards, to fit what had been produced) tended to focus attention on lateral motion. This rather primitive method of organization was to have important consequences.

Both by temperament and by virtue of the theories he professed – themselves largely the product of his temperament – Pollock was an intensely subjective artist. For him, inner reality was the only reality. Harold Rosenberg, the chief theorist of Abstract Expressionism, describes the style as a 'conversion phenomenon'. He goes so far as to call it 'essentially a religious movement'.[9] But it was a religious movement without commandments, as appears from Rosenberg's remark that 'the gesture on the canvas' was 'a gesture of liberation from Value – political, aesthetic, moral'.[10] One might add that in Pollock's case as in some others, it also seems to have been a gesture of estrangement from society and its demands. Frank O'Hara describes the artist as being 'tortured with self-doubt and tormented by anxiety'.[11]

Pollock would not, however, have made the impact he did, first in America and subsequently in Europe, if he had been completely isolated as a painter. The real father-figure of the New York school of painting during the post-war years was probably the veteran Hans Hofmann, who exercised great influence as a teacher, and whose late style, as in *Rising Moon*, shows how keen was his sympathy with what the younger men were doing. Hofmann was typical of the things which go to make up the American amalgam. He had lived in Paris from 1904 to 1914, and had been in contact with Matisse, Braque, Picasso and Gris. It was Matisse's work that he particularly admired, and it is this which can be thought of as underlying the more decorative side of Abstract Expressionist painting. That the new painters were not without roots in the past is something that can be judged from Hofmann's own career. He had begun to teach in the United States in 1932, and had founded the Provincetown Art School in 1934. His last phase, upon which he embarked when he was over sixty, was both logical in the artistic climate of the time, and in human terms wonderfully unexpected: an example of a talent at last unfolding to its full extent when the right atmosphere was provided for it. Some of these late pictures are at least as bold as the work of younger men.

The 'organizer' of the Abstract Expressionist movement, in so far as it had one, was neither Pollock nor Hofmann, but Robert Motherwell (1915–91). Motherwell was an artist whose intellect and energies ranged wide. As a painter, he too began his career

11. **Robert Motherwell**, *Elegy to the Spanish Republic No. LV*, 1955–60

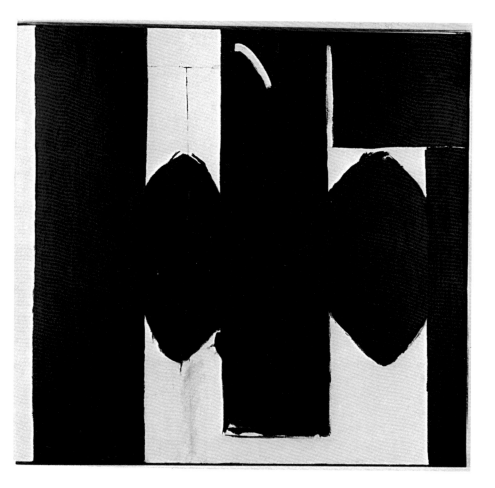

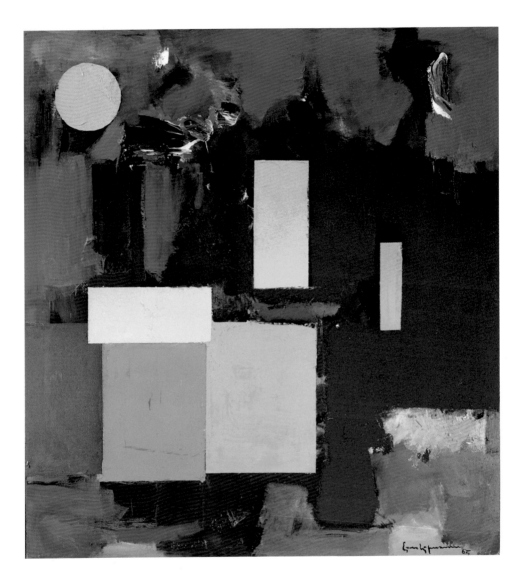

12. **Hans Hofmann**, *Rising
Moon*, 1964

under the influence of the Surrealists, and, in particular, under that of Matta, with whom he made a trip to Mexico. He had his first one-man exhibition at the Art of This Century Gallery in 1944. As the Abstract Expressionist movement got under way, the range of Motherwell's activities continued to expand. He was co-editor of the influential but short-lived magazine *Possibilities* in 1947–8, and in 1948 founded an art school with three other important painters, William Baziotes (1912–63), 13 Barnett Newman (1905–70), and Mark Rothko (1903–70). In 1951 he published an anthology of the work of the Dada painters and poets which was one of the earliest signs of the arrival of 'Neo-Dada'.

The variety of these activities did not prevent Motherwell from having a large output as a painter. His best known works are the long series of canvases known collectively as the *Elegies* 11 *to the Spanish Republic, No. LV* from which is reproduced on p. 25. These pictures serve to correct some erroneous ideas about Abstract Expressionism. It is significant, for instance, that

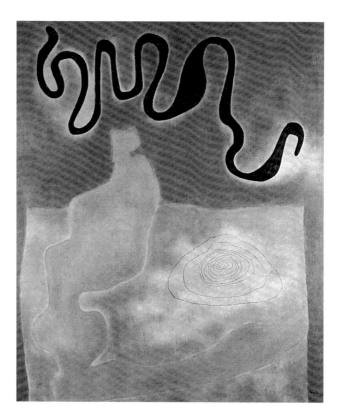

13. **William Baziotes**, *Congo*, 1954

Motherwell's theme is one drawn from the recent history of Europe: recent, but not absolutely contemporary. Motherwell was in his early twenties when the Spanish Civil War broke out, and is looking back with nostalgia on his own youth. His choice of subject suggests that the 'subjective' painting which flourished in America during the late 1940s and early 1950s was by no means incapable of dealing with historical or social issues, but that these issues had to be approached in personal terms, and obliquely. The *Elegies* are certainly far more oblique than Picasso's *Guernica*. The nostalgic rhetoric of Motherwell's paintings, sustained in painting after painting, is reminiscent of the tone to be found in a good deal of post-war American poetry: in that of poets as different from one another as Allen Ginsberg and Robert Duncan, for example. It is a mood which has few equivalents in the painting of post-war Europe, and which acts as a reminder both of the essentially American character of the style and of the fact that it was not necessarily the 'instantaneous' art which European painters at times mistook it for.

Essentially, there are two sorts of Abstract Expressionist painting, rather than one. The first kind, typified by Pollock, Franz Kline (1910–62) and Willem de Kooning (1904–97), is energetic and gestural. Pollock and de Kooning are much involved with figuration. The other kind, typified by Mark Rothko, is more purely abstract and more tranquil. Rothko's work, in particular, serves to justify Harold Rosenberg's use of the adjective 'mystic', when describing the school. Rothko, like several other leading American artists of the post-war period – Gorky, de Kooning, Hofmann – was born abroad; he came to America from Russia in 1913, when he was ten. He began as an Expressionist, felt the influence of Matta and Masson, and followed the standard pattern by having an exhibition at the Art of This Century Gallery in 1948. Gradually his work grew simpler, and by 1950 he had reached the point where the figurative element had been discarded. In *Orange, Yellow, Orange* of 1969, a few 14 rectangles of space are placed on a coloured ground. Their edges are not defined, and their spatial position is therefore ambiguous. They float towards us, or away, in a shallow space of the kind that we also find in Pollock – it derives, ultimately, from the spatial experiments of the Cubists. In Rothko's paintings the colour relationships, as they interact within the rectangle and within this space, set up a gentle rhythmic pulsation. The painting becomes both a focus for the spectator's meditations and a screen before a mystery. The weakness of Rothko's work (just as the subtlety of colour is its strength) is to be found in the relative rigidity and monotony of the compositional formula. The bold central image became one of the trademarks of the new American painting – one of the things that differentiated it from European art. Rothko was an artist of real brilliance imprisoned in a straitjacket; he exemplifies the narrowness of focus which many modern artists imposed upon themselves.

The lesson is reinforced by the work of an artist who in many ways resembles Rothko, Adolph Gottlieb (1903–74) who, in paintings such as *The Frozen Sounds Number 1*, also evokes, like 15 Rothko, or even depicts, a generalized landscape. He is also linked to Motherwell, in that he is a rhetorician – by 'rhetoric' in painting, I mean the deliberate use of vague, expansive, generalized forms. An interest in Freud led Gottlieb towards an art which he deliberately filled with cosmic symbolism. The similarity between Gottlieb's most characteristic style and the paintings done by Joan Miró in the late 1930s is something that bears investigation. Miró, too, is fond of cosmic symbols, but paints them more lightly and crisply, without too much stress on their deeper meanings. Gottlieb's work makes me feel that I am being asked to take a weighty significance on trust. This significance is not inherent in the colour or the brushwork; one has to recognize the symbol and make the historical connection.

The limitations I find in the work of Rothko and Gottlieb seem to me to be shared by the earlier work of Philip Guston, and by that of Franz Kline. Guston (1913–80) typified the boneless aspects of Abstract Expressionism, when too often his pictures were no more than a riot of lush paint and sweet colour, until he reversed direction at the end of his life and started painting in a gritty 'cartoon' style which makes a bridge between Pop art and Neo-Expressionism. *The Clock* (1956–7) is an example of this 17 earlier softly lyrical phase in Guston's work. Kline, like Rothko, is an artist who runs to rather sterile extremes, and he is speeded on his way to them by Abstract Expressionist doctrine. Unlike Rothko's, his work is gestural, and his technical affiliations are with Pollock. What he most frequently did was to create on the canvas something which looked like a Chinese character, or part of one, enormously magnified, as, for instance, in *Chief.* These 16 strong, harsh ideograms relied for their effect on the stark contrast of black strokes on a white ground. Paint seems to be used only for reasons of breadth and scale: there is little in most of the paintings that could not have been said with Indian ink and paper. When, in the last years of Kline's life (he died in 1962), colour

14. **Mark Rothko**, *Orange Yellow Orange*, 1969

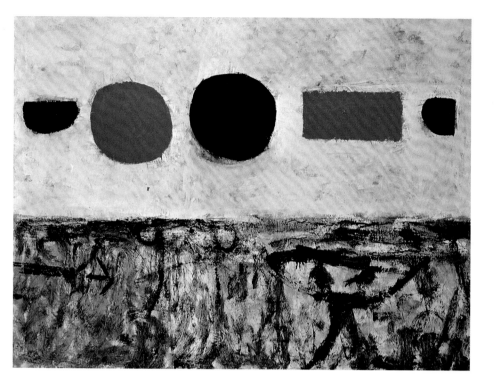

15. **Adolph Gottlieb**, *The Frozen Sounds Number 1*, 1951

began to play a part in his work, the results were not usually happy because we are never made to feel that colour is essential to the statement. Its purposes are cosmetic.

Kline was always very wary about admitting to any sort of Oriental influence in his work, yet influences of this kind have undoubtedly been important in American painting since World War II. Not only is there an element of passivity which grows increasingly powerful with each successive stylistic revolution – Rothko invites the spectator to contemplation, Morris Louis collaborates almost passively with the demands of his materials, Andy Warhol accepts the image and refuses to edit it – but the techniques of Oriental artists, as well as their philosophies, have made an important impact.

It is interesting to compare Kline's big gestural symbols with the work of an artist who had a very different sense of scale, Mark Tobey (1890–1976). Although not, strictly speaking, an Abstract Expressionist painter, Tobey pursued a parallel development, modified by different experiences and a different context. His

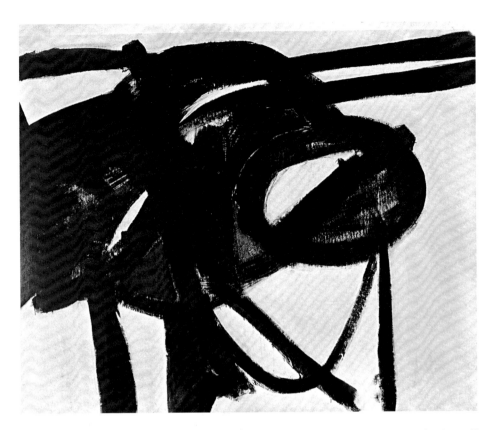

16. **Franz Kline**, *Chief*, 1950

career was centred not on New York but on Seattle – that is, until a final move to Switzerland. He visited the Near East and Mexico, besides making several visits to China and Japan. In Japan he stayed for a while in a Zen monastery, and became a convert to Buddhism (thus anticipating a similar conversion on the part of one of the most important of the American Beat poets, Gary Snyder). Tobey's journeys to the Orient were made with the specific purpose of studying Chinese calligraphy, and they had an avowed and decisive effect on his painting. He adopted a technique which he labelled 'white writing' – an excellent example of which is *Edge of August*, in the Museum of Modern Art, New York – a way of covering the picture surface with an intricate network of signs which are like Kline's hieroglyphs writ small. In many ways Tobey's work is a critique of Kline's, and of Abstract Expressionism as a whole. The thing which is impressive about Tobey's paintings, however tenuous his formal devices may sometimes appear, is the fact that what he produces is always complete in its own terms. Tobey's discoveries reinforced those

18

of Pollock: in his later work, the canvas, or 'field', is articulated from end to end by the rhythmic marks of the brush. But he, more than the true Abstract Expressionists, gives the spectator a feeling of possibility. The marks, one feels, might at any moment rearrange themselves, but would retain a sense of ordered harmony. This is not an art straining against its own limitations, but one which is exploring a newly discovered and infinitely flexible means of expression.

Yet it would be a mistake to assume that Abstract Expressionism itself was entirely inflexible. The school was at any rate flexible enough to incorporate the art of Willem de Kooning, an artist who, in his best pictures, stands next to Pollock in force and originality of talent. De Kooning was born in Holland, and did not arrive in America until he was already an adult. His style tends to emphasize the Expressionist component of Abstract Expressionism, at the price of abstraction. He deals with imagery which seems to rise up out of the texture of the paint, and then to relapse again into the chaos which momentarily gave it form.

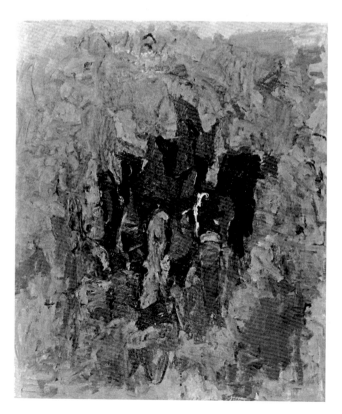

17. **Philip Guston**, *The Clock*, 1956–7

(overleaf)
18. **Mark Tobey**, *Edge of August*, 1953

19. **Willem de Kooning**, *Woman and Bicycle*, 1952–3

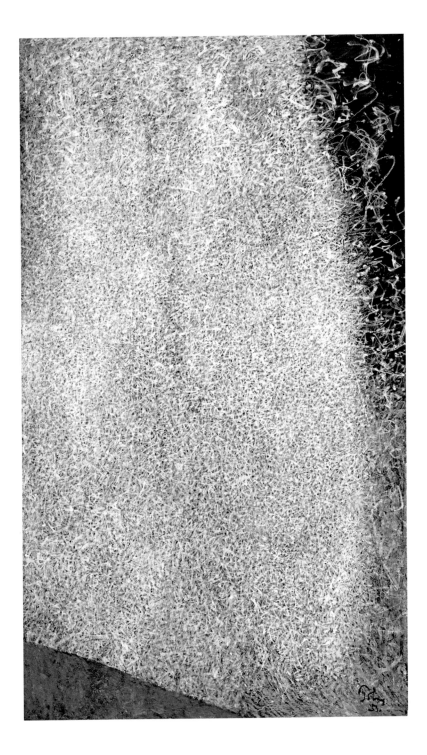

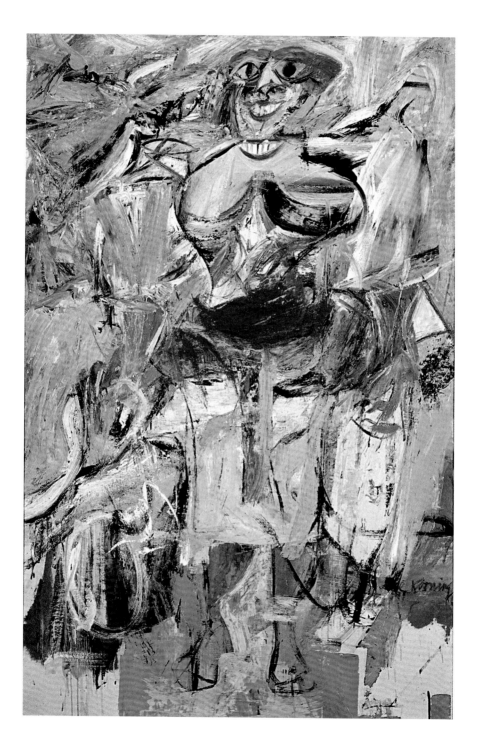

What marks him off from contemporary European Expressionists is the characteristically American boldness – one might even say rawness – and sense of scale that appear in his pictures. When de Kooning bases himself on imagery taken from landscape, the work is so broad that it seems as if he has discovered a way of using oil-paint as the boldest Chinese and Japanese scholar-painters used ink: yet his grip on the original source of the image is never quite broken. When he paints in a more directly figurative way, as in the series of *Women*, such as *Woman and Bicycle*, the whole force of the sexual impulse is there in the painting. These Kali-like figures correspond to the kind of work which Jean Dubuffet (1901–85) did in his earliest period, and again in his *Corps de Dame* series of 1950. De Kooning's work is an important point of contact, therefore, between European and American art. In addition to this, it predicts certain aspects of Pop art. De Kooning's *Women* are the forerunners of Warhol's *Marilyns*.

19

61

The enormous success scored by Abstract Expressionism was to have important consequences for the arts on both sides of the Atlantic. Pollock's legend grew with tremendous rapidity in the years between the first European showing of his work in 1948 and his death in a car crash in 1956. Some of the effects of this success were all too predictable. An attempt was made to set up Abstract Expressionism as the only conceivable kind of art. A rapid succession of yet newer and more radical adventures seemed to disprove this claim almost immediately. Ironically enough, there was something in it. Abstract Expressionism looked both forward and back. Despite the huge scale on which they worked, Pollock and Kline seem to have had perfect faith in canvas and paint as a viable means of communicating something. That faith has since been questioned, and one reason for the questioning is the degree to which the Abstract Expressionist painters strained traditional categories of art; nothing further evolved from what they did. If one compares the work of a painter such as Clyfford Still (1904–80) in, for instance, *1957-D No. 1*, to the superficially very similar work of Sam Francis (1923–94), one gets some idea of the extent to which Abstract Expressionism was at home only in America. Francis, as a Paris-domiciled American, introduces the European element of 'taste', in paintings such as *Blue on a Point* which immediately compromises the rigour of the style. And again, if one compares the work of one of the few good Abstract Expressionists of the second generation, Helen Frankenthaler (b. 1928), in her painting *Mountains and Sea*, of 1952, reproduced in Chapter 3, with that of the pioneers, one

20

21

72

20. **Clyfford Still**, *1957–D No. 1, 1957*

sees how difficult it was to build on what those pioneers had achieved. This least academic of styles made an astonishingly rapid descent into academicism. The art boom of the middle and late 1950s created a spate of bubble-reputations.

The effect of the new American art on Europe was not altogether happy. One reason for this was that Europeans misunderstood it, and tried to make use of criteria that had been suddenly outgrown. In England, for example, one still encounters a certain bitterness among early supporters of Abstract Expressionism. The British painter-critic Patrick Heron (1920– 99), who welcomed his American colleagues very generously when they first appeared, has complained of their ingratitude.[12] He too suggests that the monotony of the central, heraldic image to be found in much Abstract Expressionist painting could be remedied by a resort to more sophisticated European methods of composing the picture space. This shows that his initial enthusiasm was based on a misapprehension, as such methods of composition were just what the Americans had been most concerned to reject from the very beginning, even at the price of losing their freedom to develop and manoeuvre.

21. **Sam Francis**, *Blue on a Point*, 1958

22. **Patrick Heron**, *Manganese in Deep Violet: January 1967*

The importance of Abstract Expressionism was arguably more to culture as a whole than to painting in particular. The success made by the new painting, and its attendant publicity, drew the attention of writers and musicians who were discontented with their own disciplines. Earle Brown, one of the most radical of the new composers, claimed to have found new inspiration for his own work in that of Pollock. At first, it was the gesture of liberation which counted, rather than any specific resemblance between the disciplines of the various arts. The so-called 'mixed media' and 'intermedia' were to come later, partly as a result of experiments with assemblage and collage.

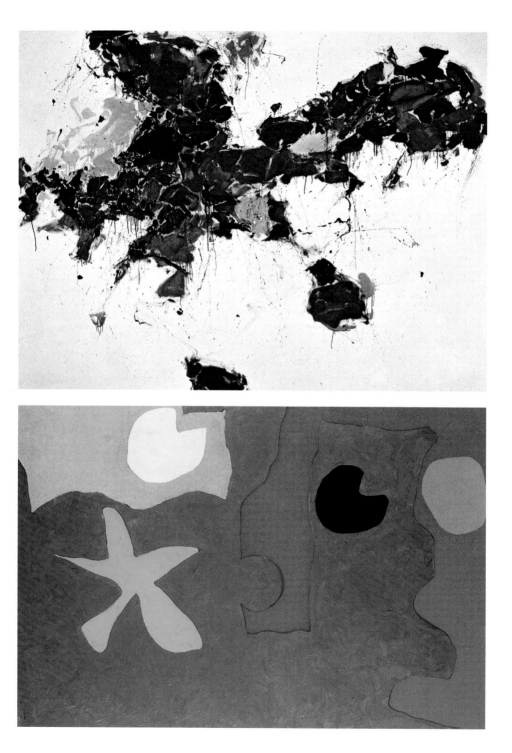

Chapter 2:   The European scene

The course of events in France, and on the Continent as a whole, was very different from that in America. Paris was naturally the place towards which Europeans looked as soon as peace was restored. Equally naturally, it was the artists of the 'great generation' who began by attracting the most attention. Indeed, the six-year gap had served to establish these artists more, rather than less, firmly in the public mind. They were no longer outsiders; they had come to seem like representatives of the civilization that the Allies had been fighting for; and the Nazi condemnation of 'decadent art' was now of some considerable service to their reputations. Picasso became as much an object of pilgrimage to American GIs in liberated Paris as their own compatriot, Gertrude Stein.

On the other hand, there was a sense in which these senior artists found themselves cut off from their roots by what had happened. A feeling of change was in the air, and they, who had been the instigators of so many changes, were not the promoters but the victims of this one. The new eminence they were accorded often brought a certain aridity to their work.

This verdict seemed to apply particularly to Picasso (1881–1973). Immediately after the war he was awarded his final status as a mortal god: the most universally acclaimed and celebrated artist since Michelangelo. It says something for Picasso's furious creativity that, even when he had been placed in this uneasy situation, it showed no sign of slackening. His production after 1945 was prodigious, and new aspects of it were almost constantly revealed to the public. In 1966, for example, his extensive but previously almost unknown work as a sculptor was shown in exhibitions in London, Paris and New York. Despite his immense celebrity, however, Picasso's work gradually fell from favour with the leaders of taste in modern art. They were encouraged to downgrade him both by his Arcadian visions of nymphs and fauns, which seemed not only frivolous, but curiously 'thirties' in style – part of the repertoire of Art Deco (then still very much out of favour) – and by the occasional propaganda pictures which expressed the painter's Communist sympathies. One such was

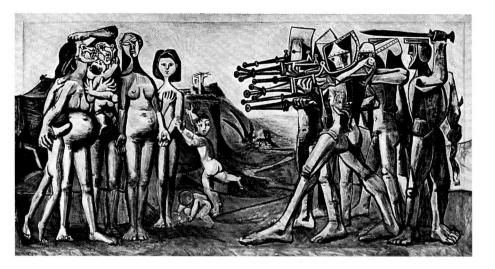

his *Massacre in Korea*, painted at the time of the Korean war. Most 23 people saw it as a rather barren paraphrase of Goya's *Dos de Mayo*.

Paraphrase was a habit which increasingly grew on the artist. Among the most characteristic works of the 'late' – but not the latest – period of his production were the series of variations on famous paintings by the great masters of the past, such as the *Las Meninas* of Velázquez, or the *Women of Algiers* by Delacroix. To these Picasso applied Monet's habit of working in series, conducting a kind of unpacking process, taking from the original work various ideas and qualities, and holding these up for our inspection, adding at the same time comments of his own. Often the spectator is conscious of a sort of hostility towards the achievements of the past; some of the versions might almost be described as rapes or dismemberments.

Picasso turned the same baleful eye on the effects of the ageing process as it applied to himself, and some of his most personal late works are a series of prints on this theme, often including self-portraits showing the artist as an aged voyeur or else as a monkey. They were produced in a great burst of creative energy between 16 March and 5 October 1968. Even more extraordinary are the very late paintings, done in the final years before the artist's death in April 1973. Painted with tremendous boldness, and even with a certain crudity, they met with incomprehension when they were first shown, but have since been hailed as the most important precursors of the new Expressionist figuration. Certainly there is a wild sense of risk about them which makes them exciting. Images are radically simplified, yet retain legibility thanks to Picasso's unsurpassed skill as a draughtsman.

Several other painters of the great generation continue to seem isolated from the main current of post-war events, though the work they did was often impressive. Georges Braque (1882–1963), for example, painted some undoubted masterpieces in his old age, such as the series of pictures devoted to the theme of the studio, such as *Studio IX*. These tranquil, monumental paintings sum up all the lessons of the painter's long lifetime. Yet it is surely significant that they are inward-turned without being truly introspective. They look, not at the world outside, nor at the psyche, but at the familiar paraphernalia of the artist's workshop. Their greatness comes, not from new invention, but from refinement of invention. Braque is giving a final polish to ideas

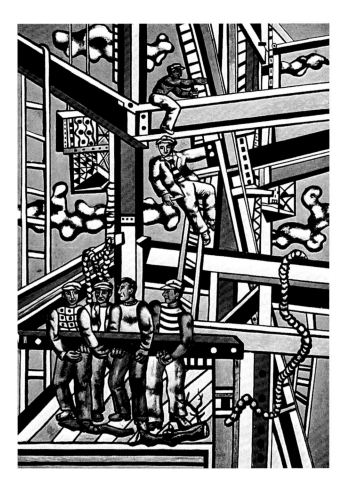

24. **Fernand Léger,**
The Constructors, 1950

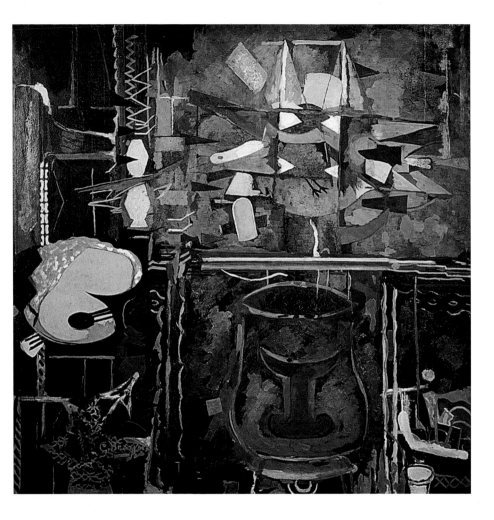

25. **Georges Braque**, *Studio IX*, 1952–6

which he first began to use in the days of Cubism, and he deploys these ideas less radically in the late than in the early work.

More willing to get to grips with the world around him was another veteran, Fernand Léger (1881–1955). In a picture such as *The Constructors*, painted in 1950, we see an attempt to bring a Poussinesque classicism to terms with properly modern and Marxist subject-matter. The results have been duly admired by Marxist critics. Nevertheless, a reversion to Poussin seems curiously eccentric and wilful even in the wilful world of post-war art.

Even the two acknowledged masters whose work seems most relevant to the post-war scene seem to have achieved this relationship almost by accident. The most conspicuous triumph was

24

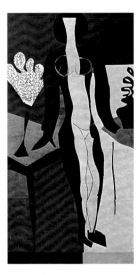

26. **Henri Matisse**, *Zulma*, 1950

that of Matisse (1869–1954), who became in his old age almost as radical an artist as he had been at the time of the Fauves. Between the wars Matisse had specialized in a fluent hedonism which made increasingly few demands on his talent. In 1941 he underwent a series of operations, and emerged from them a permanent invalid. In some ways this ordeal and even the war itself seem to have sharpened his perceptions. In the late 1940s he painted a series of splendid interiors, flooded with light and colour, which form a parallel to the *Studios* of Braque. But he was to go beyond this. By 1950, the patches of colour in his pictures (for example, the *Zulma* in Copenhagen) had begun to enjoy an autonomy of their own. It was at about this time that, because of his increasing feebleness, Matisse began to use the *papier découpé* technique which was the chief creative resource of his last years. Pieces of paper were coloured to the artist's specification, and these were then cut and used to form designs. Thus the old man could create works of considerable size without too much strain. The method encouraged extreme simplification, and helped to discipline Matisse's decorative gift. *The Snail* is one of the most abstract of all the designs of this period, severer even than the work which Matisse did around 1910. The activation of colour which Matisse achieved in these works was to mean something important to painters much younger than himself.

26

29

The other painter who had something to contribute was Miró. His great simple canvases of the Fifties were certainly close to the Abstract Expressionists, whom he influenced, and, in the 1960s even to some of the 'colour painters' whom I have yet to discuss, as in *Blue II* which plays on his characteristic ambiguity between representation and abstraction, but owes its greatest appeal to its wonderful use of colour. His sculpture, too, has links with Dubuffet. But Miró remains strangely elusive as an artistic personality: an artist who kept so many options open is difficult to interpret satisfactorily.

31

Other major artists, such as Max Ernst, continued their careers, but producing work which seemed at the time increasingly remote from the current scene. Ernst's *Cry of the Seagull*, like Miró's *Blue II*, is evocative and lyrical, both abstract and representational in its effect and by now quite remote from his earlier Surrealist work. Some important painters acknowledged this dilemma quite openly. One seems to find a confession of this ambiguity between modernist Surrealism and Realism in the powerful portraits which the British painter Graham Sutherland (1903–80) produced after the war, numbering Sir Winston

30

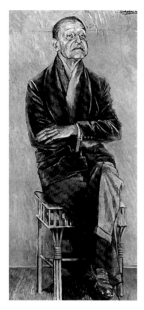

27. **Graham Sutherland**,
Somerset Maugham, 1949

Churchill and Somerset Maugham among his sitters. These seem a surprising development of style for an artist who certainly began in the Surrealist tradition, and who continued, in other paintings, to produce work which was reminiscent of Surrealism.

'Realism' itself is not, however, an irrelevant issue, where the post-war painting of Europe is concerned. In fact, the sombre mood of immediately post-war Europe did seem to produce at least a theoretical leaning towards Realist art. There was a feeling that artists should now face up to their responsibilities, that they should participate in building a new and better world, and, in particular, that they should fall into line with film-makers and authors, both of whom were attracted towards a documentary style. In Italy, for example, Rossellini's early Neo-Realist films, *Città Aperta* and *Paisa*, were important – infinitely more so than the *Manifesto del Realismo* issued by leading Italian artists in 1945.

On the whole, Social Realism took root only in those countries which could be counted as markedly provincial. In England, for example, the so-called 'Kitchen Sink' painters enjoyed a considerable vogue. Their leader, David Bomberg (1890–1957), had begun his career as a pioneer Modernist, under the influence of Vorticism, but later developed in a way which showed that his true masters were the German Expressionists, as is evident in landscapes such as *Monastery of Ay Chrisostomos, Cyprus*. Bomberg

28

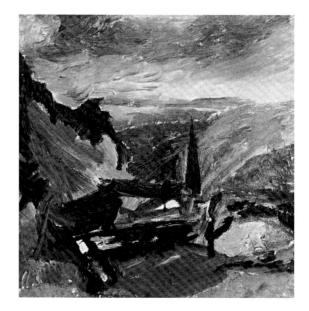

28. **David Bomberg**, *Monastery of Ay Chrisostomos, Cyprus*, 1948

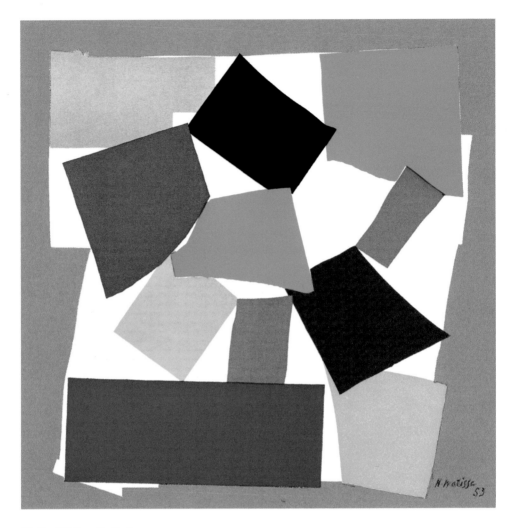

29. **Henri Matisse**, *The Snail*,
1953

30. **Max Ernst**, *Cry of the
Seagull*, 1953

31. **Joan Miró**, *Blue II*, 1961

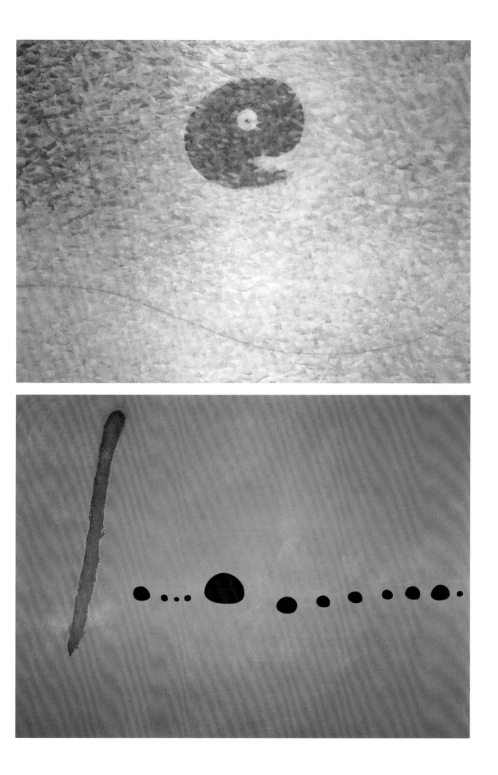

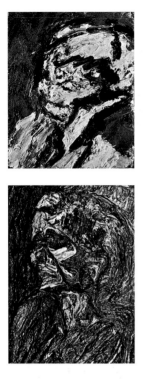

tried to create a balance: he wanted the spectator to be able to enter into his work, both in its role as a representation and in its role simply as paint. His followers tended to emphasize one of the terms of this occasion at the expense of the other. The work of Frank Auerbach (b. 1931), e.g. *Head of Helen Gillespie III*, and of [32] Leon Kossoff (b. 1926), e.g. *Profile of Rachel*, is concerned with a [33] reality that is achieved literally: by means of the solidity of paint, which is piled up on the canvas in ropes and mounds. Though the approach is different, the final result has something in common with the French 'matter painters' whom I shall discuss in a moment.

The realism of the other 'Kitchen Sink' painters (those to whom the term more properly applies) was more descriptive, and their allegiance to it proved more fragile. The early work of artists such as Jack Smith, Edward Middleditch (b. 1923), and [34] John Bratby (1928–92) dates only from the middle 1950s, and is [35]

32. **Frank Auerbach**, *Head of Helen Gillespie III*, 1962–4

33. **Leon Kossoff**, *Profile of Rachel*, 1965

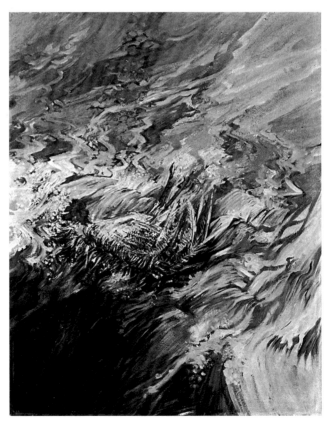

34. **Edward Middleditch**, *Dead Chicken in a Stream*, 1955

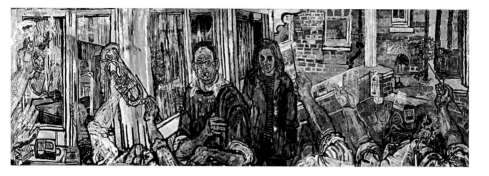

35. **John Bratby**, *Window, Self-Portrait, Jean and Hands*, 1957

36. **Renato Guttuso**, *The Discussion*, 1959–60

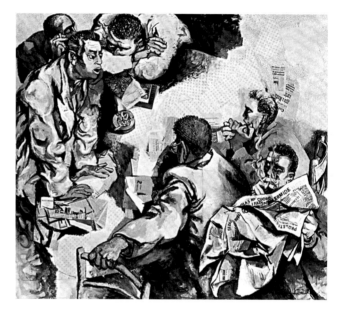

the equivalent of the kind of Realism which was then dominant in English literature and on the London stage: Kingsley Amis's novel *Lucky Jim*, John Osborne's play *Look Back in Anger*. However, none of these English painters produced work of the strength of that done by the Italian Realist Renato Guttuso (1912–87), who discovered a kind of Neo-Baroque idiom in which to describe the lives of 'ordinary people', as in his painting *The Discussion*, a typical café scene of workers engaged in political debate. Where Léger, in his late years, looked back towards the Baroque of Poussin, in trying to create an 'art of the people', Guttuso based himself on the more tactile art of the Carracci, and of Caravaggio.

36

49

There is, however, one British figurative painter who ranks among the most distinguished European contemporary artists: Francis Bacon (1909–92). Bacon and the Frenchman Balthus (b. 1908) seem to me, in fact, to be the only two artists who have managed to make figuration work in a contemporary European context. Both are so strange and individual that it is worth considering them side by side.

Bacon seems to me to represent the degree to which the demands of traditional figurative painting can be forced into a compromise with those of Modernism. By the standards of many of the artists whose work is described in this book, he was an extremely traditional figure. He worked with the old materials, oil paint on canvas, and he accepted the discipline of the old formats. In other ways he was far from orthodox. This is the way in which he described his method of work in a television interview with David Sylvester:

I think that you can make, very much as in abstract painting, involuntary marks on the canvas which may suggest much deeper ways by which you can trap the facts you are obsessed by. If anything ever does work in my case it works from that moment when consciously I didn't know what I was doing. . . . It's really a question in my case of being able to set a trap with which one would be able to catch the fact at its most living point.[1]

This leaves open at least two questions: the precise one of the 'facts' the painter feels attracted towards, and the more general one of the future of figurative art. In Bacon's case the facts seem to be mostly those of terror, isolation and anguish. A visit to any large retrospective exhibition of Bacon's work is an oppressive experience. Bacon went through a number of stylistic changes: the screaming popes and businessmen that made him famous were to give way to harder, clearer, and in a way more disturbing images. Distorted figures cower in glaringly lit rooms, which suggest both the luxury apartment and the execution chamber. These figures are not merely isolated, they are abject: man stripped of his few remaining pretensions.

Bacon's consistent, narrow art represents at least one of the positions that it is possible to take up, *vis-à-vis* mid-twentieth-century experience. But, though the unease of his work impressed both the ordinary spectator and his fellow artists, there is no such thing as a 'school of Bacon', even in England. The attitudes he took up precluded membership of any group or movement.

37

42

37. **Francis Bacon**, *Study after Velázquez: Pope Innocent X*, 1953

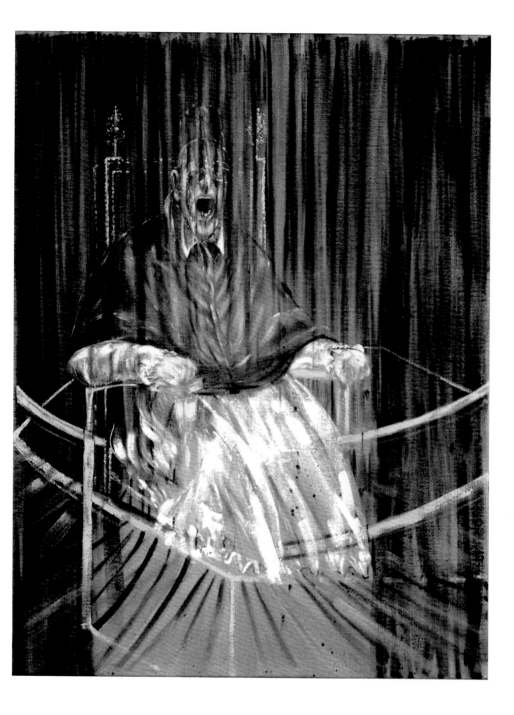

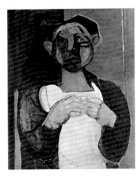

38. **Edouard Pignon**, *The Miner*, 1949

39. **Maurice Estève**, *Composition 166*, 1957

Easier to assimilate psychologically, but still isolated from the main current, is the work of Balthus. He differs from Bacon in being more naturalistic, in eschewing improvisation, in being influenced by artists such as Courbet and Piero della Francesca who could never be described as Bacon's masters (Bacon's debts were mostly to Velázquez). But they still have much in common. Like Bacon, Balthus broods on private obsessions; like Bacon, he often uses the symbolism of figures in a room which claustrophobically contains and shuts them in. If Bacon occasionally seemed to depict the aftermath of rape, Balthus gives its foretaste. Nude, adolescent girls sprawl in abandoned poses, inviting sexual violence, as in *The Bedroom*. Light gilds their contours, with a hand that is secretive and loving.

Bacon and Balthus stand out among their contemporaries because each is endowed with a very special temperament, one which overrides all considerations of style. Few artists possess the perhaps burdensome qualities which these two seem to have, and the development of European painting was to go a very different way.

41

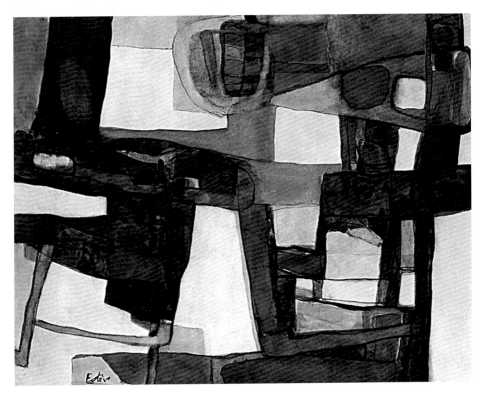

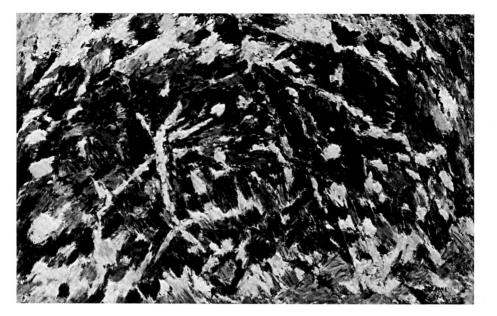

40. **Jean Bazaine**, *Shadows on the Hill*, 1961

I have spoken of the sudden attention which was devoted to the great names of the Ecole de Paris immediately following the war. For younger artists in France, the process of growing up under the shadow of these giant reputations was bound to be a difficult one. Those artists most spoken of as 'promising' in Paris at this time were the so-called 'middle generation', which consisted of Jean Fautrier (1897–1964), Maurice Estève (b. 1904), Edouard Pignon (1905–93), and Jean Bazaine (1904–75) among others. These men were expected to do several entirely contradictory things at the same time. It was their duty to maintain the impetus of the Modernist revolution; it was equally their duty to maintain the prestige of Paris, and the whole apparatus of dealers and critics that went with Paris as a centre. Naturally they found themselves in two minds. Their development was not made any easier by the vigorous promotion they received.

Of the painters whom I have just mentioned, Fautrier is without question the most original and important, as well as being the oldest. He was born in 1897, the other three in the middle of the next decade. Fautrier's first post-war show, at the Galerie Drouin in 1945, which consisted of the series of pictures called *Hostages* – one of which is reproduced on p. 58 – did have a significance for the future. The ostensible subject of *Hostages* was the mass deportations during the war, but the paintings put great stress upon the tactility of the painter's materials, the evocative quality of

44

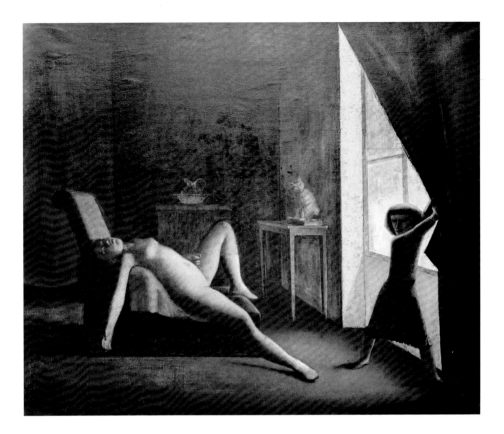

41. **Balthus**, *The Bedroom,*
1954

the surface itself, as is evident in the example reproduced. There is a narcissism in this which tells us something about the waning vitality of French painting, but it was also a genuine innovation. One sees in these pictures the first steps being taken towards *art informel* – art 'without form' – the style which was to dominate the next decade; and it is interesting to note that the step was made before the influence of the American Abstract Expressionists had reached France. Bazaine, Estève, and Pignon are lesser figures. In their work, such as Pignon's *The Miner*, Estève's *Composition 166* – both on p.52 – and Bazaine's *Shadows on the Hill* – on p. 53, Fauvism, Cubism and Expressionism jostled together to make an amalgam that had little that was new in it, save the fact of the mixture.

38
39
40

There were, however, better artists than these at work in the Paris of the late 1940s and the 1950s: men who did something, if not enough, to justify the critic Michel Tapié's claim, in his book

42. **Francis Bacon**, *One of Three*
Studies for a Crucifixion, 1962

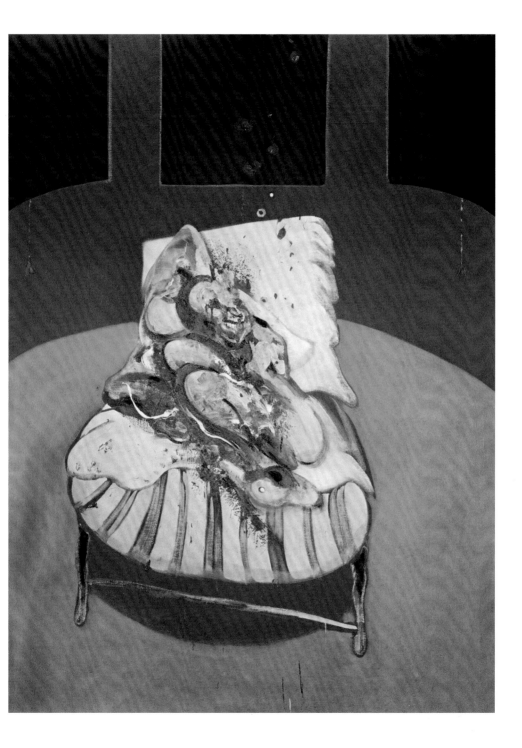

Un Art autre, that there was now a kind of painting which started from premises wholly different from the traditional ones. Most of the painters whom Tapié supported were working in a direction which paralleled that being taken by the Abstract Expressionists in America. The pioneer, almost the Arshile Gorky of this group, was the short-lived German artist Wols. Wols (1913–51) began by training as a violinist, then studied at the Bauhaus in Berlin under Moholy-Nagy (1895–1946) and Mies van der Rohe (1886–1969). In the early 1930s he moved to Paris, and formed links with the Surrealists. The rest of the decade was divided between France and Spain: at this time Wols worked mostly as a photographer. In 1939–40 he was interned, and began to achieve his mature style in a series of drawings. These were successfully shown at the Galerie Drouin in 1945, and Wols began to exercise a real influence over his contemporaries. The paintings he made in the few years that remained to him (he died in 1951), as in the characteristic *The Blue Pomegranate*, seem to blend the graphic sensibility of Klee with the new and more freely abstract way of seeing things. Wols's fascination with the actual substance of which the picture is made, as is evident even in reproduction, the thick impasto which can be scratched and carved, prompts a comparison with Fautrier.

Hans Hartung (1904–89) was a compatriot of Wols. During the art boom of the mid-1950s, he was to score a resounding success, thanks to a rather limited formula for picture-making which is correspondingly easy to recognize. Like Wols, Hartung left Germany in the 1930s, and settled in Paris, where he was encouraged by the sculptor Julio González. What he had to show now, in the years immediately following the war, was a vigorous calligraphy of bundled sheaves of lines. No picture of Hartung's is wholly without energy, but, once one has seen a group of them, it is certainly possible to wonder why a given mark, a given brushstroke, as in *Painting T 54–16*, opposite, appears in one canvas and not in another.

Another very fashionable painter in the 1950s was the French-Canadian Jean-Paul Riopelle (b. 1923). Riopelle, too, has an effective but limited formula. His work is an attempt to marry the spontaneity of 'informal' abstract painting to the rich texture and colour which are to be obtained from a heavy impasto, seen, for instance, in *Encounter*, on p. 63. Here, as in Hartung's paintings, there is vigour of rather an obvious sort. The bright colour emphasizes the mechanical roughness of the surface, but the two elements – colour and texture – do not quite coalesce. Further-

45

44

43

50

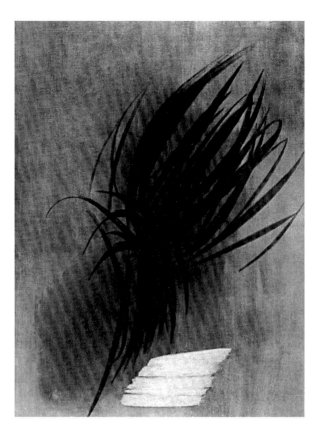

43. **Hans Hartung**, *Painting T 54–16*, 1954

more, the use of a title, like *Encounter*, suggests meaning which is not visually supported.

A stronger artist, whose work is akin to informal abstraction, but stands somewhat apart from it, was the poet-draughtsman Henri Michaux (1899–1984). Michaux seems to have turned to making drawings as a means of conveying meanings which it was impossible to catch in writing (he had been a prominent literary figure since the 1930s). Many of these meanings were connected with the altered states of consciousness induced by hallucinogenic drugs. Michaux's drawings, like *Painting in India Ink*, are so alike that, when they are seen in bulk, the effect becomes monotonous; but the best of them come surprisingly close to the look of some of Pollock's work, at least in terms of surface similarity, but lack his toughness. *Painting in India Ink* may be suggestive and elegant, but compared to a Pollock drip painting, it looks more illustrational. The marks are on the verge of resolving themselves into shorthand representations of human figures.

46

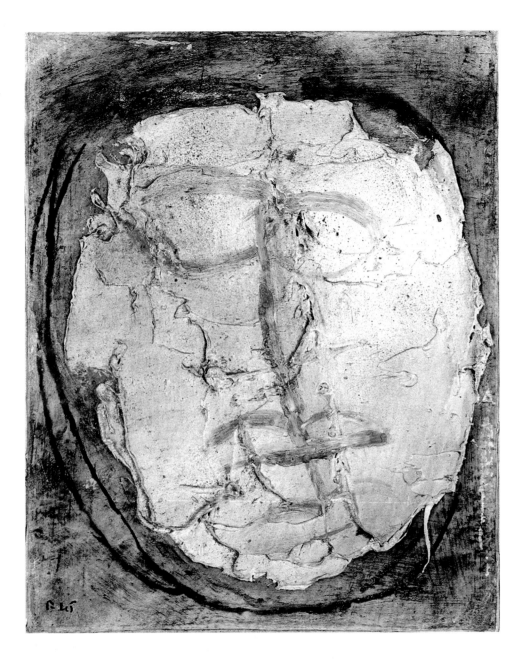

44. **Jean Fautrier**, *Hostage*,
1945

45. **Wols**, *The Blue
Pomegranate*, 1946

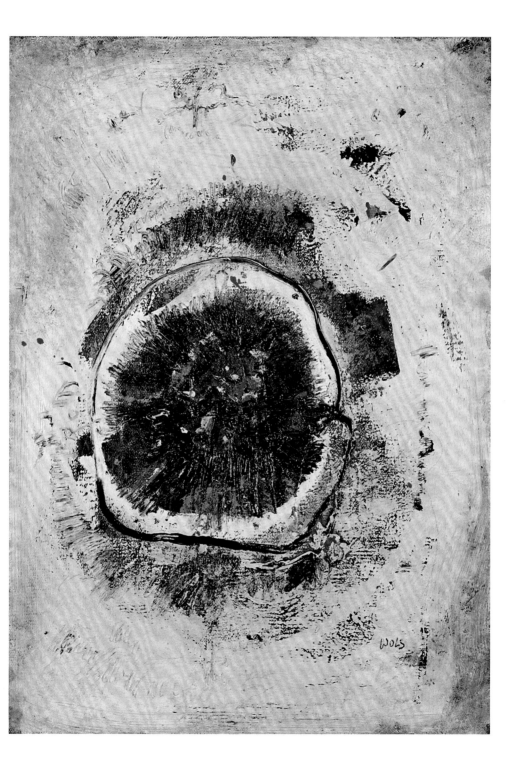

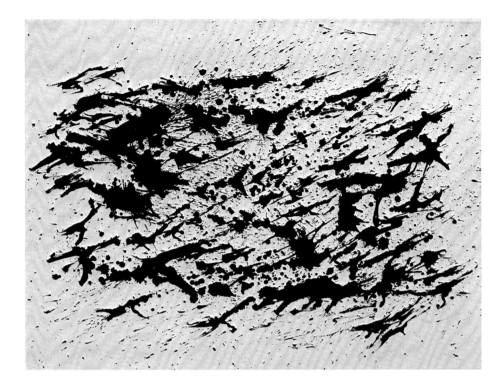

46. **Henri Michaux**, *Painting in India Ink*, 1960–7

The new abstraction scored an enormous success not only in Paris, but in the rest of Europe. Painters such as Antoni Tàpies (b. 1923) in Spain, and Alberto Burri (b. 1915) in Italy are recognizably part of the same impulse. Both are interesting because of the way in which they relate an international tendency to a national situation. Tàpies, who is self-taught, began to paint in 1946, and had his first one-man show in Barcelona in 1951. His work shows a fascination with surfaces, textures, and substances which links him closely to the French 'matter painters', such as Fautrier (see p. 58), who directly influenced him. Tàpies brings the spectator face to face with one of the paradoxes of the radical art of the post-war epoch. He is in politics a liberal, and it is not without significance that he comes from Barcelona, traditionally the centre of left-wing sentiment in Spain. Yet his work was by its nature and concepts too ambiguous to give much uneasiness to the Franco government. With its 'hand-made' textures, it tended to align itself with the products of the Spanish luxury crafts, such as fine leatherwork, as can be seen in *Black with Two Lozenges* on p. 62. This may give us the reason why Tàpies, and other Spanish artists whose work in a general way resembles his, such as

49

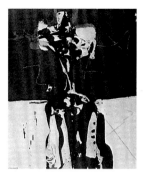

47. **Manolo Millares**, *No. 165*, 1961

48. **Alberto Burri**, *Sacco 4*, 1954

Manolo Millares (1926–72) in, for instance, *No. 165*, enjoyed a certain degree of favour in the eyes of the authorities in Franco's day. What they created became a form of prestige export, better known abroad than in its country of origin. 47

Burri is a rather similar case. He was a doctor during the war, and first began to paint in 1944, in a prison camp in Texas. When he was set free, he gave up his practice in order to continue painting. His first exhibition was held in 1947. Burri is best known for works made of sacking and old rags, e.g. *Sacco*: his reason 48 for using these materials was that they reminded him of the blood-soaked bandages he had seen in wartime. He has also made use of charred wood, of plastic foil burned and melted with a blow-lamp, and of battered plates of tin. The programme put forward to justify these works is the existentialist one of metaphysical anguish, but what strikes one instead is their good taste, their easy sensuousness.

Indeed, it is possible to feel that nearly all the European free abstractionists of the late 1940s and early 1950s suffer from a thinness of emotion and a restriction of technical means. At the same time, one must sympathize with their predicament. As can be seen from the work of Wols and Fautrier, in *Hostage* and 44 *The Blue Pomegranate*, on pp. 58 and 59, they were exploring a 45

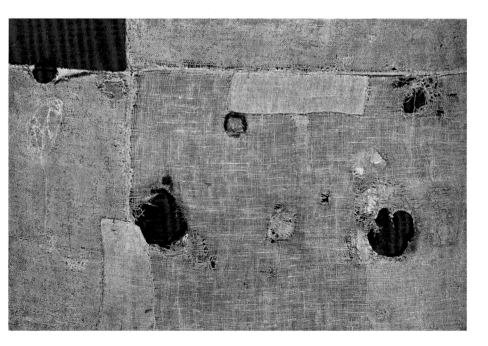

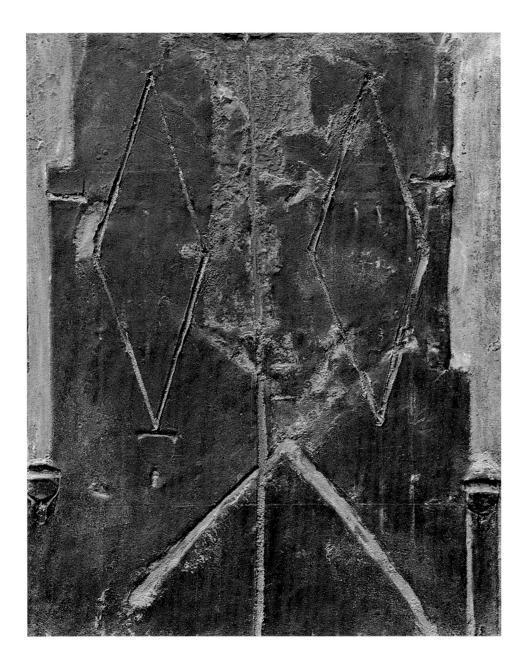

49. **Antoni Tàpies**, *Black with
Two Lozenges*, 1963

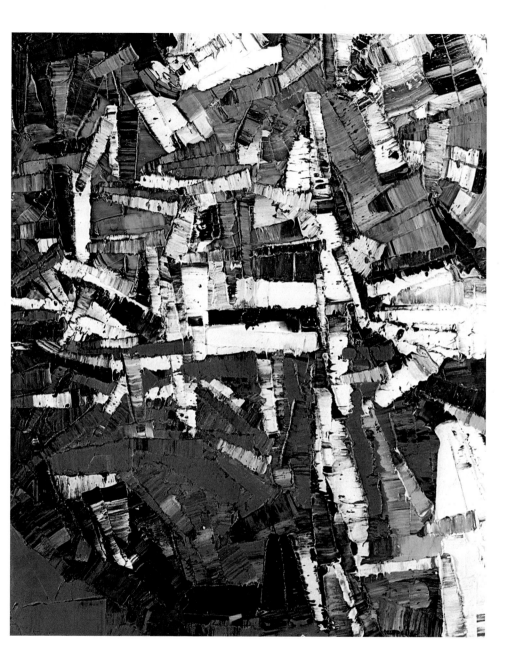

50. **Jean-Paul Riopelle,**
Encounter, 1956

kind of painting which had also attracted the leading Americans. The European experiments were, however, less radical and less sure of their direction than those being made in New York. The long-standing European (and especially French) tradition of *belle peinture* – of the painting as a beautiful and luxurious object, a bed of delight for the senses – stood in the way of radicalism. The American worship of 'rawness' is to be found, although in another form, in Picasso's *Demoiselles d'Avignon*, but it is not visible in the art that was being produced in France some forty years later. When the new Americans began to be exhibited in Europe – when Peggy Guggenheim's collection made a tour of European cities in 1948, for instance – the effect was overwhelming. One reason that the Americans triumphed so easily was to be found in the fact that their European colleagues were already partly converted – enough to understand what they were being offered – but had not yet achieved so spectacularly radical a stance. Yet European artists found it difficult to use Abstract Expressionism as a starting-point, because the American statement had a completeness of its own.

The dilemma is clearly shown in the work of Pierre Soulages (b. 1919), and in that of Georges Mathieu (b. 1922). Soulages can, on occasion, look like a sweeter and less committed version of Franz Kline, but his broad strokes of the brush, e.g. *Painting*, 51 do not have the energy or the constructional quality which one finds in the American artist. Mathieu is a more interesting figure than Soulages. His work has certain affinities with that of

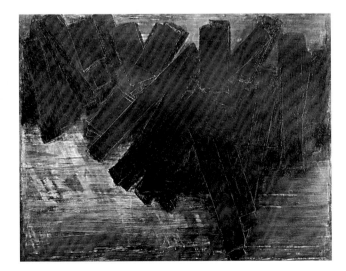

51. **Pierre Soulages**, *Painting*, 1956

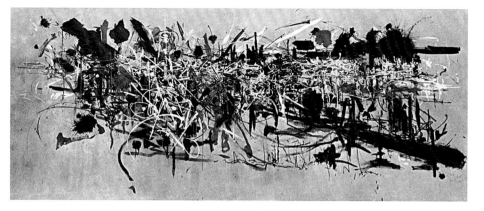

52. **Georges Mathieu**, *Battle of Bouvines*, 1954

Pollock, though he started painting in a freely calligraphic way so early (1937) that there can be no question of direct derivation. Rather, his has been an independent development along similar lines: which does not amount to a claim that Mathieu is an artist of the same stature as Pollock. For instance, his pictures, such as *Battle of Bouvines*, even the very large ones, are always far less complex than those painted by the American. Image and background have separate identities, which is not the case with Pollock; and there is in Mathieu's work little real feeling for space, even for the shallow, flattened version of it that Pollock uses. Mathieu writes on the canvas in a series of bravura scribbles. These scribbles do not blend with the ground; they dominate it. Rhythmical as they are, they express little beyond a delight in their own ease and dash. Mathieu seems very much the virtuoso, satisfied with his own tricks.

Nevertheless, he has an importance which is unconnected with the flashy triviality of so many of his pictures. He has been an efficient and intelligent publicist and organizer: it was he who arranged the exhibition in which the new French and American painters were shown together for the first time. More, he has been in all senses a forerunner, a man keenly attuned to the seminal ideas of the time. When, in 1956, Mathieu painted a twelve-foot canvas in the presence of a large audience at the Théâtre Sarah Bernhardt, he anticipated the 'Happenings' which American artists were to make fashionable a few years later, as well as recalling some of the antics of the Dadaists and Surrealists. Modern art has produced a crop of dazzling showmen, and Mathieu, like Salvador Dalí, has been one of these.

Art informel, though the best publicized of the European developments after the war, was by no means the only new

52

beginning. Even more significant, in many ways, was the short-lived Cobra Group of 1948–50. The name is taken from the names of the cities which the various participants hailed from: Copenhagen, Brussels, Amsterdam. Among its members were the Dane Asger Jorn (1914–73), the Dutchman Karel Appel (b. 1921), and the Belgians Corneille (b. 1922) and Pierre Alechinsky (b. 1927). Like the Abstract Expressionists, the artists of the Cobra Group were interested in giving direct expression to subconscious fantasy, with no censorship from the intellect, as, for instance, in Alechinsky's *The Green Being Born.* 53
But they did not rule out figuration – as the aerial view *Souvenir of* 54 *Amsterdam* by Corneille shows: in this they resembled Fautrier and Wols, rather than Hartung, Soulages, and Mathieu. Expressionism had struck deep roots both in Scandinavia (with Munch) and in Holland and Belgium. The Dutch-American de Kooning shows its impress just as clearly as Karel Appel, a Dutchman who has remained a 'European' – see, for example, his *Women and Birds* 57 on p. 69. In one sense, therefore, the Cobra Group revives and continues an old tradition, rather than making a completely fresh start. This led to a greater complexity of reference than we usually find in the art of the immediately post-war period. Jorn, for example, veered from the cheerful to the sinister. His pictures, such as *You Never Know*, on p. 68, incorporated a wide range of 55

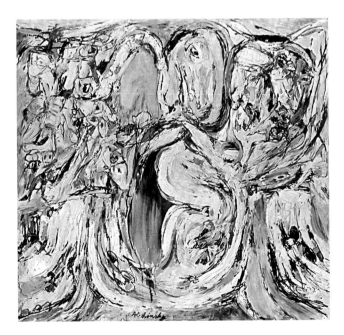

53. **Pierre Alechinsky**, *The Green Being Born*, 1960

54. **Corneille**, *Souvenir of Amsterdam*, 1956

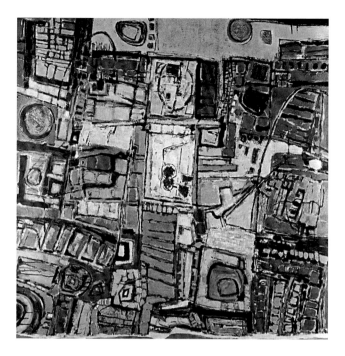

references; thanks to his interest in myths and magic, Jorn had access to a great range of signs and symbols. He was also a notably bold colourist. Yet he and his colleagues had less impact than one might have predicted. The same is true of an English artist whose work in some respects resembles theirs: Alan Davie (b. 1920) formed one of the few real bridges between English and Continental art at this period, and was exhibited in European exhibitions where English painters were seldom seen. 56

More loosely linked to the Cobra group than Davie, yet working in a parallel style, is the Austrian Fritz Hundertwasser (1928-2000). In his work, such as *The Hokkaido Steamer* on p. 72, Expressionism becomes formal and decorative, under the influence of Art Nouveau. 59

Yet there was one European artist of crucial importance who was related to the Cobra Group painters, as well as to Wols and to Fautrier. Jean Dubuffet was one of the few really major artists to have appeared in France since the war, though 'since the war' is perhaps the wrong phrase, for Dubuffet was at work as a painter long before 1945. But his first one-man show was held in 1945, a few months after the Liberation.

His painting *Corps de Dame* contains the clues to many of Dubuffet's preoccupations. He was interested in child art, in the 61

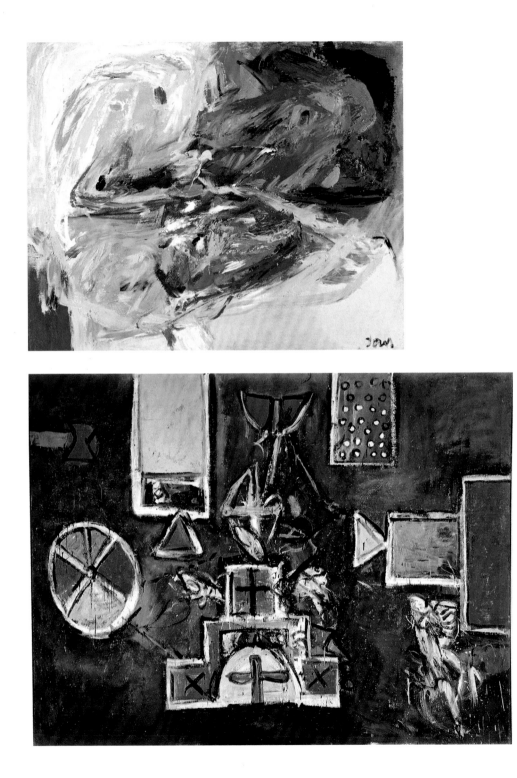

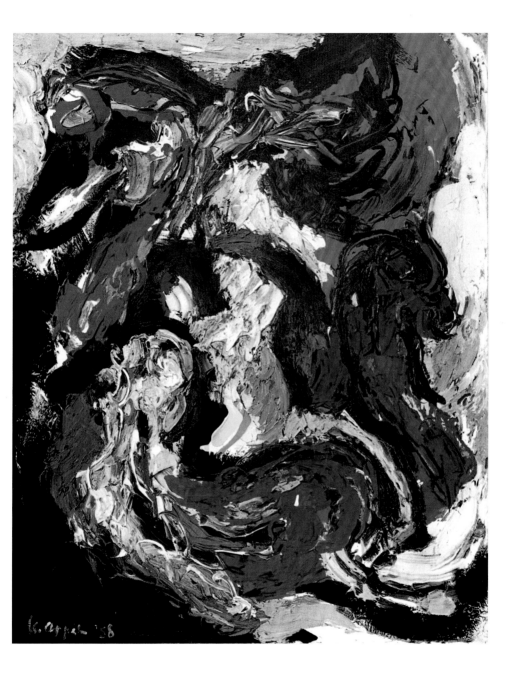

55. **Asger Jorn**, *You Never
Know*, 1966

56. **Alan Davie**, *The Martyrdom
of St Catherine*, 1956

57. **Karel Appel**, *Women and
Birds*, 1958

art of madmen, in graffiti on walls and pavements, and in the accidental markings and maculations to be found on these surfaces. Dubuffet was the most persistent explorer of the possibilities offered by materials and surfaces to have appeared during the post-war period. He wrote:

In all my works . . . I have always had recourse to one never-varying method. It consists in making the delineation of the objects represented heavily dependent on a system of necessities which itself looks strange. These necessities are sometimes due to the inappropriate and awkward character of the material used, sometimes to the inappropriate manipulation of the tools, sometimes to some strange obsessive notion (frequently changed for another). In a word, it is always a matter of giving the person who is looking at the picture the startling impression that a weird logic has directed the painting of it, a logic to which the delineation of every object is subjected, is even sacrificed, in such a peremptory way that, curiously enough, it forces the most unexpected solutions, and, in spite of the obstacles it creates, brings out the desired figuration.[2]

The artist here proclaims himself the ally of certain important creators in the other arts. There seems to be a real affinity, for example, between Dubuffet's methods and those adopted by the dramatist Eugène Ionesco. Dubuffet and Ionesco alike are heavily permeated with the idea of 'the absurd', perhaps more thoroughly so than Sartre, with whom it originated. Dubuffet appears in his statements about art as a man of culture who is sophisticatedly obsessed with the anti-cultural. His work shows how hard it is for the modern artist to break out of the prison of 'taste'. His remarks about the *Corps de Dame* series, which I have already mentioned in connection with de Kooning, show just how such considerations crept into his work, more or less by the back door:

It pleased me (and I think this predilection is more or less constant in all my paintings) to juxtapose brutally, in these feminine bodies, the extremely general and the extremely particular, the metaphysical and the grotesquely trivial. In my view, the one is considerably reinforced by the presence of the other.[3]

Dubuffet spent his life, not so much in breaking new ground, as in trying to see what could be done with the existing heritage of the Ecole de Paris, by misusing it as well as using it. He made sculpture out of clinker, foil, and papier mâché, and pictures from leaves and butterfly-wings. The result is an oeuvre in which the individual works are nearly always fascinating, either in their

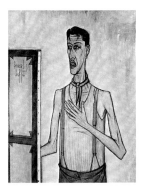

58. **Bernard Buffet**, *Self-portrait*, 1954

(overleaf)
59. **Fritz Hundertwasser**, *The Hokkaido Steamer*, 1961

60. **Nicolas de Staël**, *Agrigente*, 1954

61. **Jean Dubuffet**, *Corps de Dame*, 1950

grossness or their intricacy, or some intermingling of these two qualities. Dubuffet's creative limits are to be found in his self-consciousness, and the degree to which his work is an exegesis rather than a truly original contribution to Modernism. It comments both wittily and pertinently, but we are aware that, to savour these comments fully, we must have at least some knowledge of modern art, its theories and its controversies.

Nevertheless, Dubuffet seems to me to sum up many of the leading tendencies to be found in the visual arts in the period immediately following the war. The priority given to the inner world of the artist, and the rejection of the traditional claims of art to be more coherent, more organized, and more homogeneous than 'non-art', or 'reality', were pointers to the future.

The difficulties of a more traditional approach can be judged from the work of two other painters who made their reputations at about the same period. One of them need not detain us long, however. Dubuffet's near-namesake Bernard Buffet had a spectacular success in the 1940s and 1950s with schematic figurative paintings, e.g. *Self-portrait*, which were literal interpretations of the gloomier and more superficial aspects of Sartre's existentialist philosophy. Buffet's interest really lies in the fact that quite a large section of the public received him so eagerly as an acceptable representative of modern art.

Another, equally popular and far more gifted painter was the tragic Nicolas de Staël (1914–55). In terms of natural endowments for painting de Staël is the only French painter of the immediately post-war generation with serious claims to rival Dubuffet. The two artists pursued opposite courses. Instead of accepting absurdity and fragmentation, and exploiting them, as Dubuffet did, de Staël looked for a synthesis, and in particular for a synthesis between the claims of Modernism and those of the past. He began as an abstract painter, with certain affinities to Riopelle. Abstraction dissatisfied him, and gradually he came closer and closer to figuration, first through a series of *Football players*, and then in the late landscapes and still lifes for which he is best known. These extremely simplified paintings, such as *Agrigente*, can be seen both in abstract terms and as representations. A skilful, delicate balancing-act is going on in them; the various planes must be made to advance and recede in such a way that the 'abstract' paint surface is never broken; so that we never feel that the representation is being forced on us, but rather that it has come about naturally as the result of the play of form against form and colour-area against colour-area. In his

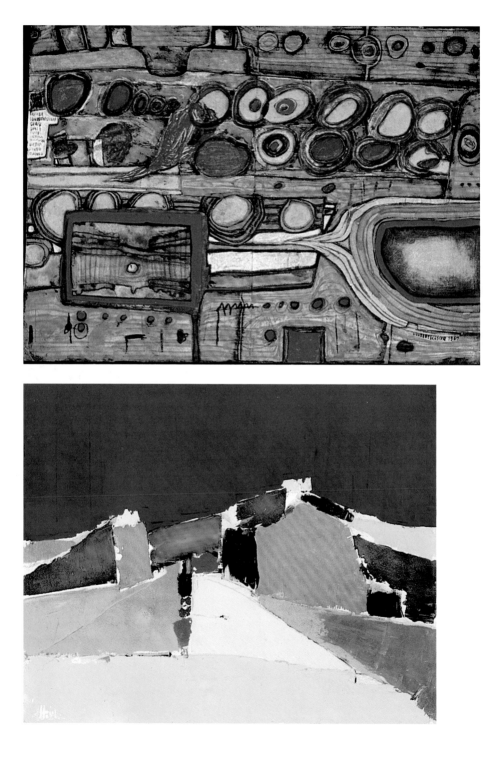

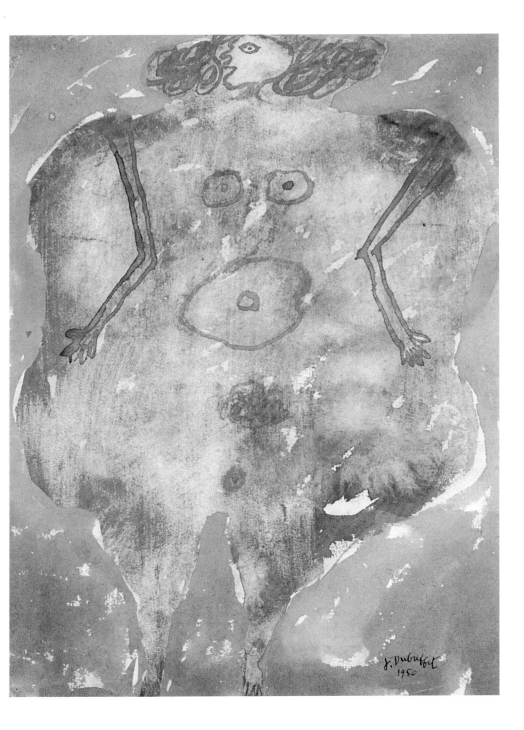

best pictures, like the one reproduced om p. 72, de Staël achieves his aim: the paint surface is placidly, creamily delicious; the colours have a sonority that reminds us of the painter's Russian ancestry.

But is this an art which lives up to the great claims that have been made for it since the painter's suicide in 1955? De Staël has been compared to Poussin (that high compliment of the academic art critic), has been called the greatest of post-war painters, and so forth. True, with his piquant combination of the traditional and the original, he appeals to many spectators: to find a Poussin-like scheme of forms under an apparently abstract and arbitrary surface is strangely reassuring. The question is if the power to reassure is enough to make a genius. De Staël's compromise between figuration and abstraction pales beside the obsessive force of Bacon or Balthus. The abrasive style of Bacon makes an especially interesting contrast, because Bacon, too, owes something to the arbitrary procedures of abstraction but tries to yoke them to a figurative vision. While it would be foolish to deny the calm beauty of de Staël's best work, it seems obsessed with a perfectionism which in the end becomes sterile. As a painter, he succeeds rather as Whistler did before him, not through the invention of new forms, but through tact and taste in the manipulation of pre-existing ones.

The path of tact and taste was certainly not the one which the post-war arts were to pursue. Abstract Expressionism and *art informel* were to be followed by a rapid succession of other initiatives, none of them owing much to traditional ideas about *belle peinture*.

Chapter 3: Post-painterly abstraction

As it turned out, however, there was one style which held its own in the wake of Abstract Expressionism, and which, while owing something to the Abstract Expressionist example, had deep roots in the European art of the 1920s and 1930s. 'Hard edge' abstraction never completely died out, even in the palmiest days of Pollock and Kline. By 'hard edge' I mean the kind of abstract painting where the forms have definite, clean boundaries, instead of the fuzzy ones favoured, for example, by Mark Rothko. Characteristically, in this kind of painting, the hues themselves are flat and undifferentiated, so it is perhaps better to talk of colour-areas and not forms.

One of the progenitors of this kind of painting in America was Josef Albers, who has already been referred to because of his importance as a teacher. Albers had been closely connected with the Bauhaus during the 1920s: in fact, as student and teacher, he worked there continuously from 1920 to 1933, when it was closed, a longer period of service than any other *Bauhäusler*. During the 1930s, when he was already living in America, Albers took part in the annual shows mounted by the Abstraction-Création group in Paris. He was thus thoroughly cosmopolitan. Albers's cast of mind is very typical of the Bauhaus atmosphere: systematic and orderly, but also experimental. He was, for instance, very much interested in Gestalt psychology, and this led him towards an exploration of the effects of optical illusion. Later he was drawn towards a study of the ways in which colours act upon one another. The pictures and prints of the *Homage to the Square* series – e.g. *Homage to the Square 'Curious'*, reproduced on p. 77 – Albers's best known works, are planned experiments with colour.

Albers is interesting not only in himself, but because he seems to stand at the point where several attitudes towards painting converged. The systematic element in his work relates it to that of two Swiss artists, Max Bill (1908–94) and Richard Lohse (1902–88): Bill was also a Bauhaus alumnus, and, in his subsequent career, he became a sort of universal genius, at once artist, architect and sculptor. The serial development of colour

63

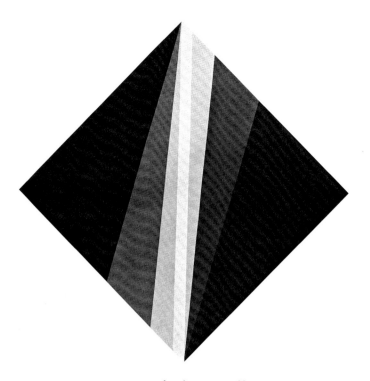

62. **Max Bill**, *Concentration to Brightness*, 1964

has been one of his interests throughout his career and *Concentration to Brightness* is but one characteristic example of austere, formal composition that makes use of optical data. Bill and Lohse are usually spoken of as exponents of 'Concrete art', and Albers is lumped in as a third member of the triumvirate. On the other hand, Albers's interest in optical illusion relates him to the so-called Op artists, while his particular treatment of form brings him into relationship with what critics labelled Post-painterly abstraction.

If one looks for a difference between Albers and his two Swiss colleagues, it seems to lie in the treatment of form. Albers's squares are free, passive, unanchored, floating, and it is this passivity which has come to seem particularly typical of a great deal of post-Abstract Expressionist painting in America. The difference between 'hard edge' and Post-painterly abstraction is precisely that it is not the hardness of the edge that counts, one colour abutting firmly upon another, but the quality of colour. It does not matter whether the colour melts into a neighbouring hue, or is sharply differentiated from it: the meeting is always passive. Albers's squares are crisp enough, but generate no energy from this crispness of outline.

63. **Josef Albers**, *Homage to the Square 'Curious'*, 1963

64. **Richard Lohse**, *Fifteen Systematic Colour Scales Merging Vertically*, 1950–67

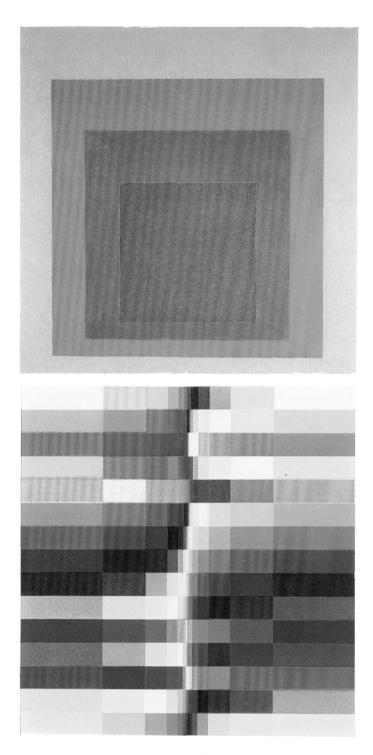

Another painter whose work has something of this quality, without qualifying as Post-painterly abstraction in the strictest sense, is Ad Reinhardt (1913–67), who made a reputation as *the* professional nonconformist of the New York art world during the 1950s, and succeeded in retaining it until his death in 1967. Influenced by the abstract decorative art of Persia and the Middle East, Reinhardt went through a phase in the 1940s when his work came close to the calligraphy of Tobey. But these 'written' marks drew together, and became rectangles which covered the whole picture surface e.g. *Red Painting*. From an orchestration of intense colours, Reinhardt moved towards black. The characteristic paintings of his last phase contain colours so dark, and so close in value to one another, that the picture appears to be black, or almost black, until it is closely studied, at which point the component rectangles slowly emerge from the surface.

It is interesting to contrast Albers and Reinhardt with 'hard edge' painters who have a more conventional, but still very American, attitude towards composition. Among these are Al Held (b. 1928) – whose large-scale *Echo* is characteristic in its

70

65

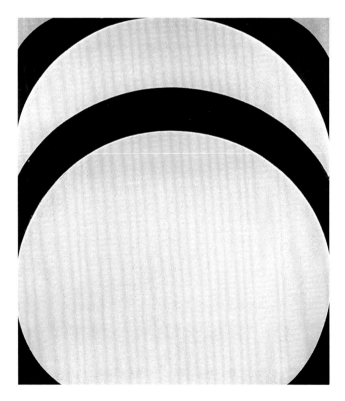

65. **Al Held**, *Echo*, 1966

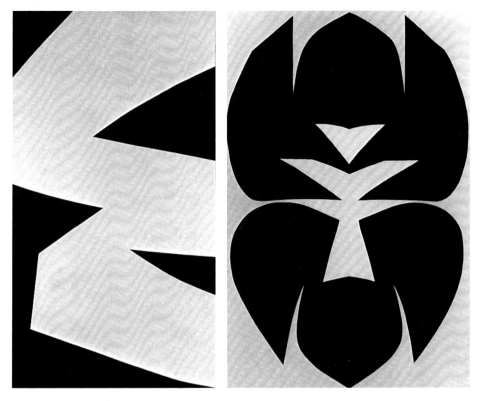

66. **Ellsworth Kelly**, *White–Dark Blue*, 1962

67. **Jack Youngerman**, *Totem Black*, 1967

simplified, schematic and geometric form – Jack Youngerman (b. 1926) – whose *Totem Black*, equally monumental as Held's *Echo*, looks like a paper cut-out painted large – and Ellsworth Kelly (b. 1923). Of these, Kelly is probably the best known. His painting consists of flat fields of colour, rigidly divided from one another. Sometimes one colour will contain another completely, so that the picture consists of an image placed upon a ground. These are usually Kelly's weakest works, especially when the image itself is derived from some natural form, such as a leaf. At other times it seems as if the canvas, already very large, has not been big enough to accommodate the form, which is arbitrarily sliced by the edge, and continues itself in the mind's eye of the spectator, as, for instance, in *White – Dark Blue*. As a device to impart energy and interest to the painting, this is quite successful, but there is something rather gimmicky and tricky about it. There is also the fact that 'energy' and 'interest' are traditional pictorial concepts which, in the sense in which I have just used them, Albers, Reinhardt, and the Post-painterly abstractionists seem alike determined to reject.

67

66

What links Albers and Reinhardt with the so-called Post-painterly abstractionists is, in part, the fascination not with pictorial means, but with aesthetic doctrine. The doctrinaire nature of Post-painterly abstraction is striking. Rather as the logical positivists have concentrated on the purely linguistic aspects of philosophy, so the painters who adhere to the movement have been concerned to rid themselves of all but a narrow range of strictly pictorial considerations. The American critic Barbara Rose notes that:

in the process of self-definition, an art form will tend toward the elimination of all the elements which are not in keeping with its essential nature. According to this argument, visual art will be stripped of all extravisual meaning, whether literary or symbolic, and painting will reject all that is not pictorial.[1]

Rising out of what Jacques Barzun on one occasion described as the 'abolitionist' nature of Abstract Expressionism (referring to its apparent desire to do away with the art of the past), the new style rejected stratagems even more completely than Albers and Reinhardt.

The two painters who can be thought of as its real originators are Morris Louis (1912–62) and the veteran Abstract Expressionist Barnett Newman, though other Abstract Expressionists, such as Jack Tworkov (1900–82), also show some characteristics of Post-painterly abstraction in their later work; an example is the use of thinned paint, which gives a 'flat' look to the canvas.

68

By 1950 – that is, while Abstract Expressionism was at the height of its success – Newman's aims were already clear. He wanted to articulate the surface of the painting as a 'field', rather than as a composition, as, for example, in *Tundra*, on p. 82 – an ambition which went considerably beyond Pollock. Newman's way of achieving the effect he wanted was to allow the rectangle of the canvas to determine the pictorial structure. The canvas is divided, either horizontally or vertically, by a band, or bands. This line of division is used to activate the field, which is of intense colour, with some small variations of hue from one area to another. The American critic Max Kozloff declares that, in Newman's work, 'the colour is not used to overwhelm the senses, so much as in its curious muteness and dumbness, to shock the mind'. He adds: 'Newman habitually gives the impression of being out of control without being in the least bit passionate.'[2] Whether one agrees with this verdict or not, muteness and lack

69

of passion – 'coolness' in the slang sense of the term – were certainly to be characteristic of the new phase of American art.

With Newman, however, we still get the sense that the canvas is a surface to which pigment has been applied. Morris Louis differs from this, in being not so much a painter as a stainer. The colour is an integral part of the material the painter has used, and colour lives in the very weave of it.

More even than the leading Abstract Expressionists, Louis was an artist who arrived at his mature method by means of a sudden breakthrough. This suddenness is one of the things which has to be taken into account when discussing his work. Louis was not a New Yorker. He lived in Washington, and New York was a place he was notoriously reluctant to visit. In April 1953, Kenneth Noland, a friend and fellow painter, persuaded him to make the trip, both to meet the critic Clement Greenberg and to see something of what was currently being done by the New York artists. Louis was then aged forty-one, and had produced no work of more than minor significance up to that point.

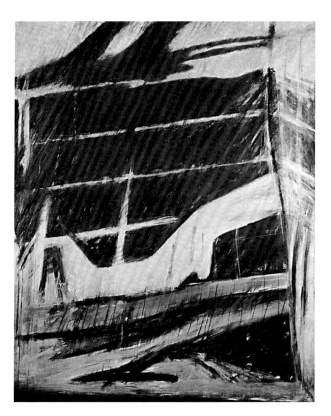

68. **Jack Tworkov**, *North American*, 1966

69. **Barnett Newman**, *Tundra*,
1950

70. **Ad Reinhardt**, *Red Painting*,
1952

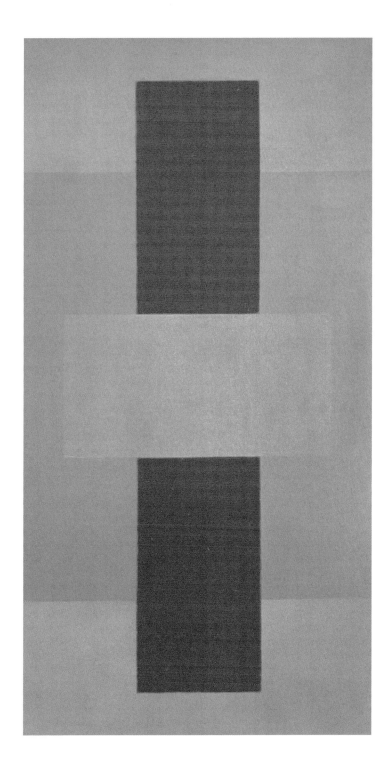

The trip was a success, and Louis was especially impressed by a painting by Helen Frankenthaler, *Mountains and Sea*, which he saw in her studio. The effect on his work was to draw him towards both Pollock and Frankenthaler as influences. Some months of experiment followed, but by the winter of 1954 he had suddenly arrived at a new way of painting. One aspect of its novelty was its technique, which Greenberg later described in this way: 72

Louis spills his paint on unsized and unprimed cotton duck canvas, leaving the pigment almost everywhere thin enough, no matter how many different veils of it are superimposed, for the eye to sense the threadedness and wovenness of the fabric underneath. But 'underneath' is the wrong word. The fabric, being soaked in paint rather than merely covered by it, becomes paint in itself, colour in itself, like dyed cloth; the threadedness and wovenness are in the colour.[3]

In fact, Louis achieved his originality partly through the exploitation of a new material, acrylic paint, which gave his paintings a very different physical make-up from those of the Abstract Expressionists. The staining process meant a revulsion against shape, against light and dark, in favour of colour. As Greenberg remarked: 'His revulsion against Cubism was a revulsion against the sculptural.' Even the shallow space which Pollock had inherited from the Cubists was henceforth to be avoided.

One of the advantages of the staining technique, so far as Louis was concerned, was the fact that he was able to put colour into colour. His early paintings after the breakthrough, such as *Untitled*, are veils of shifting hue and tone: there is no feeling that the various colour configurations have been drawn with a brush. Indeed, Louis did not 'paint' even in Pollock's sense, but poured, flooded, and scrubbed the colour into the canvas. This departure from the process of drawing was in some ways rather a reluctant one. In later experiments, Louis was to try and recover some of the advantages of traditional drawing for the stain medium. This is particularly true of the series of canvases called *Unfurleds*, which were painted in the spring and summer of 1961. Irregularly parallel rivulets of colour now appear in wing-like diagonals at the edges of large areas of canvas which are otherwise left unpainted, e.g. *Omicron*. Michael Fried remarks: 7374

The banked rivulets . . . open up the picture-plane more radically than ever, as though seeing the first marking we are for the first time shown the void. The dazzling blankness of the untouched canvas at once repulses and engulfs the eye, like an infinite abyss, the abyss that opens up behind the least mark that we make on a flat surface, or would *open up if innumerable conventions both of art and of practical life did not restrict the consequences of our act within narrow bounds.*[4]

Louis's final period of activity (he died of lung cancer in 1962) resulted in a series of stripe paintings, in which stripes of colour, usually of slightly different thicknesses, are bunched together some distance from the sides of the canvases. Fried feels that these show, as compared to the *Unfurleds* which preceded them, a further strengthening of the impulse to draw. Yet, in their strict, undeviating parallelism, the lines of colour seem inert, and this is true even where, in three paintings of this series, the stripes run diagonally across the canvas. Inertia, strict parallelism, and the constructive impulse (as shown by the paintings with diagonal stripes) were all characteristics which Louis shared with the other Post-painterly abstractionists.

Louis's friend and associate Kenneth Noland (b. 1924) was slower in making his own breakthrough, and therefore belongs to a later stage of the development of this new kind of abstract painting. Noland, like Louis, adopted the new technique of staining, rather than painting, the canvas. And like Louis, he tends to paint in series, using a single motif until he feels that he has exhausted its possibilities. The first important motif in Noland's work is a target shape of concentric rings, e.g. *Cantabile*. The pictures composed on this principle belong to the late 1950s and early 1960s. The target pattern was used, not as Jasper Johns 71

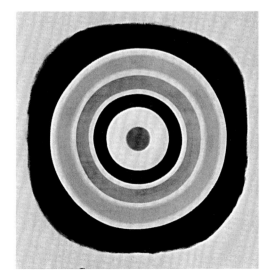

71. **Kenneth Noland**, *Cantabile*, 1962

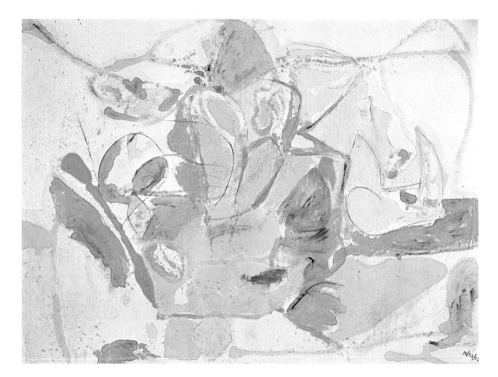

72. **Helen Frankenthaler**,
Mountains and Sea, 1952

73. **Morris Louis**, *Untitled*, 1959

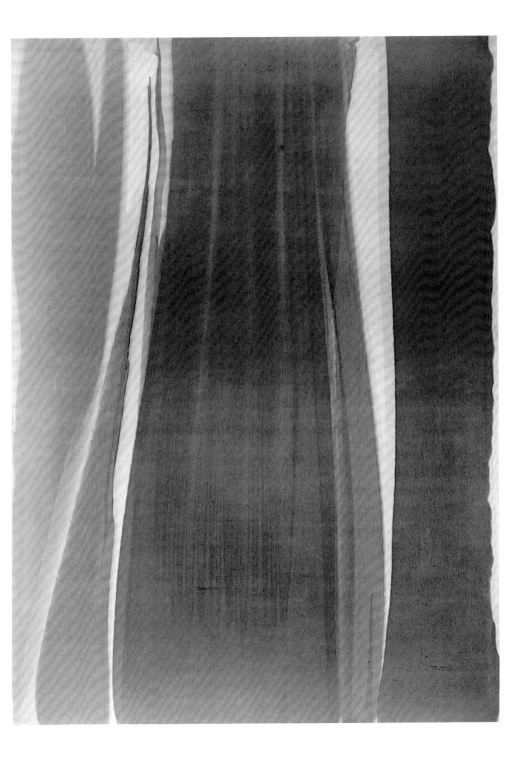

used it contemporaneously, with the deliberate intention of alluding to its banality, but as a means of concentrating the effect of the colour. Often the targets seem to spin against the background of unsized canvas, an effect produced by the irregular staining at their edges. Fried notes:

The raw canvas in Noland's concentric-ring paintings . . . fulfils much the same function as the coloured fields in Newman's large pictures around 1950; more generally, Noland in these paintings seems to have managed to charge the entire surface of the canvas with a kind of perceptual intensity which until that time only painters whose images occupy most or all of the picture-field – Pollock, Still, Newman, Louis – had been able to achieve.[5]

After experimenting with an ellipsoid shape which was no longer, in every case, in the exact centre of a square canvas, Noland began, in 1962, a series which used a chevron motif. *Grave Light* 75 is an example. This was the signal for a growing concern with the identity of the canvas simply as an object. The framing-edge began to have an importance which, on the whole, had not been accorded to it since Pollock. At first, Noland allowed the raw canvas to continue to play its part. But the chevrons suggested the possibility of a lozenge-shaped support – a kind of picture which would be wholly colour, without any neutral areas, with

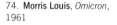

74. **Morris Louis**, *Omicron*, 1961

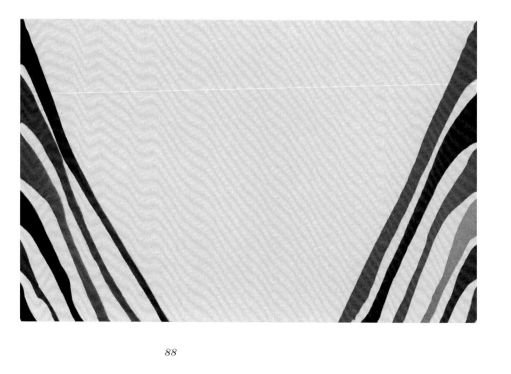

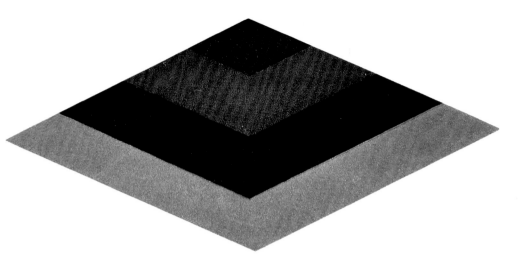

75. **Kenneth Noland**, *Grave Light*, 1965

the coloured bands moored to the bands of the frame. These canvases, like the late, diagonally striped paintings by Louis, have an obvious relationship to pictures by Mondrian, where the canvas is designed to be hung diagonally. The Abstract Expressionist and the Constructivist traditions here begin to draw together.

After a while, Noland's lozenges grew narrower and longer, and eventually the chevron pattern was abandoned for stripes running horizontally on enormous canvases, some of them more than thirty feet, nine metres, long. Colour is thus reduced to its simplest relationship, as in the late paintings by Louis, and all pretence at composition is abandoned. These late pictures show the extreme refinement of Noland's colour sensibility. As compared to his early work, the colour is paler and lighter. The tones are close together, which produces effects of optical shimmer, intensified by the sheer vastness of the field, which enfolds and swallows the eye. There is nothing painterly about the way in which the colour is applied; it does not even have the unevenness of Louis's stainings, and the colour-bands meet more crisply and decisively than Louis's stripes. Or, rather, they almost meet: on close examination they prove to be separated by infinitesimally narrow bands of raw canvas, an effect which Noland may have derived from the early paintings of Frank Stella (b. 1936).

Stella, though his work is often grouped with Louis's and with Noland's, is more of a 'structuralist' than a Post-painterly abstractionist. His concern is not so much with colour-as-colour, as with the painting-as-object, a thing which exists in its own right, and which is entirely self-referring. His work, however, does have a direct link to that of Barnett Newman.

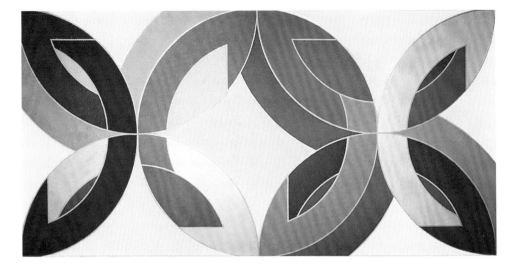

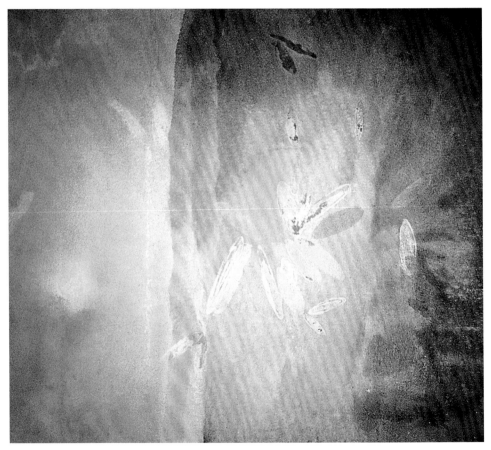

76. **Frank Stella**, *Untitled*, 1968

77. **Larry Poons**, *Night Journey*, 1968

78. **Jules Olitski**, *Feast*, 1965

The paintings which established Stella's reputation were those which were shown in the Museum of Modern Art exhibition 'Sixteen Americans' in 1960. They were all black canvases, patterned with parallel stripes about 2½ inches, over 6 cm, wide, a width chosen to echo the width of the wooden strips used for the picture support. Stella went on to execute further series of stripe paintings, in aluminium, copper and magenta paint. With the aluminium and copper paintings, Stella began to make use of shaped supports: from 1967, he turned to brilliantly-coloured shaped works interrelating semi-circles with rectangular or diamond shapes, e.g. *Untitled* reproduced in colour on p. 90. These 76 made the paintings not only objects to hang on the wall, but things which activated the whole wall-surface. There was then a period of experiment with paintings where the stripes were of different colours, followed by one where the shaped canvases fitted together in series to make serial compositions. Then came asymmetrical canvases painted in vivid colours which segmented the shapes, some of which were now curved. These works in turn developed into painted metal reliefs, with freely curved shapes attached to a background. Both these attached strips and the background itself were painted with a fluency which seemed to contradict the rigidity of Stella's earlier work, such as *New* 79 *Madrid* reproduced below, but the emphasis on structure as the subject of the painting was nevertheless still present.

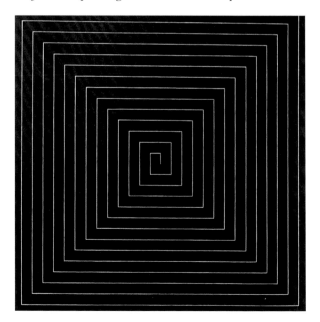

79. **Frank Stella**, *New Madrid*, 1961

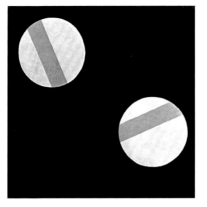

If Stella seemed inclined to flirt both with the earliest Modernism and with Pop art, another colour painter, Jules Olitski (b. 1922), experimented with what was essentially a critique of Abstract Expressionism. Olitski covered huge areas of canvas with tender stainings, e.g. *Feast*; these stained areas are often contrasted with a passage at the edge of the canvas in thick, luscious brushwork, reminiscent not so much of Pollock as of a European such as de Staël. The paintings themselves are usually vast. The paradox in Olitski's work is the hugeness of scale compared with the limitation of content – the pictures hint at an aesthetic position in order to deny it. The sweetness and prettiness are ironic, and yet at the same time truly meant and felt. More even than Noland's and Stella's work, these paintings address themselves to an informed audience.

The same might be said about the work of Larry Poons (b. 1937). Though Poons has sometimes been called an Op artist, his typical work makes it plain where his true allegiance lies. Essentially, his paintings consist of a coloured field, scattered at random with spots of contrasting colour. The eye is offered a multitude of points of focus, and skims about among them, without coming to rest. In Poons's earlier work, the optical effect is enhanced by the choice of tone and hue. The tones are close together, the hues in sharp contrast, which generates an afterimage in the eye. Later Poons enlarged the marks to eliminate this effect, as in *Night Journey*, and his work became more gestural.

Another American who was also a second-generation member of the Post-painterly abstractionist group was Edward Avedisian (b. 1936). His work, such as the one reproduced above, has close links with that of Poons of the early 1960s, and functions similarly.

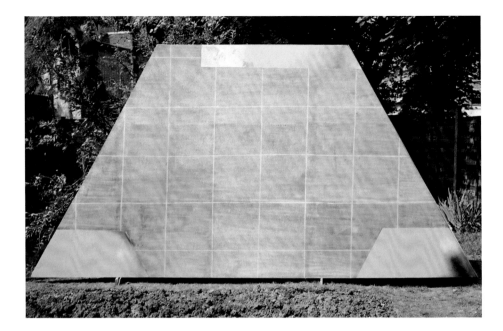

81. **John Walker**, *Touch – Yellow*, 1967

It is interesting to note that, while both Abstract Expressionism and Pop art scored very considerable triumphs in Europe, Post-painterly abstraction was not nearly so successful in making an impact on the European art scene. When Parisians spoke, sometimes rather bitterly, of the American rejection of 'our' painters, they were talking of the apparent dominance of Post-painterly abstraction in New York. The one country outside the United States where its ideas have gained a considerable foothold is Britain, and this is something which symbolizes the transfer of influence over British art.

For example, John Hoyland (b. 1934), one of the few British 85 artists with an American command of scale, is essentially in the tradition of Louis and Noland. His use of the acrylic paint medium is enough to affirm it. But Hoyland has sometimes received a hostile reaction from American reviewers for not being sufficiently *pur sang*, sufficiently reductionist. He seems to owe something important to Matisse and to Miró, and his paintings have clearly not abandoned all traditional ideas on the subject of composition. One can even detect references to de Staël, whom Hoyland at one time admired very much.

Robyn Denny's (b. 1930) paintings find their starting point in 83 the work of Josef Albers, and especially in the painting Albers produced in the 1940s. The design tends to be bilaterally symmetrical,

94

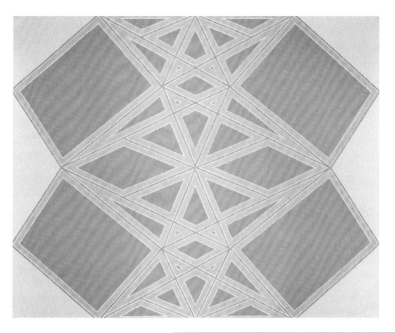

82. **Tess Jaray**, *Garden of Allah*, 1966

83. **Robyn Denny**, *Growing*, 1967

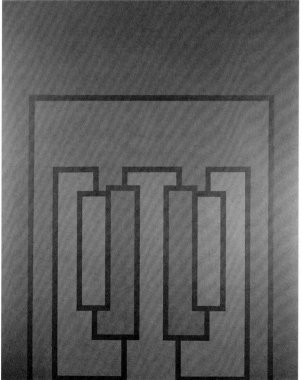

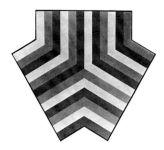

84. **Jeremy Moon**, *Blue Rose*, 1967

while the colours chosen are sharply contrasted in hue but carefully matched in tone. On a large scale, this produces a semi-optical effect, since the oblong colour-patches seem to move backwards and forwards in relationship to the main picture surface.

One of the things which seem to divide these British painters from their American colleagues is the fact that the British remain fascinated by pictorial ambiguity, and continue to juggle with effects of depth and perspective which are quite foreign to American art of the same kind. Work by painters such as John Walker (b. 1939), Paul Huxley (b. 1938), Jeremy Moon (1934–73), and Tess Jaray (b. 1939) all bears out this contention. Jaray's work makes the point particularly clearly, as one of its sources is perspective drawings of architecture.

For at least a decade, Post-painterly abstraction represented a kind of Modernist orthodoxy – it occupied the kind of position, in terms of intellectual prestige, that history painting enjoyed in the eighteenth century. Strong evidence of its success can still be seen in the work of certain Minimalist painters of the 1970s, such as Brice Marden (b. 1938) in the United States, and Bob Law (b. 1934) and Alan Charlton (b. 1948) in Britain. Because Post-painterly abstraction seemed to bring the possibilities offered by pure painting to a kind of conclusion, artists who wished to find their way forward were for a while inclined to abandon the idea of the painted canvas as a vehicle for what they wanted to do or say. This resulted in a great swing of attention towards sculpture, and also in an increasing number of experiments with mixed media.

85. **John Hoyland**, *28.5.66*, 1966

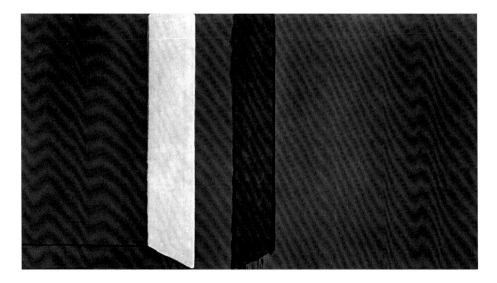

Chapter 4:   Pop, Environments and Happenings

Post-painterly abstraction, as I have described it, was a continuation of Abstract Expressionism, at least in part. Pop art was a reaction against it, and to begin with it was pop which caused a greater degree of uproar. Pop basically sprang from a shift of sources. Surrealism with its appeal to the subconscious, was replaced by Dada, with its concern with the frontiers of art. But this was not a purely intellectual choice. There were forces within Abstract Expressionism and *art informel* which propelled artists towards the new mode. For example, as Abstract Expressionism began to exhaust its impetus, the prevailing interest in texture led artists to ever-bolder experiments with materials. Some of these – with acrylic paint – were conducted by Morris Louis, and led to Post-painterly abstraction. But most consisted of a re-exploration of the possibilities of collage. Using collage involved an important philosophic step for an artist already familiar with informal abstraction. There, an interesting texture was something which the artist *created*, but collage additions came to his hand *ready-made*; and Marcel Duchamp's idea of the 'ready-made' was one of the central innovations of Dada. Collage had been invented by the Cubists as a means of exploring the differences between representation and reality. The Dadaists and Surrealists had greatly extended its range, and the Dadaists, in particular, had found it especially congenial, and in line with their preference for anti-art. In the hands of the post-war generation, collage now developed into the 'art of assemblage', a means of creating works of art almost entirely from pre-existent elements, where the artist's contribution was to be found more in making the links between objects, putting them together, than in making objects *ab initio*.

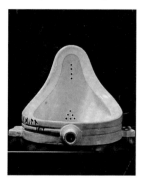

86. **Marcel Duchamp**, *Fountain*, 1951 replica of 1917 original

86

In 1961, the Museum of Modern Art in New York staged an important exhibition under the title 'The Art of Assemblage'. William C. Seitz remarked in his introduction to the catalogue:

The current wave of assemblage . . . marks a change from a subjective, fluidly abstract art towards a revised association with environment. The method of juxtaposition is an vehicle for feelings

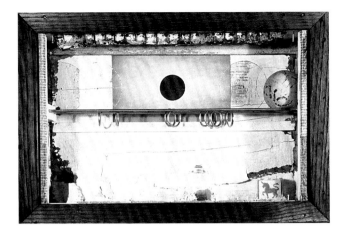

87. **Joseph Cornell**, *Eclipse series, c.*1962

of disenchantment with the slick international idiom that loosely articulated abstraction has tended to become, and the social values that this situation reflects.[1]

Assemblage was important for another reason too. It was not only that it provided a means of transition from Abstract Expressionism to the apparently very different preoccupations of Pop art, but it brought about a radical reconsideration of the formats within which the visual arts could operate. For example, assemblage provided a jumping-off point for two concepts which were to be increasingly important to artists: the environment and the Happening.

89. **Jasper Johns**, *Numbers in Colour*, 1959

88. **Enrico Baj**, *Lady Fabricia Trolopp*, 1964

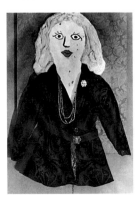

Of course, some practitioners of assemblage did not move very far beyond their original sources. The exquisite boxes made by Joseph Cornell (1903–72) – one of which, *Eclipse*, is characteristic – with their poetic, surrealistic juxtapositions of objects, and the witty collages of Enrico Baj (b. 1924), are things which explore the resources of a tradition, without seeking to enlarge them very radically. Other artists were not content with this. Most of them fall into the category which has now been rather slickly labelled Neo-Dada. One would prefer to say, rather, that they are often artists who want to explore the idea of the minimal, the unstable, the ephemeral in what they do.

87

88

In America, the two most-discussed exponents of Neo-Dada have undoubtedly been Robert Rauschenberg (b. 1925) and Jasper Johns (b. 1930). Of the two, Rauschenberg is the more various, and Johns the more elegant; elegance has a genuine, if rather uneasy, part to play in any discussion of what these two artists represent.

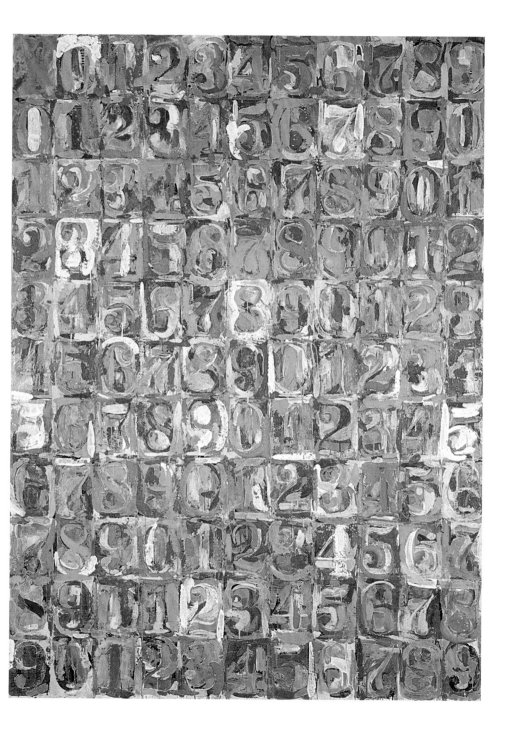

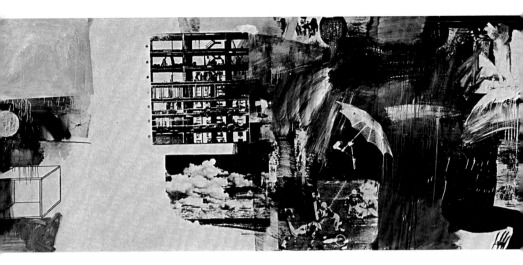

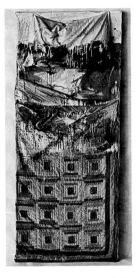

91. Robert Rauschenberg, *Bed*, 1955

Rauschenberg was born in Texas in 1925. In the late 1940s he studied at the Académie Julian in Paris, and then under Albers at Black Mountain College. In the early 1950s, Rauschenberg painted a series of all-white paintings where the only image was the spectator's own shadow. Later there was a series of all-black paintings. Neither of these developments was unique. The Italian painter Lucio Fontana (1899–1968) did a series of all-white canvases in 1946; the Frenchman Yves Klein (1928–62) exhibited his first monochromes in 1950 and, closer to home, were of course Ad Reinhardt's 'all black' paintings, also from the 1950s on. After these experiments with minimality, Rauschenberg began to move towards 'combine painting', an early example of which is *Bed*, a mode of creation in which a painted surface is combined with various objects which are affixed to that surface. Sometimes the paintings develop into free-standing three-dimensional objects, such as the famous stuffed goat which has appeared in so many exhibitions of contemporary American art. One painting makes use of a functioning wireless set, another of a clock. The artist has also used photographic images, which are silk-screened on to the canvas.

The aesthetic philosophy informing this is essentially that of the experimental composer John Cage (1919–92), whom Rauschenberg met in North Carolina. One of Cage's basic ideas is that of 'unfocusing' the spectator's mind: the artist does not create something separate and closed, but instead does something to make the spectator more open, more aware of himself and his environment. Cage says:

91

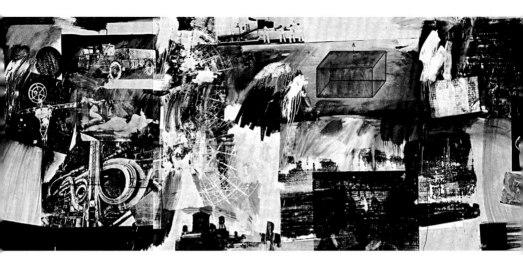

90. **Robert Rauschenberg,**
Barge, 1962

*New music; new listening. Not an attempt to understand something
that is being said, for, if something were being said, the sounds would
be given the shapes of words. Just an attention to the activity of
sounds.*[2]

A characteristic painting of Rauschenberg's, such as the enormous *Barge* painted in 1962, is a kind of reverie which the   90
spectators are invited to join; a flux of images which are not necessarily fixed and immutable. Cage remarks on 'the quality of
encounter' between Rauschenberg and the materials he uses; one
can compare this to the way in which Kurt Schwitters worked.
But Rauschenberg is a Schwitters who has passed through the
Abstract Expressionist experience.

So, for that matter, is Jasper Johns, though John's work gives
one the impression of greater discipline. Johns is also more of an
ironist. One work, entitled *The Critic Smiles*, is a toothbrush cast
in sculpmetal, placed upon a plinth of the same material. Unlike
Rauschenberg, Johns is chiefly known for his use of single, banal
images: a set of numbers, e. g. *Numbers in Colour*, a target, a map of   89
the United States, the American flag. The point about these
images is largely their lack of point – the spectator looks for a
specific meaning, the artist is largely preoccupied with creating
a surface. Where the manipulation of paint is concerned, as is
evident in *Numbers in Colour*, Johns is a master technician. The
way in which Johns operates also suggests links with other
things besides Pop art. Like Kenneth Noland, he is interested in
pictorial inertia, for example. One of the reasons for choosing

banal patterns is the fact that they no longer generate any energy. He is also interested in the idea of the painting as an object rather than as a representation. In some cases, he has used two canvases linked together, with a pair of wooden balls forced between them, so we see the wall behind at the point where they join. Other works have attachments: a ruler, a broom, a spoon.

It is clear from this description of the activities of these two artists that they represent a move away from 'pure' painting. Even to Johns, for all his virtuosity, painting is no more than a means of achieving a certain result, which might possibly be achieved some other way. Rauschenberg was for years associated with the Merce Cunningham dance company: he performed with them as well as devising props and scenery, and clearly this formed as important and central a part of his activity as painting and making objects.

One of the directions suggested by a painting like *Barge* is the move towards the tableau, the work of art which surrounds or nearly surrounds the spectator. The bulky and ferocious assemblages and installations of Edward Kienholz (1927–94) are an example.

92

Kienholz also represents one aspect of the tendency which is often called 'funk', or Funk art: the liking for the complex, the sick, the tatty, the bizarre, the shoddy, the vicious, the overtly or covertly sexual, as opposed to the impersonal purity of a great deal of contemporary art. Perhaps because if offers this kind of alternative, Funk art proved more than a passing fashion. It was responsible for some of the most alarming images of the 1960s – things such as Bruce Conner's (b. 1933) *Couch* of 1963, which shows an apparently murdered and dismembered corpse lying on a crumbling Victorian sofa, or Paul Thek's (b. 1933) *Death of a Hippie*, or various tableaux by the Englishman, Colin Self (b. 1941). A characteristic one is another corpse, a figure entitled *Nuclear Victim*.

93

95

In Europe, an equivalent of the American Neo-Dadaists was supplied by what is sometimes called New Realism, after the movement founded by the French critic Pierre Restany, in conjunction with Yves Klein and others. Restany claimed that 'the new realism registers the sociological reality without any controversial intention'. What this means one may perhaps deduce from the work of Arman (b. 1928), who was one of the adherents of the group. Arman's most characteristic works consist of random accumulations of objects, e.g. *Clic-Clac Rate*, but objects all of the same sort, encased in clear plastic. These accumulations can

94

92. **Edward Kienholz**, *Roxy's*, 1961

93. **Bruce Conner**, *Couch*, 1963

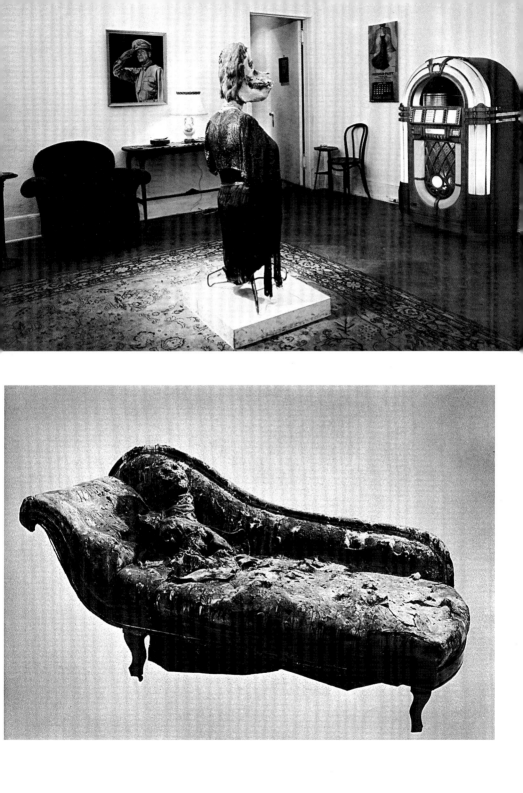

exist as panels, or can be three-dimensional. For example, Arman has made a plastic torso of a woman, filled with writhing rubber gloves. Another artist attracted by the systematic is Christo (b. 1935), who is best known for his packages, mysterious lumpish objects which sometimes suggest and sometimes wholly conceal what is wrapped up in them, and especially for his spectacular and poetic wrapped public buildings and landscapes. 96

The major personality among these European Neo-Dadaists was undoubtedly Yves Klein, an example of an artist who was important for what he did – the symbolic value of his actions – rather than for what he made. One sees in him an example of the increasing tendency for the personality of the artist to be his or her one true and complete creation.

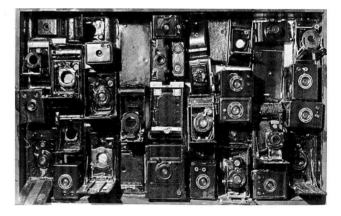

94. **Arman**, *Clic-Clac Rate*, 1960–6

95. **Paul Thek**, *Death of a Hippie*, 1967

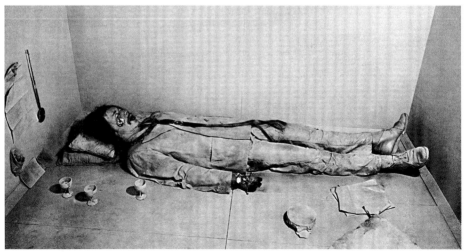

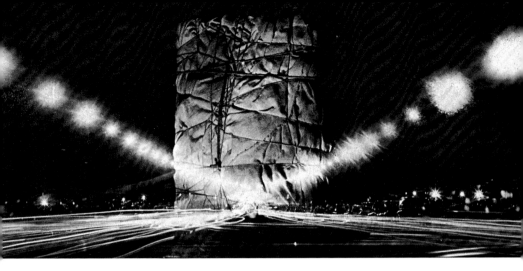

96. **Christo**, *Packaged Public Building*, 1961

Klein was born in 1928. He was a jazz musician, a Rosicrucian, and a judo expert (he studied judo in Japan and wrote a book about it which is still a standard text). In judo, the opponents are regarded as collaborators, and it is this notion which seems to underlie a great deal of Klein's thinking about art. So does the wish to 'get away from the idea of art'. Klein said:

The essential of painting is that something, that 'ethereal glue', that intermediary product which the artist secretes with all his creative being and which he has the power to place, to encrust, to impregnate into the pictorial stuff of the painting.[3]

Besides creating his monochromes (see p. 100), Klein adopted various unorthodox methods of producing works of art. For example, he used a flame-thrower, or the action of rain on a prepared canvas. (Paintings produced by the action of the elements he labelled *Cosmogonies*.) At his direction girls smeared with blue paint flung themselves on to canvas spread on the floor. The ceremony was conducted in public while twenty musicians played Klein's *Monotone Symphony*, a single note sustained for ten minutes which alternated with ten minutes' silence. The making of these *Imprints* is recorded in the film *Mondo Cane*. On another occasion – in Paris in 1958 – Klein held an exhibition of emptiness: a gallery painted white, with all the furniture removed and a Garde Républicain stationed at the door. Albert Camus came, and wrote the words 'with the void, full powers' in the visitors' book. There were thousands of other visitors to the *vernissage*, so many as to cause a near-riot. Another of Klein's ideas was to offer for sale 'zones of immaterial pictorial sensitivity'. They

100

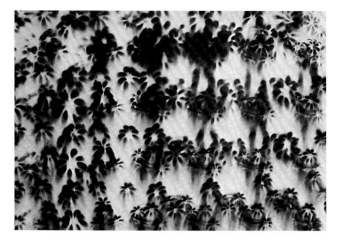

98. Lucio Fontana, *Spatial Concept*, 1960

99. Piero Manzoni, *Line 20 Metres Long*, 1959

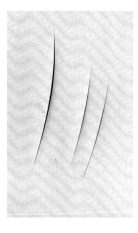

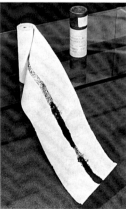

were paid for in gold-leaf, which the artist immediately threw in the Seine, while the purchaser burned his receipt.

These actions have a certain poetic rightness to them, a quality often absent from the clumsier and more elaborate happenings staged in New York. Klein, at the time of his death in 1962, seemed to stand at the meeting-point of a number of different tendencies. There is the obvious connection with the original Dadaists, and also with certain contemporary artists who stand on the fringes of Dada, such as Lucio Fontana, whose own experiments with monochromes developed into the more familiar slashed canvases. Also reminiscent of Klein's work are the 'lines' of Pietro Manzoni (1933–63): single, unbroken brushstrokes which unroll on long strips of paper. All of these, in turn, are linked in a more general way with the tendency towards minimality in sculpture. On the other hand, Klein, as much as Johns and Rauschenberg, is one of the prophets of Pop art. His use of monotony, of the undifferentiated, gives him something in common with Andy Warhol, for instance.

But only *something* in common. Neo-Dada and Pop art are not identical, though Neo-Dada includes Pop. The artists I have so far spoken of in this chapter are not, in my view, genuine practitioners of Pop, though their work has been included in exhibitions and discussed in books under that label. The factors which created Pop art were not universal, but had much to do with the urban culture of Britain and America in the years after the war. Only artists in close touch with that culture caught its special tone and idiom: of all the post-war styles, this is the one which most conspicuously has 'a local habitation and a name'.

After Pop scored its initial success, it did, very naturally, exercise an influence elsewhere. Many of the artists connected with Pierre Restany's New Realism toyed with it. There are, for instance, Michelangelo Pistoletto's (b. 1933) photographic figures fastened to mirror backgrounds in which the spectator sees himself reflected, thus completing the composition; and Martial Raysse's (b. 1936) skilful parodies of painters such as Prud'hon. In a version of Prud'hon's *Cupid and Psyche* entitled *Tableau simple et doux*, Cupid holds a neon heart in his fingers. Another Frenchman, Alain Jacquet (b. 1939), uses photographic images in a way which is reminiscent of both Warhol and Lichtenstein. The Japanese have been almost equally eager to catch up with Pop. Tomio Miki (b. 1938) has made almost as much a speciality of ears in cast aluminium as Warhol has of endlessly repeated images of Marilyn Monroe. In examining these works, however, one is aware that the involvement with the urban environment is not as immediate as it seems to be in the case of the leading British and American Pop artists.

It now seems to be generally agreed that Pop art, in its narrowest definition, began in England, and that it grew out of a series of discussions which were held at the Institute of

101

102

103

100. Yves Klein,
Anthropometries of the Blue Period, 1960

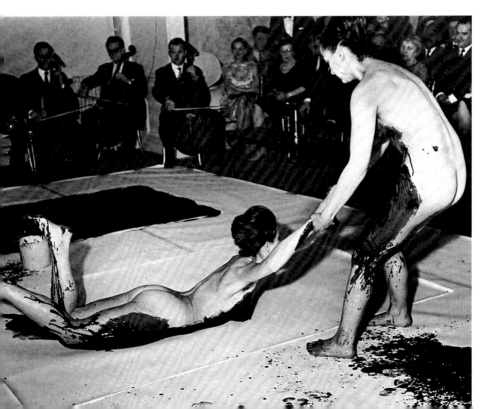

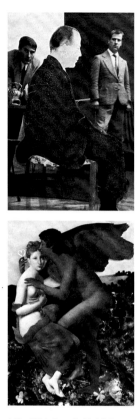

Contemporary Arts in London by a group that called itself the Independent Group. It included artists, critics, and architects, among them Eduardo Paolozzi (b. 1924), Alison and Peter Smithson (1928–93, b. 1923), Richard Hamilton (b. 1922), Peter Reyner Banham (1922–88), and Lawrence Alloway (1926–90). The group were fascinated by the new urban popular culture, and particularly by its manifestations in America. Partly this was a delayed effect of the war, when America, to those in England, had seemed an Eldorado of all good things, from nylons to new motor-cars. Partly it was a reaction against the solemn romanticism, the atmosphere of high endeavour, which had prevailed in British art during the 1940s.

In 1956 the group was responsible for an exhibition at the Whitechapel Art Gallery, 'This Is Tomorrow'. The show was designed in twelve sections to draw the spectator into a series of environments. In his book on Pop art, Mario Amaya points out that this probably owed something to Richard Buckle's exhibition of the Diaghilev Ballet, held in London in 1954, and which seized on the excuse of a theatrical subject to provide a brilliantly theatrical display.[4] From the point of view of the future, however, probably the most significant part of 'This Is Tomorrow' was an entrance display provided by Richard Hamilton – a collage picture entitled *Just What is it that Makes Today's Homes so Different, so Appealing?* In the picture are a muscle-man from a 104

101. **Michelangelo Pistoletto**, *Seated Figure*, 1962 (with Pistoletto)

102. **Martial Raysse**, *Tableau simple et doux*, 1965

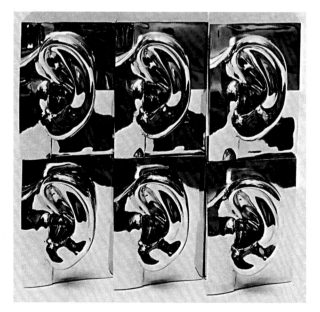

103. **Tomio Miki**, *Ears* (detail), 1968

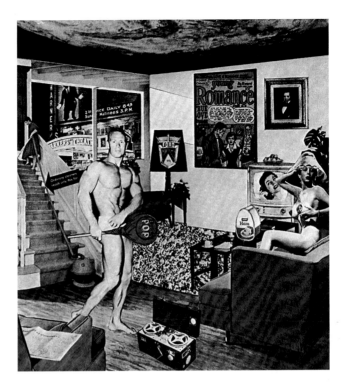

104. **Richard Hamilton**, *Just What is it that Makes Today's Homes so Different, so Appealing?*, 1956

physique magazine and a stripper with sequinned breasts. The muscle-man carries a gigantic lollipop, with the word pop on it in large letters. With this work, many of the conventions of Pop art were created, including the use of borrowed imagery.

Hamilton already knew clearly what he thought a truly modern art should be. The qualities he was looking for were, so he said in 1957, popularity, transience, expendability, wit, sexiness, gimmickry, and glamour.[5] It must be low-cost, mass produced, young, and Big Business. These were the qualities that British Pop artists of the 1960s were afterwards to worship. But granted Hamilton's priority, and that of the Independent Group, it is still a little difficult to prove that Pop art sprang directly from their activities. Of all the artists who belonged to the group, Hamilton himself is the only one who can be classified as a Pop painter. In addition, there is the fact that he has always been a very slow worker, and that, at this period, little of his work was to be seen in England.

There were two other British painters who might be labelled 'transitional', both of them, as it happens, among the most interesting that Britain has produced in recent years. Both were

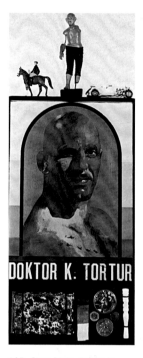

105. **Peter Blake**, *Doktor K. Tortur*, 1965

106. **Richard Smith**, *Soft Pack*, 1963

students at the Royal College of Art in the mid-1950s. One is Peter Blake (b. 1932), who would classify himself unhesitatingly as a 'realist'. Blake's work represents a reversion to the tradition of the Pre-Raphaelites in the middle of the twentieth century. Like the Pre-Raphaelites, he is nostalgic, but not for the Middle Ages. What he looks back on is the popular culture of the 1930s and 1940s. Unlike other Pop painters, Blake is always concerned to be a little out of date. His house is crammed with memorabilia – postcards, seaside souvenirs, toys, knick-knacks of every sort – and out of these is distilled a very personal poetry.

Richard Smith (b. 1931) represents an attitude that is almost the opposite of this. As a student, he painted in a figurative style which was influenced by the Euston Road School and the Kitchen Sink painters. He was still at the Royal College at the time of 'This Is Tomorrow', and on him, at least, the show had a demonstrable influence. During 1957–9 he shared a studio with Peter Blake, but in 1959 he left for America, and at first divided his time between England and the United States before settling there permanently. Smith's earliest characteristic works were based on packaging. He was also influenced by colour photography, the kind of thing to be found in magazines such as *Vogue*.

His colour sensibility remained unaltered through subsequent changes of direction. He himself describes his colour as 'sweet and tender', and speaks of wanting to give 'a general sense of blossoming, ripening, and shimmering', but the work itself has shed any overt association with Pop. What Smith has done is to pass through the experience of Pop art in order to arrive at a position which approximates to that of the American colour painters. His change to acrylic paint in 1964 was an important step in this process. So was his abandonment of conventional formats in favour of canvases stretched over three-dimensional frames, and his adoption, later, of shapes constructed like kites.

Smith, because he had successfully established himself in New York, meant a lot to his English colleagues, both as an example and as an influence. When he returned to England in 1961, he brought with him on-the-spot information about the activities of artists such as Jasper Johns which had an impact on artists such as Peter Phillips (b.1939) and Derek Boshier (b. 1937). Smith had already absorbed the American indifference to conventional limitations of format, and the American sense of scale, for example.

The key date in British Pop was 1961, not so much because of Smith's resumption of contact with British artists, but because of the Young Contemporaries exhibition which was held in that

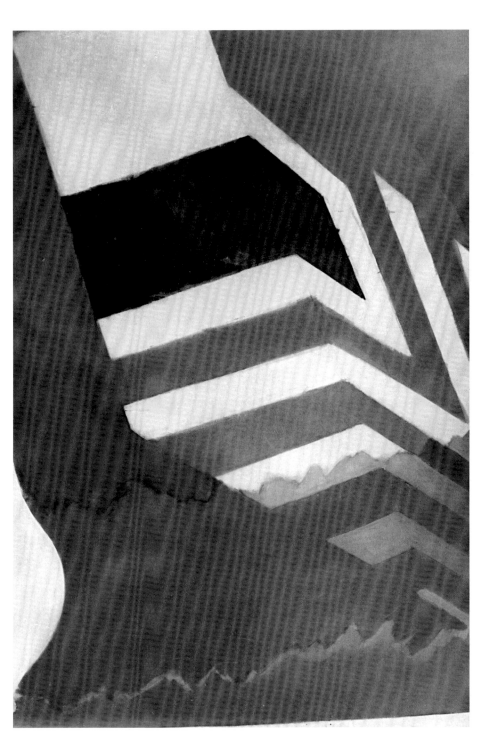

109. **David Hockney**, *Rubber Ring Floating in a Swimming Pool*, 1971

110. **Richard Smith**, *Tailspan*, 1965

107. **Peter Phillips**, *For Men Only Starring MM and BB*, 1961

108. **Derek Boshier**, *England's Glory*, 1961

year. This caused perhaps the greatest sensation of any student show held since the war. The reason was the presence of a group of young artists from the Royal College of Art: Phillips, Boshier, Allen Jones (b. 1937), and David Hockney (b. 1937). Exhibiting with them was a slightly older American student, R. B. Kitaj (b. 1932) who, like Smith, had a first-hand knowledge of American techniques, and he fostered the new obsession with popular imagery among his fellow students.

One of the weaknesses of British Pop art was its easy and rapid success. England, so far as the visual arts were concerned, was at last moving out of its phase of insularity (in literature, insularity was to last much longer). The hedonism of the late 1950s had taken root, and the new artists seemed to offer precisely the gay, impudent, pleasure-centred art which fitted the mood of the times. But modern artists of any talent were still thin on the ground, and the young lions of Pop did not meet with much competition.

It soon became clear that the artists who were grouped together after their spectacular début at the Young Contemporaries were temperamentally very different. Phillips was the most genuinely interested in popular imagery, but used it in a rigid and

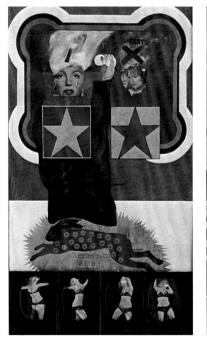

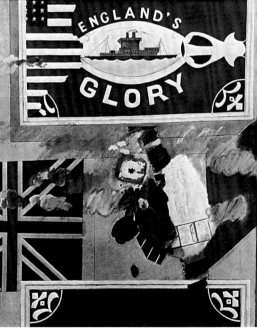

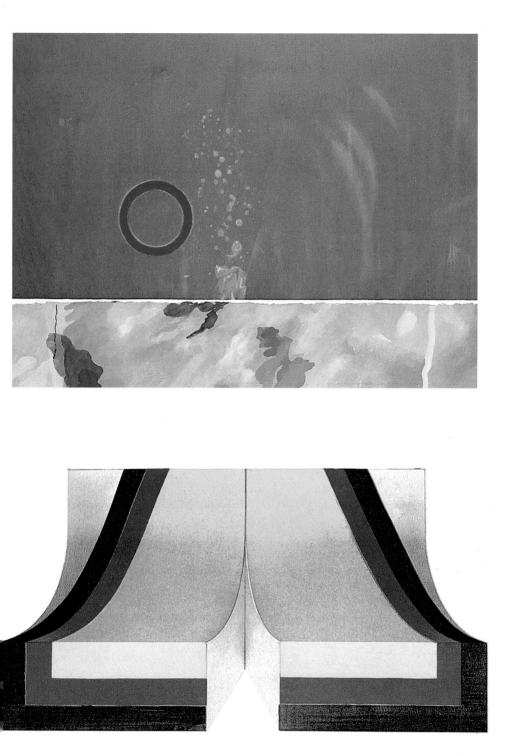

boringly dogmatic way. Boshier came under the influence of Richard Smith and veered away from figurative imagery in the direction of Op art. More capricious and personal than either of these two were Hockney and Jones.

Hockney is an artist who has had an interesting if slightly erratic development. He began as the *Wunderkind* of British art. His life-style was instantly famous; his dyed blond hair, owlish glasses, and gold lamé jacket created – or contributed to – a persona which appealed even to people who were not vitally interested in painting. In this sense, he forms part of the general development of British culture which was symbolized by the sudden and enormous fame of the Beatles. But it was also clear that Hockney was precociously gifted. In his early work, he adopted a cartooning, *faux-naïf* style which owed a lot to children's drawings. Often these early pictures have a delightful deadpan irony.

Some of Hockney's most characteristic work at this time was to be found in his prints. The suite of etchings entitled *The Rake's Progress* chronicles his reactions to the dream-world of America, which he visited for the first time in 1961. They reflect profoundly

109
111
112

111. **David Hockney**, *Picture Emphasizing Stillness*, 1962–3 (inscription: THEY ARE PERFECTLY SAFE, THIS IS A STILL)

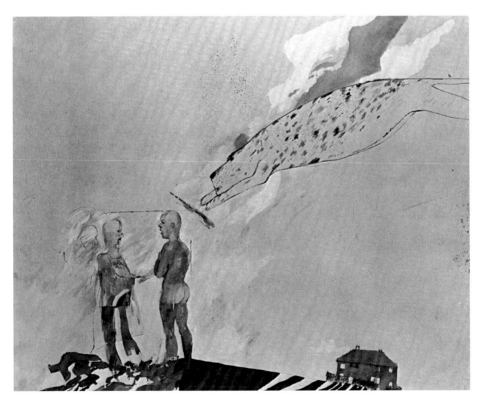

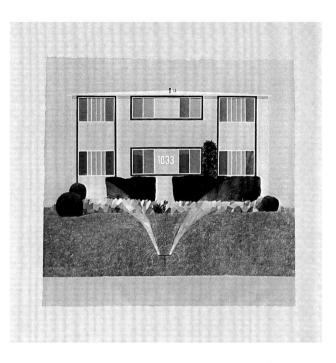

ambiguous attitudes. The comment is often sharp – the *Bedlam scene*, for instance, shows a group of automata governed by the pocket transistor radios which have become part of their anatomy – but the overall tone of the series is one of avid enjoyment.

Soon, the precarious poise of these early works was threatened. Hockney's painting became increasingly dry, increasingly pre-occupied with naturalism. Some middle-period paintings of the Californian landscape have, it is true, become classics – American critics have compared them to Edward Hopper (1882–1967). Others are disconcertingly dull. Eventually Hockney found naturalism confining, and he made a series of paraphrases of classic modern art, paying especial attention to Picasso. At the same time he became increasingly pre-occupied with photography, made a large series of photo-collages, which he called *Cameraworks*, and through his photographic experiments which raised issues about the representation of space; later still he returned to quasi-abstract paintings where the viewer wanders in space.

Allen Jones, like Hockney, is an artist whose early work was captivating because it radiated an air of enjoyment not unspiced with satirical humour. The most 'painterly' of all the British Pop painters, he seems to have learned a great deal from Matisse

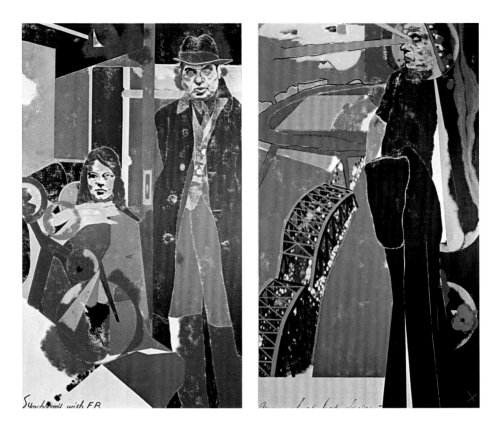

113. **R.B. Kitaj**, *Synchromy with F.B. – General of Hot Desire (diptych)*, 1968–9

where colour is concerned. There is also a debt to the Orphism of Robert Delaunay. Jones is a less narrative artist than Hockney: he is interest in metamorphoses, transformations, visual ambiguities. A series of *Hermaphrodites* (male/female images melting into one another on the same canvas) seem particularly characteristic of his work. Jones has shown a particularly deft and ingenious fancy with shaped canvases: a series of paintings of *Marriage Medals*, done in 1963, is made up of tall vertical canvases to which octagonal canvases are attached.

Jones resembles Hockney rather less happily because he too seems to have had trouble in deepening and developing his work. It has had a tendency to grow increasingly harder and more strident; the colour has left the comfortable 'fine art' tradition of the Fauves. This shows up the extreme thinness of content. The artist insists that the subject-matter of his work has always been of secondary interest to him, but one becomes more and more aware of its insistent banality, a banality that does not seem to have been adopted with any doctrinaire purpose in mind.

114

114. **Allen Jones**, *Hermaphrodite*, 1963

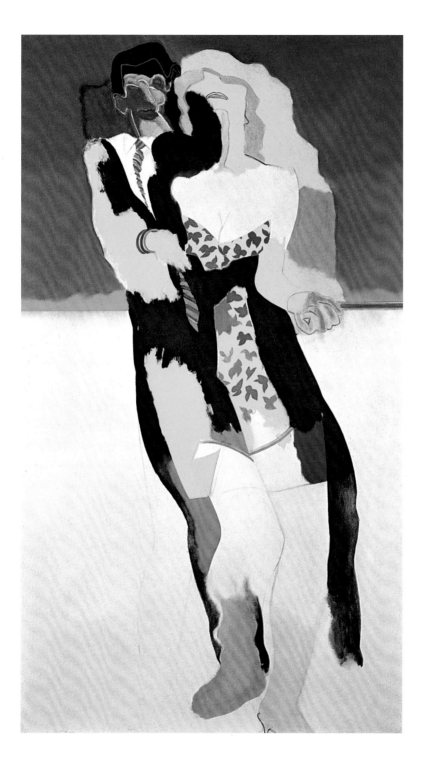

No one could accuse R. B. Kitaj's work of lack of complexity. The term 'Pop' has to be stretched rather far to cover his work. Kitaj is a hermetic artist; the best comparison is a literary one, in that his paintings are often rather like the *Cantos* of Ezra Pound. In them, one finds dense patterns of eclectic imagery. Often the painter requires that the spectator should try and match his own experience. The catalogue of one of Kitaj's exhibitions tends to pile footnote on footnote, in the endeavour to explain the complexity of his source material. These sources are more likely to be *The Journal of the Warburg Institute* than a favourite comic strip. One's approach to Kitaj's work must be intellectual. He is a dedicated and increasingly excellent draughtsman, and a rather dry colourist. Because his painting is so nearly a form of literature, it sometimes seemed that his prints were more successful than his paintings, and in the 1960s and early 1970s a good deal of his production was graphics, mostly silk-screen prints which used this flexible medium with great ingenuity. From the 1970s his work deepened in meaning and allusion to autobiographical and Jewish themes in increasingly narrative paintings executed in a looser, expressive manner.

115. **Patrick Caulfield**, *Still-life with Red and White Pot*, 1966

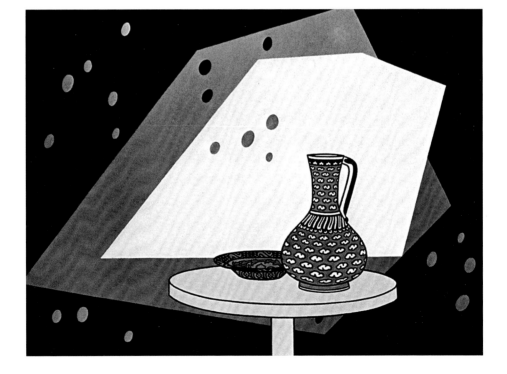

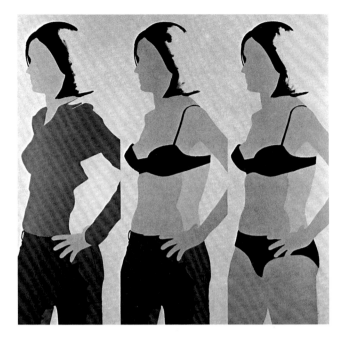

There are one or two other artists in Britain who have also been associated by critics with the Pop movement, though they stand a little apart from the rest. One is Anthony Donaldson (b. 1939), who uses Pop imagery – nude or near-nude girls – as components in pictures which are closer to 'hard edge' abstract painting than they are to Pop itself. This is because the girls are usually no more than silhouettes, and the silhouettes take their place among the other shapes in the composition. When the girls are omitted, the effect is still much the same. Another is Patrick Caulfield (b. 1936), who is a little younger than the other members of the 'Pop generation'. He did not leave the Royal College of Art until 1963. Caulfield is better described as a cliché painter than as a Pop painter. His characteristic subject is the department store reproduction, the kind of image that commonly appears in cheap prints, on plastic trays, or in the kits which invite the amateur to 'paint by numbers'. Every shape he uses, every object he depicts, is described by a hard unvaried line, which looks as if it has been printed rather than painted. The colour is equally without modulation. Caulfield is intent on exploring the relationship between fine art and mass culture, and particularly the debased ways of seeing which mass culture seems to encourage. He is thus not fully committed to the Pop ethos, but is, rather, a pitiless critic of it.

116

115

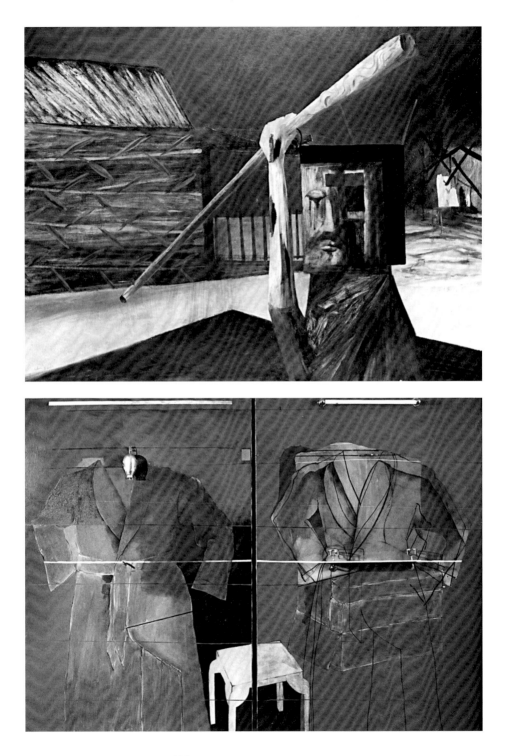

Before moving on to discuss the American Pop artists, who are in several ways very different from their British counterparts, I must say something about a group of Australian artists who have a much greater relevance to the genesis of Pop art than is generally admitted. The success of contemporary Australian art in London in the years after the war was one of the phenomena of art-dealing. The spearhead of this success was Sidney Nolan (1917–92), and the pictures which created his reputation were a series devoted to the career of the Australian outlaw Ned Kelly. 117 The earliest *Ned Kelly* paintings date from the 1940s, and thus antedate Pop by some years. In them, Nolan, who had been an abstract painter, established a new, *faux-naïf* style as a vehicle for a fairly sophisticated Australian nationalism.

Nationalism contributed to the sudden and overwhelming success of American Pop art. Americans found in it a truthful reflection of the society which surrounded them, and they also saw an assertion of the uniqueness of the American vision. It is not too much to claim that Pop led to the construction or reconstruction of American art history, so as to make a larger place for artists such as Hopper, and even (further back) for paint-

117. **Sidney Nolan**, *Glenrowan*, 1956–7

ers like Frederick Edwin Church (1826–1900).

The American Pop artists were discovered and promoted by collectors and dealers. The critics and theorists lagged a long way behind these enthusiasts. Indeed, the American art establishment considered, and to some extent still seems to consider, the triumph of Pop art as a rejection of itself and of the direction it had chosen to encourage. A leading advocate of Abstract Expressionism, Harold Rosenberg, had this to say about the new direction:

Certainly, Pop art earned the right to be called a movement through the number of its adherents, its imaginative pressure, the quantity of talk it generated. Yet if Abstract Expressionism had too much staying power, Pop was likely to have too little. Its congenital superficiality, while having the advantage of permitting the artist an almost limitless range of familiar subjects to exploit (anything from doilies to dining-club cards), resulted in a qualitative monotony that could cause interest in still another gag of this kind to vanish overnight. . . . Abstract Expressionism still excels in quality, significance and capacity to bring out new work; adding the production of its veterans to that of some of its younger artists it continues to be the front runner in the 'What next?' steeplechase.[6]

118. **Jim Dine**, *Double Red Self-portrait (The Green Lines)*, 1964

In effect, Pop art challenged Abstract Expressionism – or seemed to challenge it – in three different ways. It was figurative, where

Abstract Expressionism was mostly abstract; it was 'newer' than Abstract Expressionism; and it was 'more American'.

The principal American Pop artists – Dine, Oldenburg, Rosenquist, Lichtenstein, and Warhol – differed fairly widely from one another. Jim Dine (b. 1935) and Claes Oldenburg (b. 1929) were the closest to the Neo-Dadaists whom I have already discussed. Dine, in particular, has two qualities which link him very closely to Rauschenberg and Johns: he is essentially a combine or assemblage painter, and his subject is the different varieties of reality. In a characteristic work by Dine, a 'ready-made' object or objects – an article of dress, a wash-basin, a shower, some tools – is fastened to canvas, and an environment is created for it with freely brushed paint. Often, whatever is presented is carefully labelled with its name.

Oldenburg, too, experimented with efforts of displacement. His objects hover between the realms of sculpture and painting. These objects range from such things as giant hamburgers to squashy models of wash-basins and egg-beaters. Often these things are made of vinyl stuffed with kapok. Oldenburg said:

I use naïve imitation. This is not because I have no imagination or because I wish to say something about the everyday world. I imitate 1. objects and 2. created objects, for example, signs, objects made without the intention of making 'art' and which naïvely contain a functional contemporary magic. I try to carry these even further through my own naïveté, which is not artificial. Further, i.e. charge them more intensely, elaborate their reference. I do not try to make 'art' of them. This must be understood. I imitate these because I want people to get accustomed to recognizing the power of objects, a didactic aim.[7]

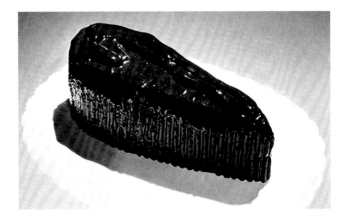

119. **Claes Oldenburg**, *Study for Giant Chocolate*, 1966

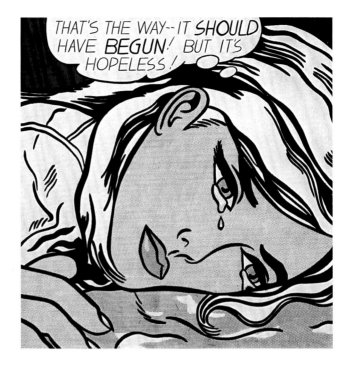

Therefore he, too, is interested in reality, with an element of totemism added.

James Rosenquist (b. 1933) and Roy Lichtenstein (1923–97) differ from Dine and Oldenburg because to a large extent they accept the limitations of the flat surface, and because they are formalists. At the moment, it seems to be Lichtenstein who has been elevated to a status above the others. He was not as hostile to the word 'art' as Oldenburg. He said, for example, that 'organized perception is what art is all about'. He added that the act of looking at a painting 'has nothing to do with any external form the painting takes, it has to do with a way of building a unified pattern of seeing'.

Lichtenstein's earlier work was based on comic strips, as in *Whaam!* and *Hopeless*; even the dots which are part of the process of cheap colour printing are meticulously reproduced. The artist once said to an interviewer:

I think my work is different from comic strips – but I wouldn't call it transformation. . . . What I do is form, whereas the comic strip is not formed in the sense I'm using the word; the comics have shapes, but there has been no effort to make them intensely unified. The purpose

121
120

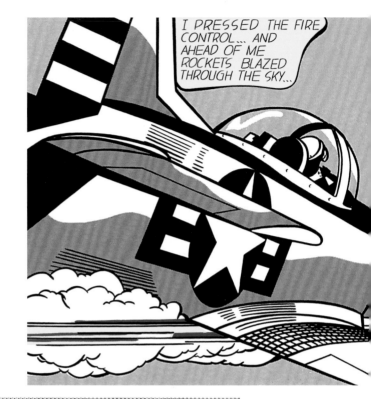

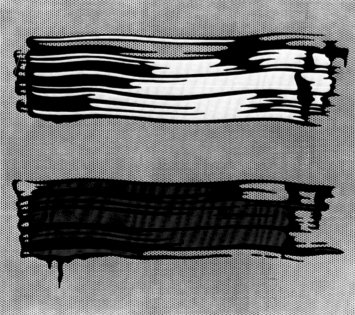

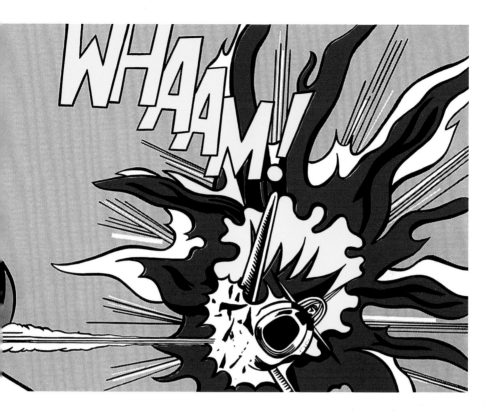

121. **Roy Lichtenstein**, *Whaam!*, 1963

is different, one intends to depict and I intend to unify. And my work is actually different from comic strips in that every mark is really in a different place, however slight the difference seems to some.[8]

That is, the imagery is in part a strategy, a means of binding together the picture surface. Another aim can be seen most clearly in the series of *Brushstrokes*, e.g. *Yellow and Red Brushstrokes*: meticulous, frozen versions (in comic-strip technique) of the marks which an Abstract Expressionist artist might have made with one sweep of the brush. The series is an experiment in 'removal': a word which crops up fairly often in Lichtenstein's discourse. It is also an attempt to make the audience question its own values.

    This raises the question of the values put forward by the Pop artists themselves. One of the most characteristic and disturbing aspects of Pop art is the fact that, though figurative, it often seems unable to make use of the image observed at first hand. To be viable, its images must have been processed in some way. Rosenquist declared: 'I treat the billboard image as it is. I paint

122. **Roy Lichtenstein**, *Yellow and Red Brushstrokes*, 1966

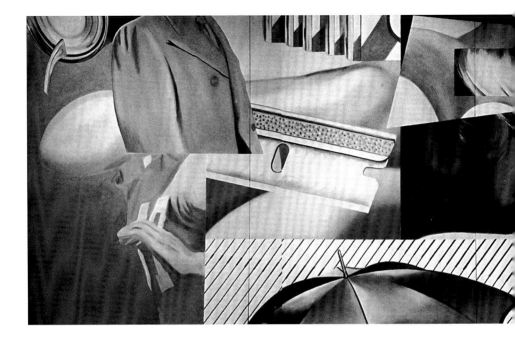

it as a reproduction of other things. I try to get as far away from it as possible.'[9] His fragments of billboard imagery were rearranged into virtual abstractions, as in *Silver Skies*. Similarly, the still lifes and nudes of Tom Wesselmann (b. 1931), e.g. *Still-life No. 34* and *Great American Nude No. 44*, are assemblages, or collages of flat, found photographic images of consumer goods; the faceless nudes are silhouettes from which the human presence fades.

123
124
126

Larry Rivers (b. 1923) is an artist who may be thought of as 'near-Pop'. Yet he paints in a way which might delight admirers of the Impressionists, of Manet in particular. The imagery he uses sometimes recalls Pop subjects, such as product packaging or the design of banknotes. His rendering of such images, however, is always painterly, not flat, not like a mechanical reproduction. And he also paints directly from nature. Some of his paintings, such as *Parts of the Face*, are treated as a vocabulary lesson – a female nude is carefully labelled with the names of the parts of the body, in French, not in English. Other paintings are fragmented accounts of a particular experience, for example a street accident. The outstanding visual characteristic of his work is a kind of glancing obliqueness, as if the artist were unable to focus on the actual subject for very long at a time.

125

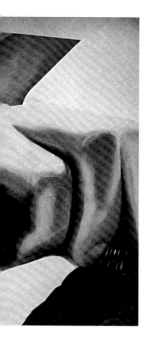

George Segal (1924–2000) showed much the same helplessness when confronted with an objective reality. His sculptures were made, not by a process of modelling, but by making life-casts of the subjects, almost as if the artist didn't trust his own vision of them.

The most controversial, as well as the most famous, of all the American Pop artists is Andy Warhol (1928–87), whose activities go far beyond the conventional boundaries of painting: he made numerous films, he directed a night-club entertainment, the Velvet Underground, and the kind of notoriety he enjoyed was like that accorded to a famous actor or film star. When the first retrospective of Warhol's work was held, in Philadelphia in 1965, the crush at the private view was so great that some of the exhibits had to be removed, for fear of damage. It was clearly the artist himself, and not his products, whom the visitors wished to see.

Yet Warhol's attitudes towards the notion of 'personality' are ambiguous. On the one hand, he labelled the performers in his films 'super-stars', on the other hand he declared that he himself wanted to be a machine, something which made, not paintings, but industrial products. Samuel Adams Green, in his introduction to the catalogue of the Philadelphia exhibition, remarked of Warhol:

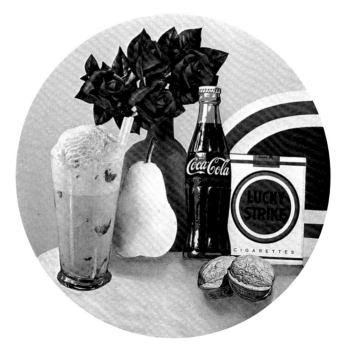

124. **Tom Wesselmann**, *Still-life No. 34*, 1963

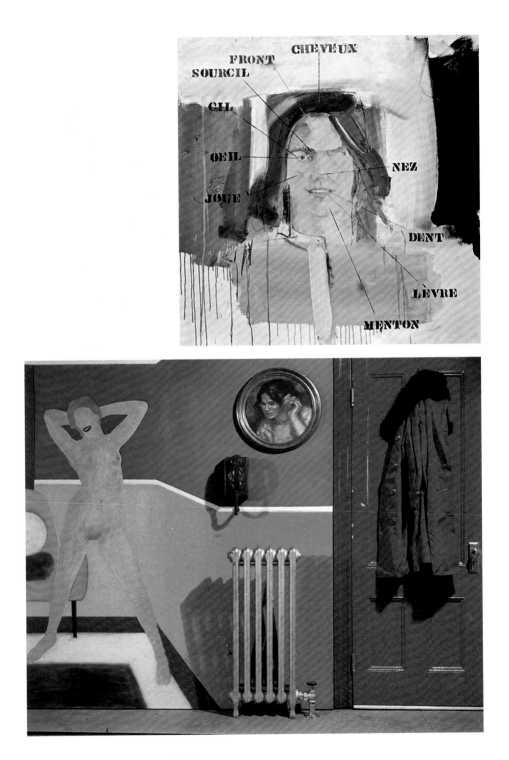

125. **Larry Rivers**, *Parts of the Face*, 1961

His pictorial language consists of stereotypes. Not until our time has a culture known so many commodities which are absolutely impersonal, machine-made, and untouched by human hands. Warhol's art uses the visual strength and vitality which are the time-tested skills of the world of advertising that cares more for the container than the thing contained. Warhol accepts rather than questions our popular habits and heroes. By accepting their inevitability they are easier to deal with than if they are opposed. . . . We accept the glorified legend in preference to the actuality of our immediate experiences, so much so that the legend becomes commonplace and, finally, devoid of the very qualities which first interested us.[10]

In fact, more than most Pop artists, Warhol seemed concerned to anaesthetize our reaction to what is put in front of us. Many of his pictures have morbid associations: Mrs Kennedy after the assassination of her husband, Marilyn Monroe after her suicide, 'mug shots' of criminals, automobile accidents, the electric chair, gangster funerals, race riots. The images are repeated over and over again in photographic enlargements which are silkscreened on to canvas. The only modification is an overlay of crudely applied synthetic colour. The repetition and the colour are the instruments of a moral and aesthetic blankness which has been deliberately contrived. We are aware of Warhol's narcissism when we look at his pictures, but even this scarcely touches us.

127
129

126. **Tom Wesselmann**, *Great American Nude No. 44*, 1963

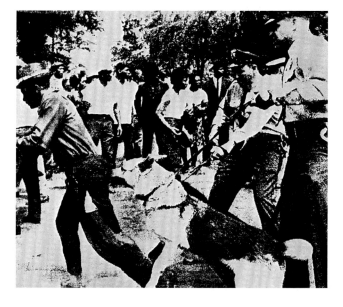

127. **Andy Warhol**, *Race Riot*, 1964

Frank O'Hara, the poet and art critic, once remarked that much Pop art was essentially a 'put on', a poker-faced attempt to discover exactly how much the audience would swallow. Lichtenstein also said, speaking of the beginnings of Pop in America, 'It was hard to get a painting which was despicable enough so no one would hang it – everyone was hanging everything.'[11] Warhol carried this attitude to extremes, so that much of what he did was contemptuously private and aristocratic. This appears in his obsessive concern with boredom, for example. He made a film of a man sleeping – that and nothing else – which lasts for more than six hours.

With the rise of Pop art, both the environment and the Happening took on a new and special importance. There were several reasons for this. One was that Pop specialized in the 'given'; this led artists to experiment with the literal reproduction of reality. Edward Kienholz's more ambitious works fall into this category. There was, too, the consuming interest taken by Pop artists in the phenomena of popular culture, among them such enfolding experiences as amusement arcades and side-shows in circuses: the 'Tunnel of Love', for example. Yayoi Kusama's

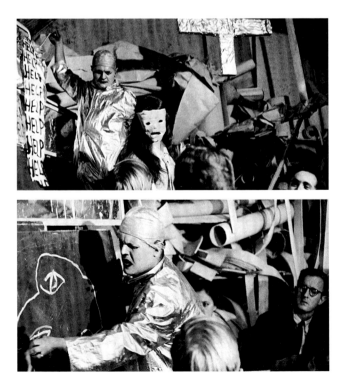

128. **Jim Dine**, *The Car Crash*, 1960

129. **Andy Warhol**, *Green Coca-Cola Bottles*, 1962

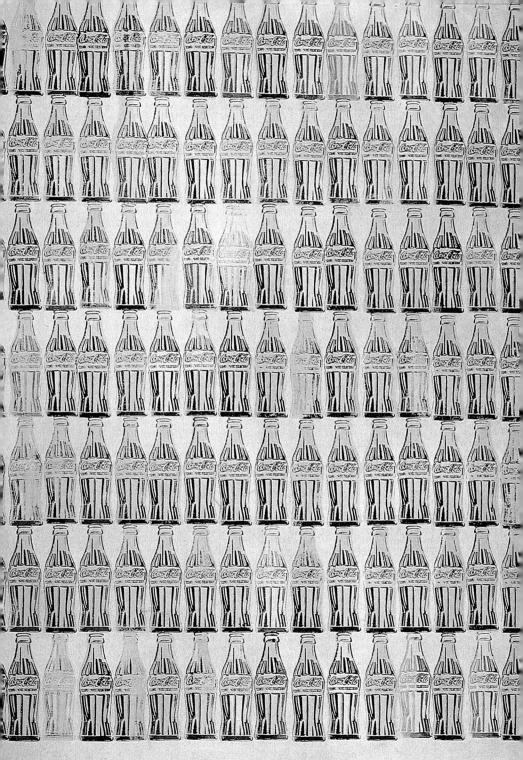

(b. 1940) *Endless Love Room* of 1965–6 uses pure fairground techniques, with a space bewilderingly enlarged by multiple mirrors. 133

The classic Pop art Happenings, such as Jim Dine's *The Car Crash* and Claes Oldenburg's *Store Days*, took place in environments specially constructed by the artists. The Happening involved the extension of an 'art' sensibility – or, more precisely, a 'collage-environment' sensibility – into a situation composed also of sounds, time-durations, gestures, sensations, even smells. Its roots remained in the artist's studio and not in the theatre. The spectator was not supplied with a matrix of plot and character; instead, he was bombarded with sensations which he had to order on his own responsibility. *The Car Crash* was a subjective reconstruction of the sensations produced by a traffic accident, and in this is comparable with the very different environmental piece by Beuys illustrated in Chapter 6 on p. 165. 128 134 161

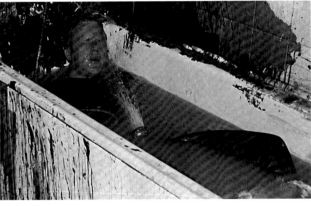

130. **Stuart Brisley**, *And For Today – Nothing* 1972

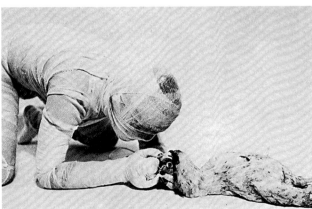

131. **Rudolf Schwarzkogler**, *Action*, May 1965, Vienna

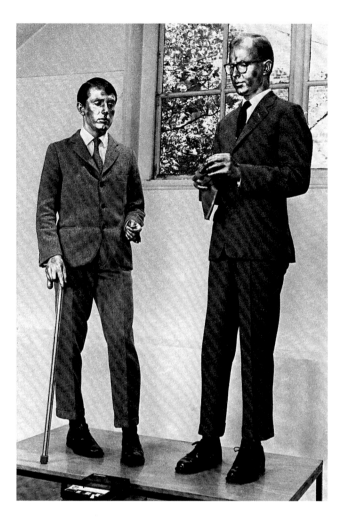

132. **Gilbert and George**,
Singing Sculpture, 1970

The events put on by Europeans differed from the American Happenings which preceded them in several ways. They were more abstract, less specific even than their predecessors. Much of their energy went into the exploration of extreme situations. Sometimes, indeed, the artists who took part in them seemed to engage in a desperate search for the unacceptable, for behaviour that would restore them to a position as rebels and enemies of society. At the same time there was less disposition to regard this kind of activity as a kind of art-world romp. For one event, the English artist Stuart Brisley (b. 1933) spent many hours almost motionless in a bath full of water and animal entrails. Even more extreme was the work done by various members of

130

133

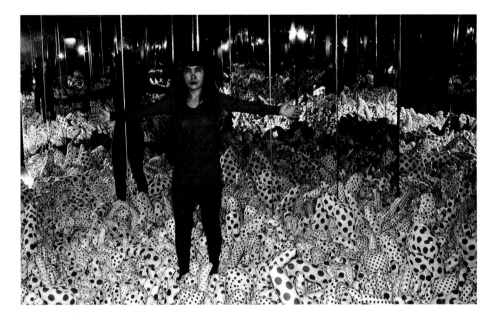

133. **Yayoi Kusama**, *Endless Love Room*, 1965–6

134. **Claes Oldenburg**, *Store Days*, 1965

the Vienna Group in Austria – among them Hermann Nitsch (b. 1938), Otto Muehl (b. 1925), Gunter Brüs (b. 1938) and Rudolf Schwarzkogler (1941–69). Many of their events and actions were unbridled expressions of sado-masochistic fantasy. Nitsch claimed that he took upon himself 'the apparent negative, unsavoury, perverse, obscene, the passion and the hysteria of the act of sacrifice so that YOU are spared the sullying, shaming descent into the extreme.'[12]

But not all the work done in Europe was deadly serious. The Englishmen Gilbert and George (Gilbert Proesch b. 1943 and George Pasmore b. 1942) made their names with a piece called *Singing Sculpture* in which the two participants, with gilded faces, stood on a plinth and mimed to the music-hall song 'Underneath the Arches'. The point was a concern with the idea of style and stylishness. Style was plucked from its context and examined as a separate entity. And, finally, the question of the division, or the lack of it, between the creator and what he creates was brought up. Gilbert and George described themselves as 'living sculptures', and there was more than an implication that everything they did was to be looked upon as art.

131

132

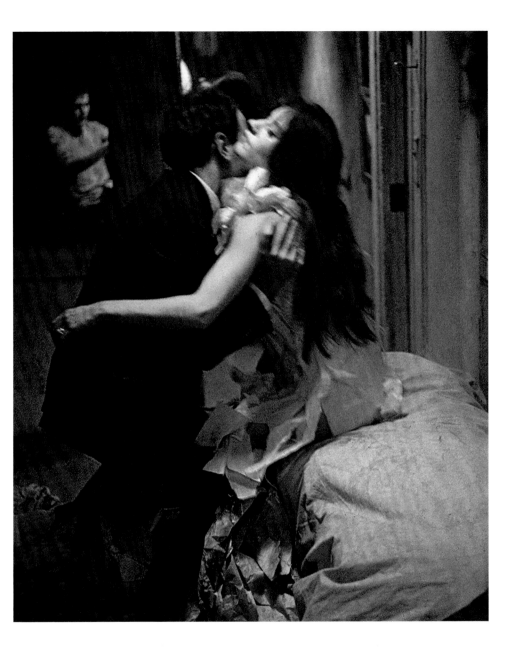

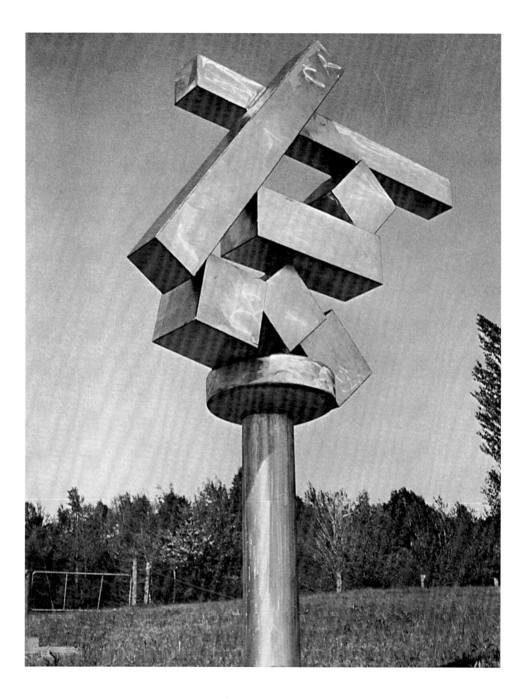

Chapter 5: Abstract sculpture, Minimal art, Conceptual art

During the 1960s radical changes took place in the development of contemporary sculpture. Concurrent with the creation of Pop objects by such artists as Claes Oldenburg, there was the rise to prominence of David Smith (1906–65), whose career as a sculptor in many ways paralleled that of Jackson Pollock in painting. Smith began his career as a painter, a close associate of Arshile Gorky and Willem de Kooning, who were to become leading Abstract Expressionists. He did not view his abandonment of painting for sculpture in the early 1930s as marking a sharp break in his career. Yet there is also a striking opposition between Smith's attitudes and those of the Abstract Expressionist painters. Pollock's work was an assertion of the rights of the individual, of the interior world of dream opposed to the exterior world of fact; the paintings themselves were a rejection of the mechanistic. Smith's mature work, on the contrary, could be the product only of a highly developed technological civilization. He relied heavily on industrial techniques, borrowing these from the metal sculptures of Picasso and Julio González, which he knew only from books and magazines, but adding an element of American industrial know-how. As the poet and critic Frank O'Hara said of him:

From the start, Smith took the cue from the Spaniards to lead him towards the full utilisation of his factory skills as an American metal-worker, especially in the aesthetic use of steel glorifying rather than disguising its practicality and durability as a material for heavy industry.[1]

By the end of World War II, Smith was already a respected artist in mid-career. In January 1946 there was a full-scale retrospective of his work, shared by the Willard and Buchholz galleries in New York. His originality became even more apparent, however, in the late 1950s, when his work became larger in scale and broke free of the conventions of contemporary American sculpture. The techniques he now adopted enabled him to work very rapidly and freely, even when using massive forms and heavy materials such as steel. In 1962, he was invited by the organizers of the

135. **David Smith**, *Cubi XVII*, 1964

137

Spoleto Festival to spend a month in Italy, and was offered an old factory as a workshop. He made twenty-six sculptures in thirty days, many of them gigantic. He was one of the first sculptors to think not in terms of individual works but of the permutations of a single idea in a series, until the artist felt that it had been taken far enough. Initially, he still made references to the human figure, as in the *Agricola* and *Tank Totem* series of the 1950s. Later, he moved towards a more completely abstract style, in the series he labelled *Zig* (1961–4) and *Cubi* (1962–5). The *Cubi* series, in particular, has an unstable, dynamic quality which characterizes Smith's most accomplished work.

135

Smith was a revolutionary artist in a number of ways. His work, despite its massive scale, has a lack of sculptural density which can seem disconcerting, with basic shapes taken ready-made from industrial forms, placed in seemingly provisional arrangements. One sculpture, seen in isolation, is usually less effective than several from the same series, viewed together or in sequence. The fact that Smith sometimes painted his work, or at other times gave it a rough polish, the raw glitter of metal which is only part of the way through the process of manufacture, reinforces these reactions. Like the Post-painterly abstractionist painters of the 1960s, Smith tended to eschew associations; in this he is very different from a sculptor such as Moore, who seems to want to summon up the powers of nature – rocks, water and wind – to help him in his task. All these procedures and preferences were to be influential upon younger men.

The only other sculptor to enjoy anything like Smith's international prestige and influence in the 1960s and early 1970s was the British Anthony Caro (b. 1924), who made similar use of ready-made steel parts – I-beams, sheet-steel, pieces of coarse metal mesh – assembled in sprawling compositions. His welding together of industrial elements, the original identity of which remained intact, followed on from the assemblages made by artists in the 1950s, but now treated in a more purely abstract way. Caro said, in an interview with Andrew Forge in 1966:

136

I would really rather make my sculpture out of 'stuff' – out of something really anonymous, just sheets maybe, which you cut a bit off . . . Much of the sculpture that I'm doing is about extent, and might even get to be about fluidity or something of this sort, and I think one has to hold it from becoming just amorphous.[2]

From this statement, and from the appearance of the work itself, it is clear that Caro did not share Smith's sculptural preoccupa-

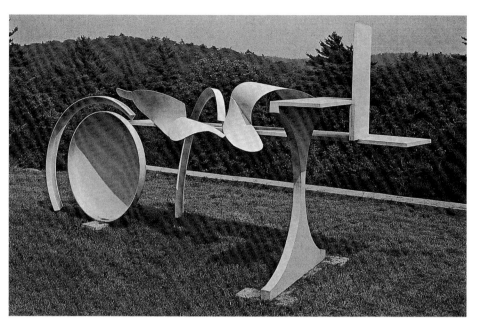

136. **Anthony Caro**, *Sun-feast*, 1969–70

tions, despite the debt he owed to him. To take the most obvious difference first: Caro's work of the 1960s usually has a horizontal emphasis, as opposed to the verticality of most of Smith's late sculpture. Caro's sculptures could be described as being both space-devouring and ground-devouring. The traditional base has been abolished, and each piece has taken possession of a certain territory and modifies the spectator's reactions to the surrounding space. While Smith preferred to have his work shown in the open air, Caro, on the contrary, favoured enclosed spaces that could be occupied and activated by the sculpture.

At the time when they were made, Smith's late sculptures, and contemporaneous and slightly later ones by Caro, seemed to indicate the main line of sculptural development for the future. This, however, did not prove to be the case, and it is perhaps significant that Caro, in work made in the 1980s and early 1990s, has more and more tended to revert to traditional techniques, such as bronze-casting, and to the incorporation of figurative references, as in a recent series, *The Trojan War* (1993–4), devoted to the personages and events of Homer's *Iliad*. The series consists of semi-abstract representations of the Olympian Gods (*Athene, Aphrodite, Apollo*), of Greek and Trojan actors in the story (*Ajax, Hector, Paris, Helen*), of groups of people (*The Achaians*), and even of landscape (*Mount Ida*). The materials are ceramic, bronze and wood as well as steel, and the organic forms look back to the sculpture of the early 1950s – to early sculptures by Eduardo Paolozzi or even by the French sculptor César (1921–98).

There were, nevertheless, features significant for the future in the work of both men, and in that of Caro in particular. For instance, though both were still interested in creating complex forms, these forms were often composed of very simple industrial units. Both, but Caro in particular, tended to abolish the bases traditional with sculpture, and to turn each piece into another object added to a pre-existing world of objects. Caro, too, tended, during the 1960s and 1970s, to 'dematerialize' his sculptures by choosing to paint them a unifying and often tonally ambiguous colour, one which heightens our uncertainty about the object's visual weight.

Neither sculptor, however, is the primary source of the radical changes which were to overtake sculpture, and with it all of avant-garde art, in the course of the 1960s and 1970s. The development of Pop art was paralleled by continuing radical changes in the realm of abstraction. At the height of Pop art's popularity, commentators were inclined to oppose it to a phenomenon which they labelled Op art – that is, to a kind of abstraction, operating in both two-dimensional and three-dimensional form, which relied on optical and kinetic effects. What the viewer saw, when confronted with works of this kind, was either something which relied on the physiological reactions of the eye – the mechanism of seeing – to contrasts of hue and tone which produced an illusion of motion; or else objects which actually made use of real motion. Both of these ways of working had deep roots in the history of Modernism. Their real originators were the Russian Constructivists, such as Aleksandr Rodchenko (1891–1956), who made a series of suspended *Spatial Constructions*, based on the forms of armillary spheres, in 1920–21; and artists who had been associated with the Bauhaus, such as Moholy-Nagy (*Light-Space Modulator*, 1921–30; a *Kinetic Sculpture*, using glass rods filled with mercury, 1930–36).

If post-war optical painting is to be traced back to a single source, that source is unquestionably Victor Vasarely (1908–97), who had studied in 1928–9 at the Mühely Academy (the Budapest offshoot of the Bauhaus, directed by Alexander Bortnyik), and who then settled in France. Characteristically, Vasarely remarked that it was during this period at the Budapest Bauhaus that 'the functional character of plasticity' was first revealed to him. Kineticism was important to Vasarely for two reasons, one

137

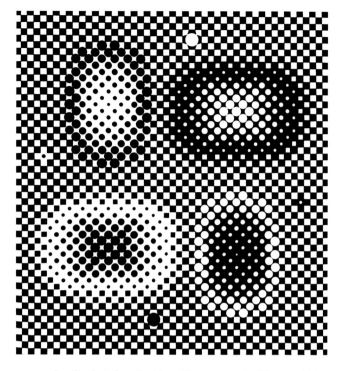

137. **Victor Vasarely,**
Metagalaxy, 1959

personal – the fact that the idea of movement had haunted him from his childhood; the other the more general idea that a painting that lives through optical effects exists essentially in the eye and mind of the spectator, not merely on the wall. Vasarely concerned himself with paintings, with works composed in separate planes, and with screens and three-dimensional objects. Static works rely for their kineticism on the action of light and on well-known optical phenomena, such as the tendency of the eye to produce after-images, when confronted with very brilliant contrasts of black and white, as in *Metagalaxy,* or the juxtaposition of certain hues. The completion of the painting through the act of looking was in line with the view taken earlier in the century by Duchamp concerning the interdependence of the object and the spectator within the framework of the creative act, and foreshadowed what came to be called Conceptual art. Vasarely's chief rival for dominance in this field is the British artist Bridget Riley (b. 1931). Her black-and-white painting *Crest* is typical of her earlier work. A much less austere, more deeply instinctive artist than Vasarely, her work often seems to attempt to render natural forces, in this case the flow of water, without making specific landscape references. Her development has led her through

137

139

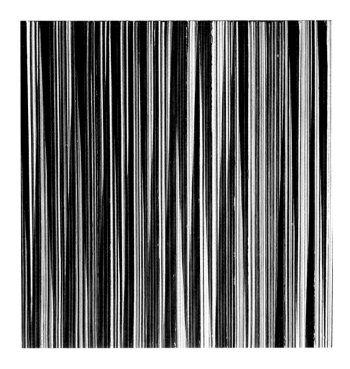

138. Carlos Cruz-Diez,
Physichromie No. 1, 1959

austere black-and-white, through muted grey and pastel hues, to her current interest in brilliant colour.

Three-dimensional kinetic art objects made a wider range of choices available to the artist. They could either, as did optical painting, remain static, while relying on the action of light and on well-known optical phenomena to produce an illusion of movement, or they could actually move, with or without the aid of mechanical power. 'Mobiles', which move at random, without mechanical aid, were essentially the invention of two men – first made by the Russian Constructivist Aleksandr Rodchenko, they were then, after a lapse of some years, re-invented and perfected by the American Alexander Calder (1898–1976). Mechanically-powered art objects can be traced back to Duchamp (who made use of a gramophone turntable), and to another Russian Constructivist, Naum Gabo (1890–1977).

The revival of objects of this type was largely the work of Latin American artists, among them the Argentinian members of the Madí Group, founded in Buenos Aires in 1944, and Venezuelans such as Carlos Cruz-Diez and Jesús Rafael Soto. The political situation in Venezuela, then under the Pérez Soto dictatorship, brought the Venezuelans in particular to Europe, and these experiments, made in Latin America in the 1940s and 1950s, at a time when Constructivism was out of favour in Europe and the United States, became widely influential in the 1960s. The 'physichromies' of Carlos Cruz-Diez (b. 1923), such as *Physichromie No. 1*, are works in very slight relief. Often this extra dimension is used to provide planes of colour which move as the spectator shifts his position in relation to them.

138

A more important artist who sometimes made use of effects of somewhat the same kind is Jesús Rafael Soto (b. 1923). Soto's original influences were Mondrian and Malevich. In the early 1950s he made paintings which created their effect by repetition of units. The units were so disposed that the rhythm which linked them came to seem more important to the eye than any individual part, and the painting was therefore, by implication at any rate, not something complete in itself, but a part taken from an infinitely large fabric which the spectator was asked to imagine. Soto then became interested in effects of superimposition, just as Vasarely did. Two patterns painted on perspex sheets were mounted very slightly apart, and seemed to blend together in a new space which hovered between the front and back planes supplied by the sheets. Later, Soto began a series of experiments

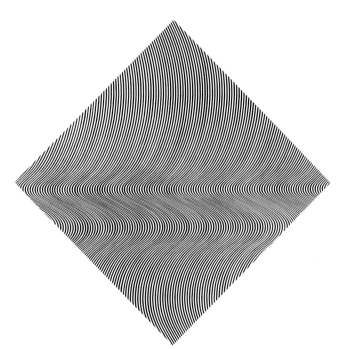

139. **Bridget Riley**, *Crest*, 1964

140. **Jesús Rafael Soto**, *Petite Double Face*, 1967

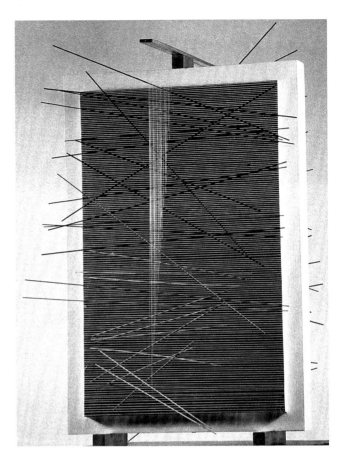

140. **Jesús Rafael Soto**, *Petite Double Face*, 1967

with lined screens. These had metal plaques which projected in front of them, or else metal rods or wires are freely suspended before this vibrating ground, such as *Petite Double Face*. The vibration tends, from the optical point of view, to swallow up and dissolve the projecting or suspended solids. Each instant, as the spectator moves his eyes, a new wave of optical activity is set up. The most intense of all Soto's works are large screens of hanging rods. Hung along the length of a wall, these layers of rods seem to dissolve the whole side of a room, calling into question all the spectator's instinctive reactions to an enclosed space.

Because Op art is so commonly treated as a completely closed, self-contained phenomenon, little has been made of its possible relationship to other developments in the abstract art of the period. Essentially, these developments were the two related phenomena which came to be labelled Minimal and Conceptual art.

Minimal art once again can be traced to the experiments made by the Russian artists of the early Revolutionary period – to the work of the Constructivists, and even more precisely to the Suprematism of Malevich, most notably to paintings such as his *White on White* of 1917. These experiments were taken up again in the 1950s and early 1960s – by the young Robert Rauschenberg, with a series of all-white canvases, made when he was at Black Mountain College in the early 1950s; by Ad Reinhardt, most radically in paintings of 1960–66 producing an all black effect through a subtle layering of dark colours; and in Europe by Yves Klein (1928–62) with completely monochrome works in IKB (International Klein Blue), and by Piero Manzoni (1933–63) in his series of *Achromes*. Other painters working in minimal or near minimal ways included Robert Ryman (b. 1930), who experimented both with unstretched canvases and with baked enamel on copper, and Agnes Martin (b. 1912), who used almost invisible grids on monochrome grounds.

In the United States, Minimalism made its greatest impact, and established itself as a major new art phenomenon, through the activity of artists working in three dimensions rather than in two. A kind of transitional stage, with Minimal overtones but still some relationship to the work of David Smith, is represented by the work of Richard Serra (b. 1939). Serra's weighty leaning pieces of 1968–71 have a dynamic quality which derives from their apparent physical instability. They are also often asymmetrical in form. His outdoor sculptures, notably the notorious *Tilted Arc* (1981), have been a focus of controversy because the public found them threatening. There is a suppressed element of Expressionism in much of Serra's work which makes it untypical of Minimal art taken as a whole. The main line of descent in American Minimalism must be looked for elsewhere. The architect-turned-sculptor Tony Smith (b. 1912), who had been an apprentice of Frank Lloyd Wright, was one of the first to make an impact. He gave up architecture for sculpture because he felt that buildings were too impermanent and vulnerable to alterations contrary to their creators' intentions. His sculptures have been described in an oversimplified way as examples of the 'single unit Gestalt' which came to be thought of as typical of Minimal art, but the artist himself spoke of some of them as:

141

Part of a continuous space grid. In the latter voids are made up of the same components as the masses. In this sense they may be seen as interruptions in an otherwise unbroken flow of space. If you think of space as solid, they are voids in that space. While I hope they have form and presence, I don't think of them as being objects among other objects; I think of them as being isolated in their own environments.[3]

Much of Smith's work seems to reflect his experience of architecture. He said of one piece, called *Playground* (1962): 'I like shapes of this kind; they remind me of the shapes of ancient buildings made with mudbrick walls.' Characteristically, many of the sculptures consist of rectangular boxes fitted together; sometimes this is varied by using tetrahedrons. One, called *The Black Box* (1962), was suggested by a box for index cards which the artist saw on a friend's desk. Seen one night, the shape became an obsession, so

142

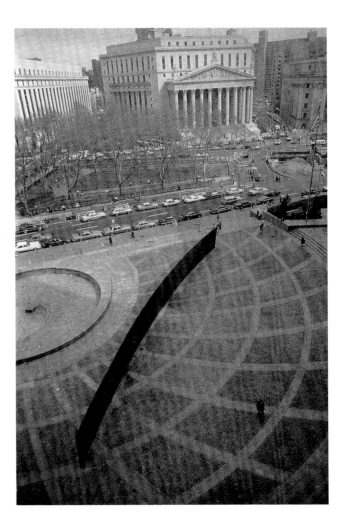

141. **Richard Serra**, *Tilted Arc*, 1981, Federal Plaza, New York

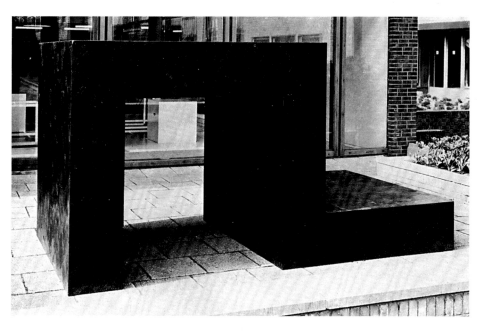

142. **Tony Smith**, *Playground*, 1962

Smith telephoned his friend the next morning and asked for the dimensions.

I asked him to take his ruler and measure the box. He was so out of it that he didn't even enquire about why I wanted to know the size. I multiplied the dimensions by five, made a drawing, took it to the Industrial Welding Co. in Newark, and asked them to make it up.[4]

Obviously, there is in this a strong element of the Conceptual as well as of the Minimal. The sculpture existed notionally as a set of measurements written down on paper, before it is given material form by the fabricator whom the artist employed to make the object to his specification. There is, in addition, a concentration on the deliberately inexpressive, which is not present in the work of Tony Smith's namesake David, nor in that of Caro. These two characteristics indicated the direction that the new American sculpture more and more tended to take.

(overleaf)
143. **John McCracken**, *There's No Reason Not To*, 1967

144. **Carl Andre**, *Plain*, 1969

145. **Robert Morris**, *Untitled (circular light piece)*, 1966

Minimal art was not simply a question of the activity of one artist, but of a whole school of artists, among them Carl Andre (b. 1935), Dan Flavin (1933–96), Robert Morris (b. 1931), Sol LeWitt (b. 1923) and John McCracken (b. 1934). One of the most articulate of these artists was Donald Judd (1928–94), who spoke of his practice thus:

144

149

145

143

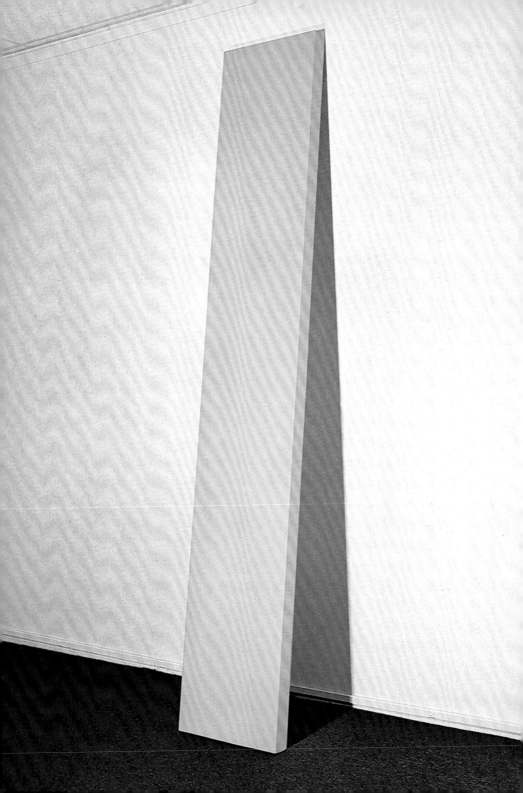

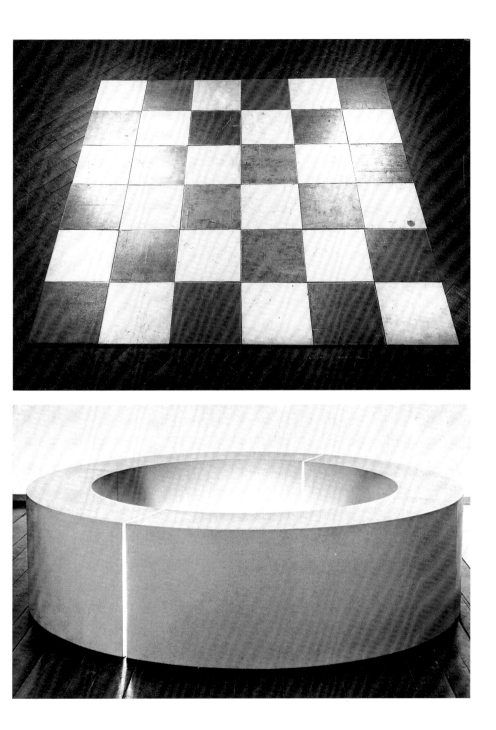

Three dimensions are real space. That gets rid of the problem of illusionism and of literal space, space in and around marks and colours – which is one of the most salient and objectionable relics of European art. The several limits of painting are no longer present. A work can be as powerful as it is thought to be. Actual space is intrinsically more powerful and specific than paint on a flat surface.[5]

Judd's interpretation of this credo was less liberal than the words themselves might lead one to suppose: a string of galvanized iron boxes strung out at regular intervals across a wall.

146

Judd's colleague, Robert Morris, defended Minimal art in equally emphatic terms:

Simplicity of shape does not necessarily equate with simplicity of experience. Unitary forms do not reduce relationships. They order them. If the predominant, hieratic nature of the unitary form functions as a constant, all those particularising relations of scale, proportion, etc., are not thereby cancelled. Rather they are bound more cohesively and individually together.[6]

These justifications are in some ways beside the point, because it became increasingly clear that the Minimal artist did not really wish to express himself, or express some meaning, in the old way. There was, it is true, a sense of *ordering*, which often took the form proposed by Tony Smith: the artists provided a partial image of a complete order throughout all the space that could be imagined, and left the spectator to fill in the rest.

This is exactly what happens, for example, in much of the work of Sol LeWitt. In April 1968 LeWitt had an exhibition in New York which consisted of a single sculpture, descriptively entitled *46 Three-part Variations on Three Different Kinds of Cubes*. The cubes were boxes of standard size. Some were closed, some open on one side only, some open on two facing sides. These were piled together in groups of three. The cubes were regularly aligned in stacks, and the stacks regularly aligned with one another. Each of the eight rows set out the possible solutions in a fixed order of permutation, beginning with a row which established all the possible permutations when each stack contained just one of each of the three kinds of cubes (see p. 152 for a later variation). 147

Another form of Minimal art relies not on placing unitary objects within a space, but on the alteration of the space itself. One of the best-known examples is the work of the Frenchman Daniel Buren (b. 1938), who makes use of patterns of stripes to

146. **Donald Judd**, *Untitled*, 1965

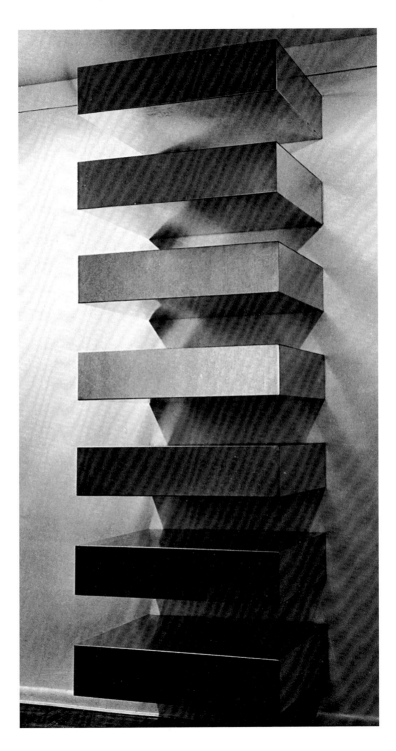

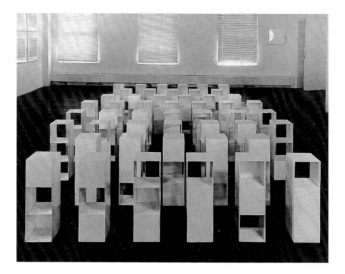

147. **Sol LeWitt**, *49 Three-part Variations*, 1967–70

emphasize the character of a room or a set of rooms, or to alter the visitor's perception of their character. Thus Buren's installation *On Two Levels with Two Colours*, made for the Lisson Gallery, London, in 1976, emphasizes the irregularity of the spaces available, and their slightly unexpected relationship (due to the fact that they formed part of two adjacent converted buildings with floors on slightly different levels), by providing them with striped skirtings in contrasting hues.

148

Some Minimal art is less dour – and perhaps also less naïve. Dan Flavin's work, for instance, makes use of straight lengths of fluorescent tubing, and is the point at which Minimalism meets Kinetic art. Flavin regards not only light, but space, as his material, and in this sense his work is related to that of Buren. 'I knew,' he says, 'that the actual space of a room could be broken down and played with by planting illusions of real light [electric light] at crucial junctures in the room's composition.'[7] His *Untitled (to the 'Innovator' Wheeling Beachblow)* of 1968 is an example of this. A framework of fluorescent tubes, pink, gold, and 'daylight', are set in a corner of the gallery space. Some of the tubes are shielded, and reflect light back on the adjacent walls; others are bare. The space is washed with different hues, which alter the visitor's perception of the space he or she stands in.

149

148. **Daniel Buren**, *On Two Levels with Two Colours*, 1976

149. **Dan Flavin**, *Untitled (to the 'Innovator' Wheeling Beachblow)*, 1968

Taking Flavin's art as a point of reference, it is possible to look in several directions. One direction points towards the California artists of the so-called 'Light and Space' group, one of whose members is Larry Bell (b. 1939), who has made glass

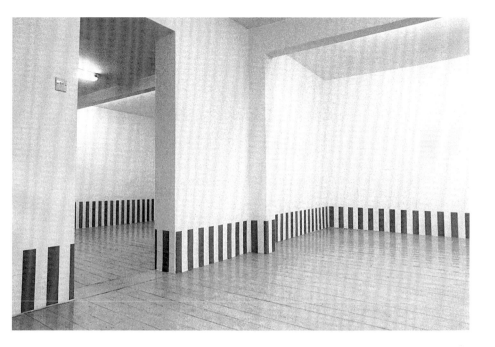

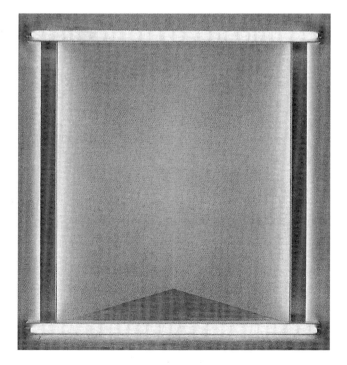

cubes and also larger sculptures consisting of coated glass sheets placed at right angles. The coatings used are the product of the California aerospace industry. The specially treated glass both reflects the spectator and allows him or her to see what is beyond, revealing and concealing reality in unexpected ways. The art object is not the cube itself, or the glass screen, but fleeting effects of reflection and transparency. An example of this was the untitled installation Bell exhibited at the Hayward Gallery, London, 150 in 1971. Basically, this consisted of a number of large sheets of glass placed in pairs, at right angles to one another, together creating a labyrinth though which the visitor was invited to wander. The installation was animated, and at the same time made mysterious, by other visitors in the space, reflected or concealed by the coated glass.

Other artists of the same group, such as Robert Irwin (b. 1928) and Eric Orr (1939–98), made works where the effect of de- 151 materialization was almost complete, and the spectator's perceptions were manipulated by the subtle use of light. One of the most ambitious practitioners of this genre is James Turrell (b. 1943), best known for his on-going *Roden Crater* project, which 152 involves the excavation and alteration of an extinct volcano at Sedona in the Arizona desert. Work on this started in 1972 and is still in progress. Turrell's aim is to create a series of experiences

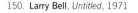
150. **Larry Bell**, *Untitled*, 1971

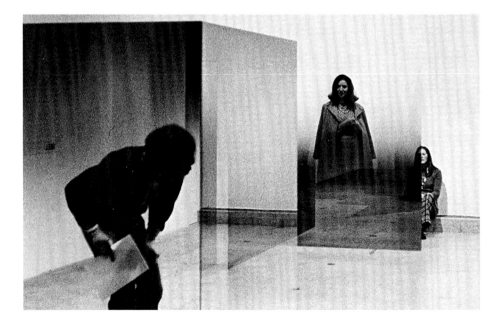

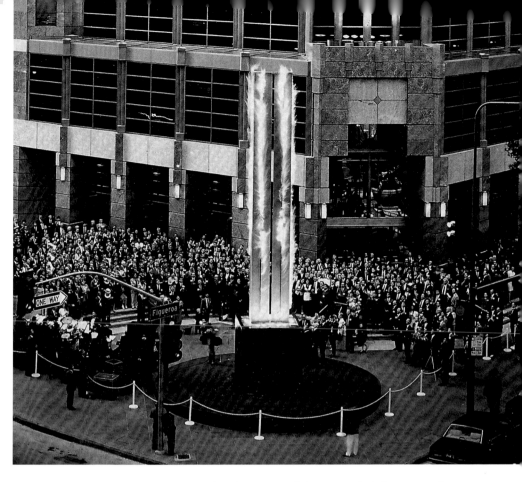

151. **Eric Orr**, *Prime Matter*, 1990

which, while relying on well-known optical phenomena, have a quasi-mystical impact on the viewer. For example, the crater, while retaining its outward appearance intact, is being excavated in such a way as to turn it into a giant camera obscura, which will throw the image of the moon or the sun on to the walls of an underground chamber.

Turrell has created similar, if less ambitious light effects by making installations in museums and commercial galleries – for example, a series of rooms (entitled *Light Spaces*), each filled with a different colour of light, made for the Stedelijk Museum in Amsterdam in 1976. Later, for example at the Venice Biennale of 1988, he devised enclosed spaces divided by an illusory diagonal plane – a shimmering wall which seems solid until the spectator walks up to it and tries to touch it.

Turrell's work, while bordering on the mystical and reliant on the action of light, also has links with the form of expression

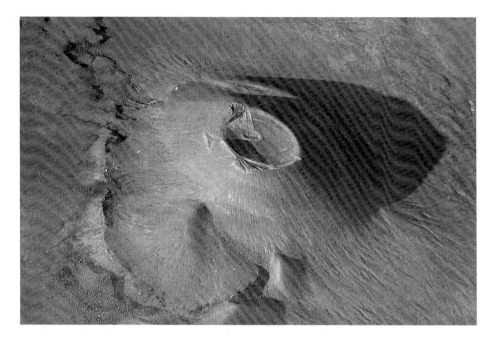

152. **James Turrell**, *Roden Crater*, work in progress, conceived 1974

which has been labelled Earth art. Much of this is Minimal art executed on a gigantic scale. The best-known example is Robert Smithson's (1928–73) *Spiral Jetty* of 1970 – a giant spiral structure of stones and earth projecting from the shore of the Great Salt Lake in Utah. The remote location, and the fact that the lake itself has now risen to swallow up the structure, means that the piece, for all its gigantism, is in fact known almost entirely through the photographic documentation made of it when it was new. 153

A similar situation exists with many other examples of Earth art, either created on distant sites, or deliberately ephemeral, or both. Some of the better-known artists in this field are British, and their work can perhaps be seen as an extension of the tradition of Romantic landscape which has played such an important role in the history of British art. Richard Long's (b. 1945) work 154 consists of a range of activities, including direct interventions in the landscape, often on remote sites, and installations such as stone circles, made in galleries using material found in a particular location; like another British artist, Hamish Fulton (b. 1946), he also uses photographs, diagrams and/or written texts to document his movement through a particular tract of country. Andy Goldsworthy (b. 1956) works in a related fashion, piling up 155 a cairn of loose stones, or covering a rock in a stream with a blanket of leaves of a particular colour, and then photographing the result. In each case, it is the pattern of activity which counts, far more than the actual physical result.

Long's work in particular, since it can consist simply of a diagram or a map, or even of a simple written statement, has as many links with what has been called Conceptual art as it does with Minimalism. Conceptual art is a form of expression which tries to abolish the physical as completely as possible, and which aims to bypass optical stimulation in favour of intellectual processes which the audience is invited to share with the artist. That is, it is essentially an art of mental patterns, embodied by any means which the maker sees fit to employ. Like Minimal art, it first made its appearance in the second half of the 1960s. A classic early example is Joseph Kosuth's (b. 1945) *One and Three Chairs* of 158 1965. It consists of a wooden folding chair, a photograph of a chair, and the photographic enlargement of the dictionary definition of a chair. The artist asks his audience in which of these three the true identity of the object is to be found – in the thing itself, the representation, or the verbal description? Can it be discovered in one, some, all, or in the end none of them?

Sometimes, paradoxically, Conceptual art became totally physical – an idea expressed in the most literal sense through flesh and blood. Dennis Oppenheim's (b. 1938) *Reading Position* 156

153. **Robert Smithson**, *Spiral Jetty*, 1970

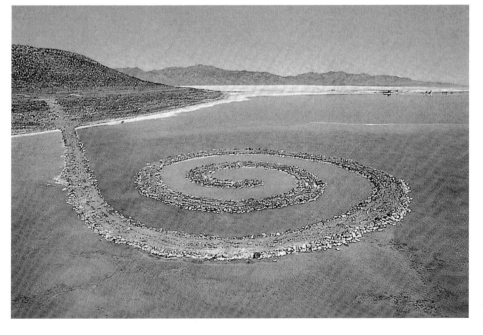

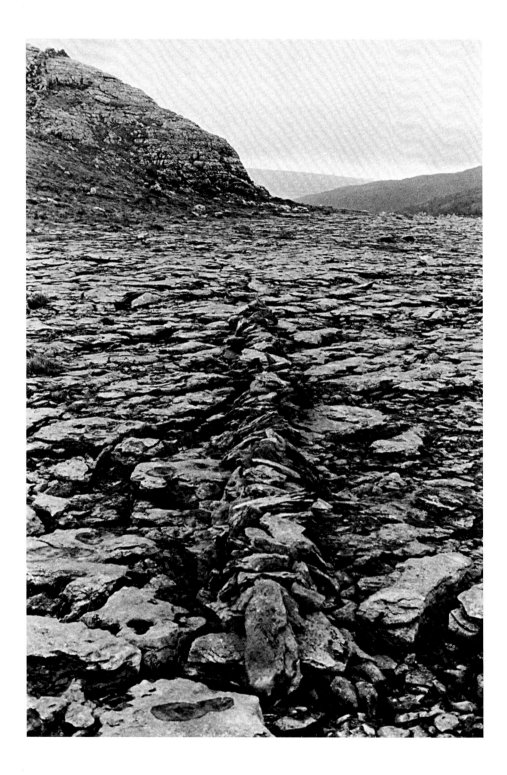

of 1970 consists of two photographs which record the effects of sunburn on the artist's own torso – part of it sheltered by an open book, and part left exposed. This kind of expression is often classified as body art or performance art. To create his piece Oppenheim had to do something at least mildly painful. Masochism is a frequent characteristic of body art – something it shares with the post-pop 'actions' or Happenings of such artists as Stuart Brisley or the Austrian Rudolph Schwarzkogler. The idea of artistic dematerialization here comes full circle, and is linked to physical actions and gestures which in turn are often yoked to the old Romantic notion of art as an expression of personal suffering or sacrifice. When this happened it was difficult to say that the art so created remained 'subjectless'. Its subject is the artist – his or her relationship to both the idea of making art and the idea of society.

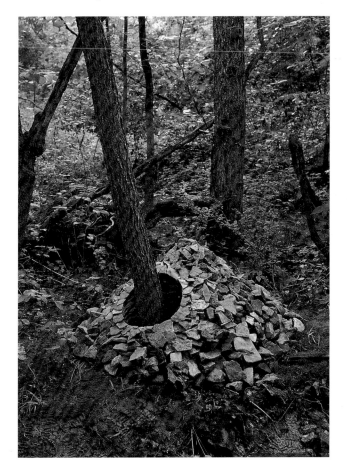

154. **Richard Long**, *A Line in Ireland*, 1974

155. **Andy Goldsworthy**, *Tree Cairn*, June 1994

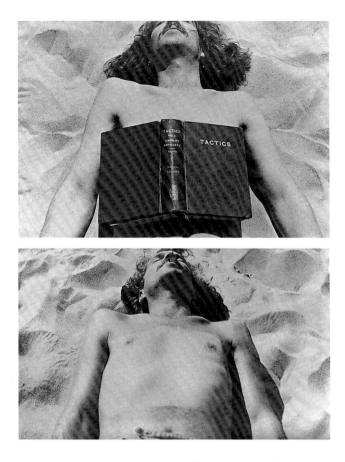

Because its basic material was ideas – and also language –
Conceptual art experienced a strong revival at the end of the
1980s, when the attention of the avant-garde art world turned to
issue and content based work. The activity of Jenny Holzer
(b. 1950) spans both periods. Her *Truisms*, which owe something to
the text-based work of Lawrence Weiner (b. 1942), date from the
end of the 1970s; her work with light-emitting diodes (as seen at
the Venice Biennale of 1990) is a further elaboration typical of the
late 1980s. Holzer's work, with its often feminist content, is related
to that of Barbara Kruger (b. 1945) whose photomontages also
rely heavily on language rather than visual imagery for their effect.

157

202

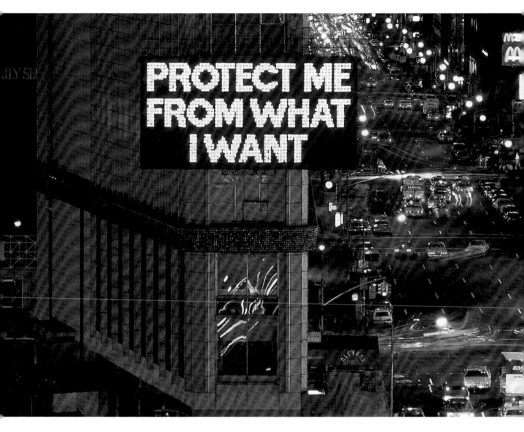

157. **Jenny Holzer**, *The Survival Series: Protect Me From What I Want*, 1985–6

158. **Joseph Kosuth**, *One and Three Chairs*, 1965

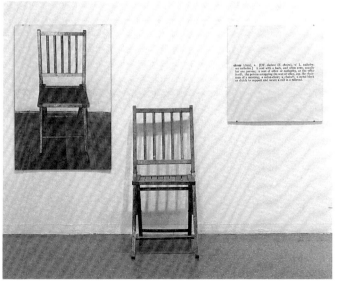

Chapter 6:   An age of pluralism

The mid 1970s probably marked the furthest point when it was possible to talk in terms of a simple succession of styles. The past twenty-five years have witnessed an almost unparalleled upsurge of creative activity in art. They also witnessed radical changes in how art itself was defined and in the way that artists function within contemporary society.

The seeds of these changes had already been sown in the 1960s. In the United States, for example, while Minimal Art and Conceptual Art seemed at first sight to possess characteristics in common with the developments which had immediately preceded them, in the sense that their preoccupations remained largely aesthetic. Minimal art, in particular, seemed to invite the spectator to concentrate on art alone, to the exclusion of everything that could be categorized as 'not art'. Its proposal was that art and the world existed in separate universes. This added greatly to the power of the museum, since museums, now, by implication, became powers in their own right, which the unqualified spectator could only successfully navigate with the aid of professional guides and interpreters. However, Minimal art also had one novel quality whose implications were largely missed at the time of its emergence. In its determination to strip away all quirks and complications of form, it stripped away the very things through which a particular style generally made itself recognized. Conceptual art carried this process still further with its proposition that art could be reduced to documentation or a series of written statements and/or diagrams, and that physical embodiment, even of the reductive kind found in Minimalism, was therefore essentially superfluous. Contrary to what was intended, however, this allowed aesthetic content in through the back door, since the propositions put forward in the name of Conceptual art soon began to stray from the realm of pure aesthetics.

These developments, which were essentially identified with the United States, found a parallel, but one of a slightly unexpected kind, in Europe. In 1962 the first Fluxus concerts took place. Fluxus and its activities have always been difficult to describe coherently, chiefly because the participants were only loosely linked and, in addition, because they themselves culti-vated a kind of incoherence. Some of Fluxus's roots were in the original Dada movement, and Dada survivors, such as Raoul Hausmann (1886–1971), associated themselves with it – this in contrast to the disapproval expressed by veteran Dadaists con-cerning Pop art in its original guise . There were, nevertheless, striking similarities between Fluxus 'events' and the Pop art acti-vities of the early 1960s – for example, the 'Happenings' devised by Claes Oldenburg and Jim Dine – though Fluxus incursions into live performance often had more overtly intellectual, politi-cal or philosophical overtones than their Pop counterparts.

Much of the impetus for Fluxus came from outside the strict limits of the art world – for example, from the work and philosophy of the composer John Cage, who had been close to the original American Neo-Dadaists, such as Rauschenberg, but who was much less so to leading practitioners of Pop, such as Warhol and Lichtenstein. There was also an element of social criticism and provocation that had almost vanished from American art. Pop, when it provoked, did so lightheartedly. Within Fluxus, as within the later offshoots of Dada, which flourished in Germany in the years immediately following World War I, there was a determina-tion to make changes in society itself. One lasting achievement of Fluxus was to provide a platform for the early activities of Joseph Beuys. However, Beuys soon outgrew the movement that had sheltered him, and became a power in his own right.

One of the best ways of describing and quantifying the change which Beuys caused in the world of contemporary art is to compare him with some of the Modernist artists who were already solidly established when he first appeared on the scene. Beuys always described himself as a sculptor, and he had certainly trained as such under the artist Ewald Mataré (1887–1965). He was, however entirely different in his approach from the cele-brated Modernist sculptors of the generation preceding his own – Constantin Brancusi (1876–1957), Hans Arp (1888–1966), Alberto Giacometti (1901–66), Marino Marini (1901–66), Henry Moore (1898–1986) and Barbara Hepworth (1903–75). Their theme was humankind and its fate, and they expressed their concern with this by creating objects that were visual meta-phors – see, for example, Hepworth's *Two Figures* and Moore's 159 *Locking Piece* – set apart from the rest of the environment, gener- 160 ally by the simple device of placing them on pedestals.

Beuys, as his career progressed, had less and less to do with objects of this traditional type. He increasingly tended to see

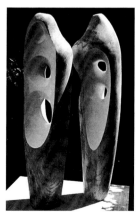

159. **Barbara Hepworth**, *Two Figures*, 1947–8

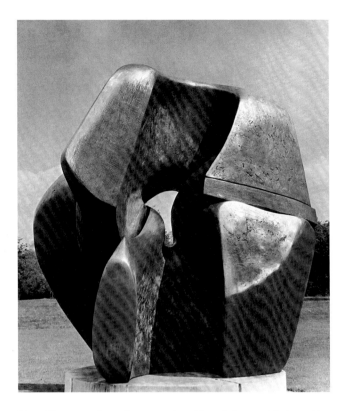

160. **Henry Moore,**
Locking-piece, 1963–4

himself as a modern shaman, who affected the world about him through enacting rituals – the difference between his version of shamanism and the traditional one being twofold; first, that he existed within a modern industrial society; second that the rituals were self-invented, as in *Action in 7 Exhibitions.* It is true that he sometimes created an embodiment for his ideas by making objects, but these could hardly be said to possess formal values in any accepted sense. Their power lay, not in shapes or relationships of shapes, nor in their metaphoric relationship to forms found in nature, but in the fact that they were ritual collocations, often involving materials which Beuys thought had magical or therapeutic power – felt, fat, gold leaf and honey were some of those he employed. Compared with him, sculptors like Giacometti and Moore belong to a different and much more traditional world.

As his career progressed, Beuys more and more tended to separate himself from the art-making process, as this had been formerly understood. Museums became arenas where his shamanistic rituals could be staged, or, more simply, platforms from which Beuys could project a political programme. Politics itself he defined as 'social sculpture'. Where he continued to use objects this was often because they had a directly autobiographical significance. For example, in *Dernier espace avec introspecteur*, an installation of 1982, the kernel is the wing-mirror of a car in which the artist suffered a near-fatal car-crash. This functions like a relic within an elaborately constructed reliquary. The surviving products of Beuys's process of self-mythologization seem, now that he is dead, more like miraculous tokens – a thorn from the Crown of Thorns, a hair from the Prophet's beard – than like works of art in any conventionally definable sense.

162

It was Beuys above all who opened the doors to a new perception of the way in which art functioned – or might function – within contemporary society. Art was in future to be defined in two ways – through its relationship to the personality of the artist, of which it was simply a visible manifestation, and through its content. In other words, it offered a definition of the artist's relationship to the world, one that continually changed as the artist himself or herself developed. It showed the deformations which occur when the subjective impinges on the objective, and vice versa.

The artist who is most usually put forward as Beuys's true heir, especially by American critics, is Bruce Nauman (b. 1941). In fact, Nauman is deeply rooted in aspects of American culture

161. **Joseph Beuys**, *Action in 7 Exhibitions*, 1972

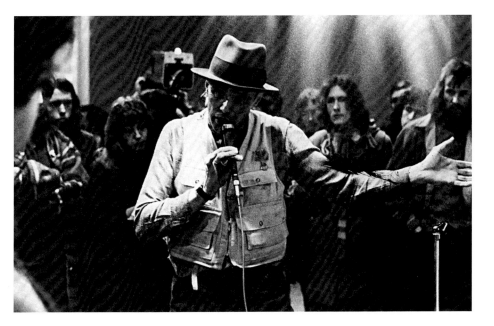

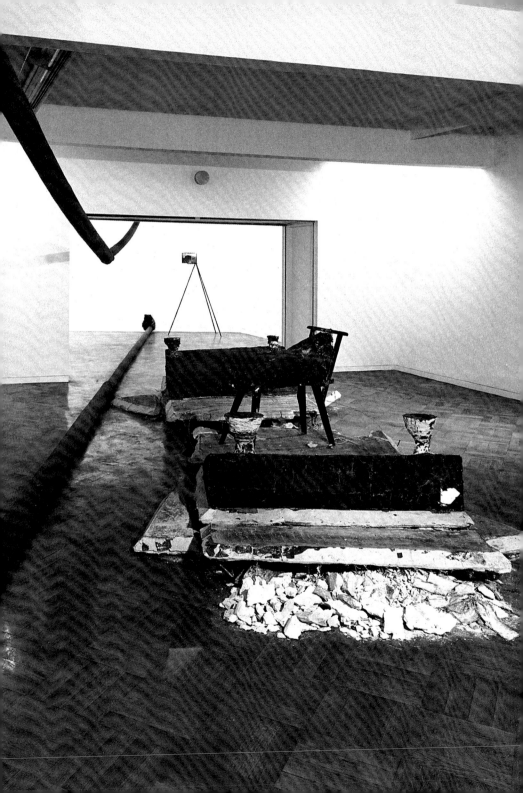

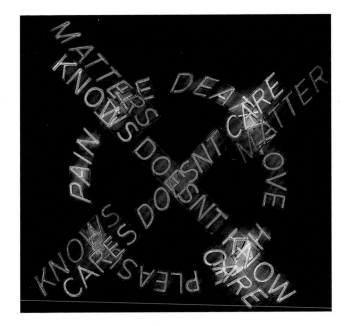

which Beuys disliked and opposed. For example his neon pieces, which are some of his most typical works, are a kind of hybrid: a compromise between Conceptual and Pop impulses. *Life Death/ Knows Doesn't Know* (1983) uses a technique familiar from advertising signs to pose a universal question which reaches well beyond any aesthetic framework. Nauman's work in this vein provided themes for a number of other artists, chief among them Jenny Holzer, (b.1950) with her elaborate installation pieces using light-emitting diodes which formed phrases and sentences – these works are an example, like Nauman working in a similar way, of advertising technology moving across into the territory of high art.

Nauman was a pioneer in the use of video for art-making, and employs the medium in a peculiarly personal way. *Clown Torture* (1987) is one of several videos by Nauman which seem to express a nihilistic anger against the world, mixed with unresolved sadism. Their essential pessimism makes them very different from anything done by Beuys, just as, in the realm of personal life, Nauman's withdrawal to his New Mexico ranch contrasts with Beuys's perpetual accessibility.

An important aspect of Nauman's work, looking at it in a broader context, is its extreme variety of means. Unlike the work of Pop painters like Warhol, or even that of Minimal sculptors

163

162. **Joseph Beuys**, *Dernier espace avec introspecteur*, 1982

such as Judd, Nauman's work possesses no immediately recognizable stylistic signature, not even one created by a particular and characteristic choice of materials. Each piece exists as an independent entity. In this Nauman resembles an earlier artist of major stature, Marcel Duchamp. He constantly questions the stylistic straitjacket which was a salient characteristic of both Pop art and Minimalism.

Scepticism about style as an end in itself became increasingly apparent in Europe at the beginning of the 1970s, not only through the increasing prominence of Beuys, but with the appearance of Arte Povera. This took its name from an exhibition organized in 1970 by the Italian critic Germano Celant. Celant characterized the kind of art he selected for the show as anti-formal, private, elusive and interested in the essential nature of the materials used.

There was, however, more to it than simply this. The originators of Arte Povera saw it as being as much the child of American Pop art as it was that of the Minimal and Conceptual influences which were the contemporaries and rivals of Pop. The Italian critic Marco Meneguzzo notes that Pop was read, in Europe, as something which had 'a direct contact with the social'.[1] That is, art was endowed with a new moral and political significance: 'The new subject [was] no longer only the artist, but who brings life into being, who retrieves the militant "poverty" of art vis-à-vis an opulent and alienating society.'[2] There was, as he points out, a repudiation of the sanctity of the object and a feeling of alienation which was strengthened by the rebellious anarchist upheavals that swept Europe in 1968 and 1969. Treating Arte Povera, as its name suggests, as primarily an Italian rather than a totally pan-European phenomenon, Meneguzzo notes that it was significant that its main centres were Turin and Rome. Turin, one of the chief industrial cities of Italy, was, at the end of the 1960s and the beginning of the 1970s, the theatre of violent social conflict. Rome, the capital, was less tense, but here the artists had constantly before their eyes the example of the Baroque with its promiscuous intermingling of forms and materials and its refusal to make firm distinctions between artistic genres.

Celant, in a history of the Arte Povera movement published in 1985, notes that it was this complex, heterogeneous quality that tended to upset American observers. He cites the attacks on European 'complexity' which were being launched as early as 1964 by artists such as Frank Stella (then still in a Minimalist

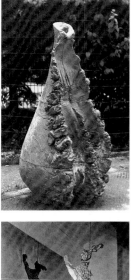

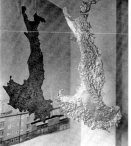

164. **Giuseppe Penone**, *Breath*, 1978

165. **Luciano Fabro**, *Golden Italy*, 1971

166. **Alighiero e Boetti**, *Bringing the World into the World*, 1973–9

phase), and Donald Judd. For supporters of American Minimalism, the new European art seem muddled and compromised. Celant retorts: 'In reality one has the affirmation of artistic variety and relativism, and of the wonder and coherence of the incoherent, where what counts is the overflowing sense of fusion and metamorphosis with history.'[3]

Among the artists closely associated with various phases of the Arte Povera movement were Giovanni Anselmo (b. 1934), Alighiero e Boetti (1940–94), Luciano Fabro (b. 1936), Jannis Kounellis (b. 1936), Mario Merz (b. 1925), Giuseppe Penone (b. 1947) and Giulio Paolini (b. 1940). Each of these interpreted the already vague credo of the movement in his own way. Anselmo and Penone make installations in which rough or 'poor' materials are used to evoke the poetry of nature. Kounellis's work often has a darker, more deliberately industrial tone, but he also makes use of 'natural' elements, including live animals and birds. One of his most famous early pieces was a work staged at the Galleria l'Attico in Rome, in 1969. In this, twelve live horses were tethered to the walls (*Untitled*, 1969). Kounellis saw in this both a conjunction between the formal (the horses spaced at regular intervals) and the completely unpredictable (the actual movement of the animals), and also as a way of turning the work into a complete sensuous experience which appealed to the spectator's hearing, touch and sense of smell, as well as to the sense of sight. Paolini alludes both to Greek myths and to modern interpretations of them. Merz has produced a long series of works which are variations on the theme of the Fibonacci series – a sequence of numbers in which each number is the sum of the previous two. Fibonacci, otherwise known as Leonardo of Pisa, was an Italian mathematician of the thirteenth century, who is said to have anticipated a number of the scientific and mathematical discoveries usually attributed to the Renaissance.

166
165
168
164
169
167

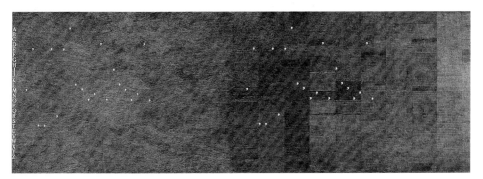

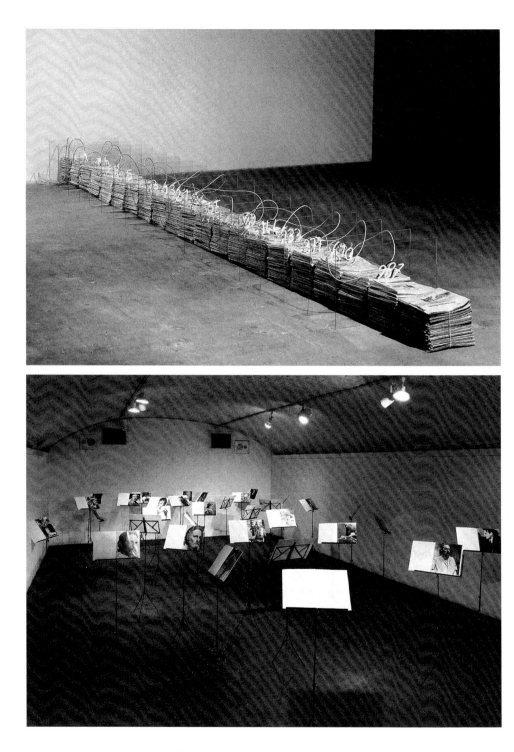

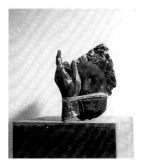

169. **Jannis Kounellis**, *Work Incorporating Classical Fragments*

167. **Mario Merz**, *610 Function of 15*, 1971–89

168. **Giulio Paolini**, *Apotheosis of Homer*, 1970–1

The link between the work of the Arte Povera group and that of Joseph Beuys, made of similarly 'poor' or humble materials, is often noted. Less commonly noticed in their link to the British sculptors of the 1970s and 1980s, such as Tony Cragg (b. 1949), Richard Deacon (b. 1949), Richard Wentworth (b. 1947), Bill Woodrow (b. 1948) and Anish Kapoor (b. 1954). The link is the more interesting because Arte Povera, despite a considerable success within Europe, and eventual acceptance in the United States, did not seem to make much impact in the British Isles. There are similarities between artists like Anselmo and Penone and the work of British Land art sculptors such as Long and Goldsworthy, but these have often been ignored on the grounds that Arte Povera, for all its improvised quality, remained an essentially gallery-based art – where it alludes to nature, this continues to be seen within an essentially Claude-like framework, poeticized but also deliberately constructed. Even more significant, however, is the affinity between some of the early sculptures of Cragg, made from fragments of urban detritus (scraps of plastic, for instance) and Arte Povera. Cragg expresses social concerns similar to those of the Italian artists, and demonstrates a like-minded rejection of the consumer society; and he does so in much the same fashion, by rescuing or 'redeeming' materials formerly considered too degraded for artistic use.

In the work of Wentworth and especially Woodrow, there is a more specific relation to Pop, through the employment of items of familiar domestic use. Woodrow, and the Scottish sculptor David Mach (b. 1956) both transform junked consumer durables – items such as television sets, washing-machines or supplies of unsold magazines – into fantastic new images, often with considerable wit, but also with some loss of the moral force that characterizes Cragg's best inventions. Items which the original Pop artists of the 1960s set up as icons of contemporary culture were now treated with sardonic contempt by a newer generation of artists.

Anish Kapoor, half-Jewish and half-Indian, brought up in India, but living and working in Britain, has used the legacy of both Arte Povera and Minimal art in a different fashion. His early sculptures – simple shapes covered in intense powdery colour – are often reminiscent of ritual objects connected with Hindu Tantrism (the most refined and mystical form of Hindu worship). Kapoor is also fascinated with the idea of absence – of the sculptural form being essentially a container for a mysterious void – he seems indebted in this sense to Lucio Fontana (1898–1968). Efforts have been made to align Kapoor's work with that of other

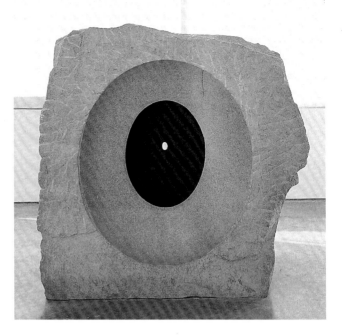

contemporary artists of Indian origin, but Kapoor has always resisted any tendency to categorize his work in this way, pointing out that his affinities are essentially European. In fact, the most striking similarity is with the work of artists like Anselmo and Penone. He represents a renewal of some of the basic ideas of Arte Povera within a British context.

One aspect of Arte Povera, largely ignored when it was new, and little analysed since, was the way in which it displaced the spectator's attention from the single object to the setting. Environmental or installation art had been practised as early as the 1920s by the Dadaist Kurt Schwitters (1887–1948), and further elaborated by the Surrealists and by the pioneers of Pop. The practitioners of Arte Povera took matters a stage further: since their materials were so often so flimsy, or at least so lacking in solid presence, it was the total ambience which counted. The link between the Roman branch of Arte Povera and the Italian Baroque, shrewdly noted by Meneguzzo, is something that deserves further investigation. From the appearance of Arte Povera onwards, spectators increasingly came to think of avant-garde exhibits as a hall of mirrors, places to enjoy a series of illusory effects, with or without some thought-provoking moral or philosophical dimension. Arte Povera can be perceived not as

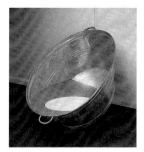

171. **Richard Wentworth**, *Jetsam*, 1984

172. **Richard Deacon**, *Two Can Play*, 1983

a closed 'art movement', organized very much along the lines of the other art movements of the same epoch (the later 1960s and early 1970s), but rather as the initial phase of an attempt to alter the nature of art, and to change its relationship with the public.

Since the birth of Arte Povera, and the appearance on the contemporary art-scene of Joseph Beuys, the word 'sculpture' has been released into a whole new series of meanings, unknown to the pre-Modern era and equally unknown to the pioneer Modernists of the first half of the twentieth century. This has given a special prominence to artists who have used their activity as a way of making points about their own obsessions or past histories, creating a series of private but deliberately theatrical effects. Not surprisingly, many of these artists are female, since women have often been either excluded or marginalized, and art of the kind I am describing is often a reaction to feelings of marginalization.

An important precursor in this respect was the short-lived Eva Hesse (1936–70). Though her work is generally associated with that of the Minimalists and Land artists, such as Smithson and LeWitt who were her New York contemporaries, her soft sculptures and ladder-like structures seem like mysterious echoes of her own psychological traumas. An artist who has a resemblance to Hesse in some of her output is another foreign-born

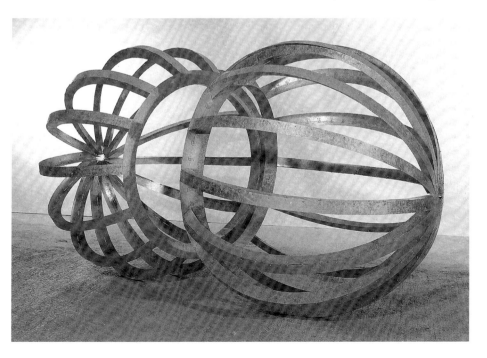

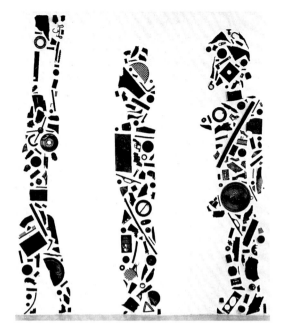

but American-domiciled sculptor, Louise Bourgeois (b. 1911), who was selected, when she was already in her early eighties, as the American representative at the Venice Biennale of 1993. Bourgeois's work is a meditation on the past, and also a release of anger – chiefly, it seems from her own account, anger about a blocked and frustrated childhood, the sadistic teasing to which she was subjected by an anglophile father, and (most of all) the presence in her childhood home of her father's mistress, a young Englishwoman who officially served as governess to Louise and her sister. Bourgeois has made these feelings the subject matter of a series of quasi-Surrealist allegorical tableaux, replete with sexual allusions of various kinds.

Also concerned with ideas of memory and loss is the American environmental artist Ann Hamilton (b. 1956). Hamilton, like Hesse and Bourgeois, makes use of organic materials, but her choice of such substances as honey and wax also makes reference to Beuys. Rebecca Horn (b. 1944), the German installation, performance, action and video artist, similarly evokes in her work the transformative power of material such as carbon and mercury, and features the interaction of the body and complex, often deliberately malfunctioning machines in metaphoric narratives about desire and vulnerability. In her work, the influence of Beuys is even more clearly evident than it is in that of Hamilton.

174. **David Mach**, *Thinking of England*, 1983

175. **Bill Woodrow**, *Self-Portrait in the Nuclear Age*, 1986

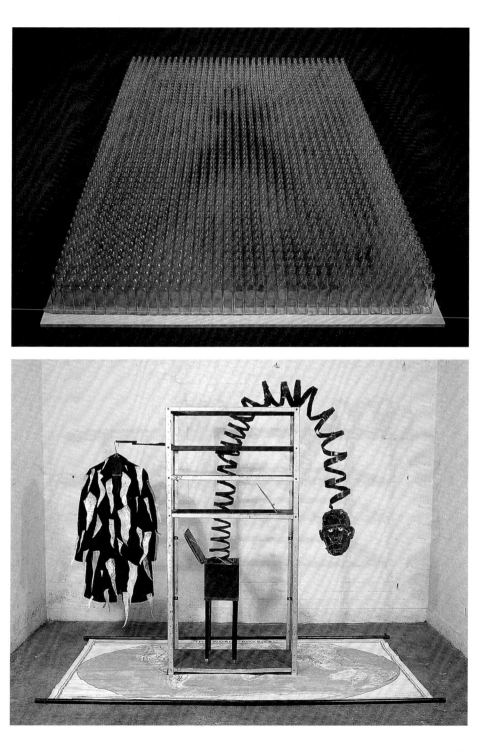

Chapter 7:   Neo-Expressionist tendencies

The radical assaults made on traditional painting by Arte Povera, Conceptual art, Performance art, Video art and other developments aroused resistance both within and without the art world. While promoters of the avant-garde now proclaimed that painting, the chief medium of expression in Western art since the Renaissance, was now dead and buried, many leading artists of the 1970s and 1980s rebelled against this new orthodoxy. The at least momentary return to an atmosphere receptive to painting was marked by an important survey exhibition held at the Royal Academy of Arts in London from January to March 1981. Its title, 'A New Spirit in Painting', carried polemical overtones for the cognoscenti, if not for the public at large.

The exhibition consisted four main tendencies. First, there were abstract painters who were practitioners on canvas of varieties of Minimalism, among them artists like Robert Ryman, Brice Marden and Alan Charlton. There were survivors from the various art movements that had flourished in the immediate past – Willem de Kooning and Cy Twombly carrying on the traditions of Abstract Expressionism; Andy Warhol and David Hockney as standard-bearers for Pop. There were, in addition, isolated 'masters' of figurative painting who were aligned with no particular movement, among them Bacon, Balthus and Lucian Freud.

The rediscovery of Lucian Freud (b. 1922), as the result of a retrospective organized in 1974 by the Arts Council of Great Britain, was an example of the way in which important artists could drop from view when their work did not fit the vision of the avant-garde currently held by those who had the power to shape opinion in the world of contemporary art. Freud's inclusion in 'A New Spirit in Painting' was part of a long process of rehabilitation which culminated in an exhibition held at the Hirshhorn Museum and Sculpture Garden, Washington, DC, in September to November 1987. It was later seen in Paris, London and Berlin. This international touring retrospective turned Freud from an artist of strictly local reputation to one of world rank. He himself remained what he had always been – a figurative painter of a traditional kind, dependent on the presence of the model in

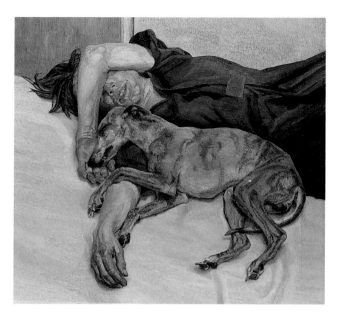

the studio, interested only in what could be observed in those circumstances.

Freud's rehabilitation was not a completely isolated event. The period from the late 1970s to the early 1990s was marked by a series of similar re-emergences. Another example (in this case a painter not included in 'A New Spirit') is the work of the French artist Jean Rustin (b. 1928). Six years younger than Freud, Rustin was the subject of a major retrospective exhibition at Oberhausen, near Düsseldorf, in January 1994. Rustin's extraordinary nudes – geriatric, sexually obsessed, making obscene gestures – are not painted from life, as are Freud's figures. Yet they are the reflection of a somewhat similar world: bleak, isolated, seemingly deprived of hope. His work, like Freud's, has found a response with contemporary audiences because it seems to offer a truthful reflection of important aspects of the world as they know it. In a certain sense they are the precursors of the depressive art of the 1990s, though this expressed itself through very different technical means.

The main thrust of 'A New Spirit in Painting', however, was not represented by Freud. The exhibition devoted itself to the promotion of a Neo-Expressionist tendency in art which was closely identified with the culture of the Federal Republic, the larger, more prosperous, committedly capitalist portion of a Germany which was at that point still politically divided. It was

177

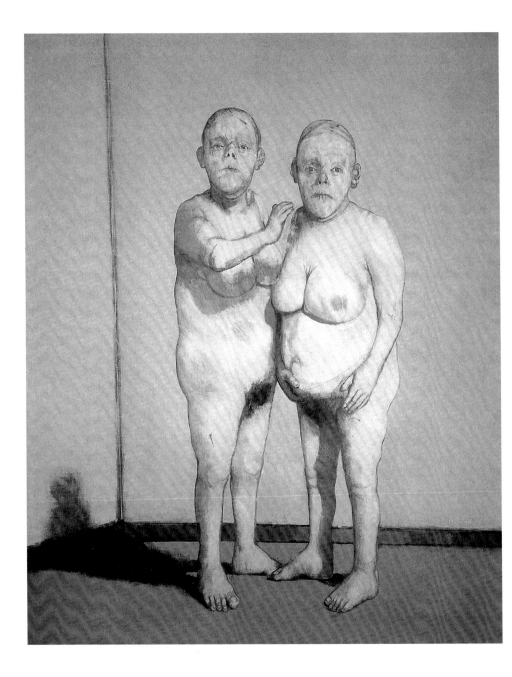

significant that, though the exhibition was held in London, much of the funding came from West German sources. Neo-Expressionist painting was not, in 1981, a new invention. One of the leading figures in German Neo-Expressionism, Georg Baselitz (born Georg Kern, 1938), had begun his career in the DDR, moving to West Berlin in 1956, and evolving a fully formed Expressionist figurative style in the early 1960s. Though Baselitz had proved a rebellious student when in the DDR, his Neo- Expressionism was to some extent based on East rather than West German practice. In the years immediately after World War II, Expressionism had been favoured as the 'official style' by the Communist East German regime because of the hostility shown by the Nazis to the original German Expressionists, who flourished both before World War I and during the Weimar period. Baselitz's close friend and ally, A. R. Penck (born Ralf 178
Winkler, 1939) was also from East Germany, and, while he never formally attended an art school, was subject to the same cultural influences.

Baselitz and Penck, though pioneers of the new tendency, were at least in some respects untypical of it. Both were interested in the 'how' of painting rather than the 'why', in method rather than in content. Penck created a language of graphic signs which owed something to Picasso, and which looked forward to the work of artists connected with the New York Graffiti movement, such as Keith Haring. In 1967 Baselitz began painting his images upside-down, in order, so he claimed, 'to set the imagination free'. A characteristic example is *Die Mädchen von Olmo* of 179
1981. The effect was to focus attention on the somewhat perverse way in which the work was done rather than on what the pictures actually represented.

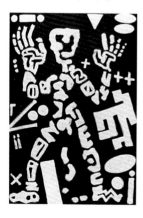

178. **A. R. Penck**, *T3 (R)*, 1982

Other members of the Neo-Expressionist group used their work to examine Germany and her problems. Anselm Kiefer (b. 1945) evolved a complex system of imagery which incorporated elements from German legend, from esoteric philosophy, from the history of World War II, and from the poetry of the great Romanian-Jewish poet Paul Celan (who wrote in German). Some of his most effective images, for example, his *Untitled* of 1978, were inspired by the designs of Hitler's Inspector-General 181
of Buildings (and later Minister for Armaments) Albert Speer. Since Speer in turn was the heir of the great German classicist Karl Friedrich Schinkel (1781–1841), this enabled Kiefer to set up a series of cultural variations and parallels which in turn illuminated some of the darker corners of recent German history.

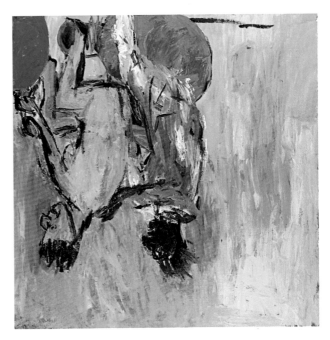

181. **Anselm Kiefer**, *Untitled*, 1978

179. **Georg Baselitz**, *Die Mädchen von Olmo*, 1981

180. **Jörg Immendorf**, *Eigenlob stinkt nicht*, 1983

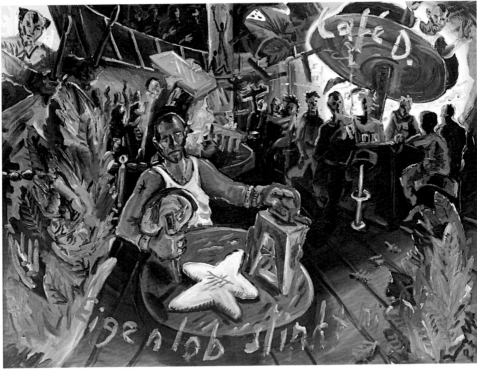

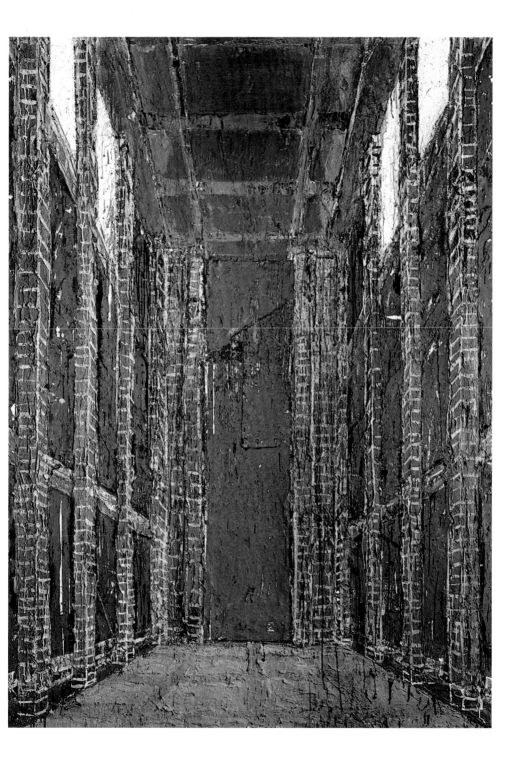

His work can be compared to the political paintings made by some of the artists of the early Romantic epoch, and perhaps most fruitfully to Théodore Géricault's *Raft of the Brig 'Medusa'*, which is similarly ambiguous and complex in its use of traditional formulations (for example, gestures and poses familiar from religious art) in order to comment on contemporary events.

German Neo-Expressionism also embraced overtly political art, such as Jörg Immendorf's (b. 1945) *Café Deutschland* series, 180 initiated in the late 1970s, which comments directly on the division of Germany, and a nostalgic revival of motifs used by the original Expressionists. Rainer Fetting's (b. 1949) *Dancers III* 182 (1982) is a reprise of imagery first used by Emil Nolde (1867–1956) in paintings inspired by his visit to the German Pacific colonies, shortly before the outbreak of war in 1914.

The insistent stylistic language of the leading German Neo-Expressionists contrasts sharply with the tactics adopted by two other German painters whose reputations have survived the art-boom of the 1980s in rather better shape than those of their contemporaries. Gerhard Richter (b. 1932) is now universally recognized as being one of the quintessential figures in one version of Post-Modernism – the version that makes room for traditional technical procedures, albeit with a Conceptual orientation. Rather than proceeding in a series of stylistic leaps, as Picasso once did, Richter has simultaneously pursued several different ways of working. He has made 'photo-paintings' based on found photographs, such as *Three Candles* (1982); 'Colour 183 Chart' paintings featuring groups of flat colour samples; 'Colour

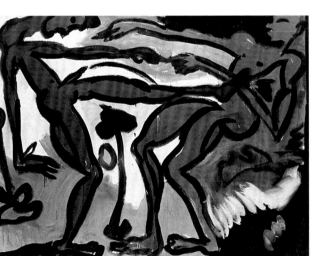

182. **Rainer Fetting**, *Dancers III*, 1982

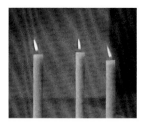

183. **Gerhard Richter**, *Three Candles*, 1982

Streaks', which are near-Minimal abstractions; and even paintings which are analyses of the work of the Old Masters, such as the *Annunciation after Titian* series (1972), in which a celebrated Titian altarpiece is progressively dissolved into pure abstraction.

Another German artist, once a collaborator of Richter, whose work demonstrates the same hostility to the idea of fixed style is Sigmar Polke (b. 1941). Polke's work shows the influence of American Pop art, but also that of Francis Picabia, the Dadaist whose late work is one of the sources of Pop. *Liebespaar II* (1965), 184 an early work, shows Picabia's influence very clearly. Polke has sometimes participated in group exhibitions devoted to German Neo-Expressionism, but it is possible to think that his contributions to these events were intended as parodies of other artists linked to the tendency – for example, Anselm Kiefer.

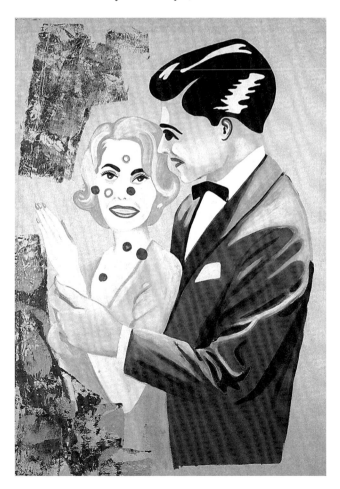

184. **Sigmar Polke**, *Liebespaar II*, 1965

Richter and Polke are both by temperament ironists, and in both cases their work has a strongly Conceptual base. It is these characteristics, as well as their mutability of style, which mark them off from most of their German contemporaries.

Though Neo-Expressionism, for obvious reasons, became firmly associated in the public mind with the post-war revival of German art, it was paralleled by developments elsewhere, notably in the United States and in Italy. In the USA the seminal figure is Philip Guston (1913-80), originally a member in good standing of the Abstract Expressionist movement. In the late 1960s Guston shocked the American art world with a sudden return to figurative work, making paintings that were deliberately bold and rough: their cartoon-like simplicity of line serves as a reminder that Guston began his artistic career as a young boy by taking a correspondence course in cartoon drawing. The cartoons his later paintings most resemble, however, are those produced from the mid-1960s onwards for 'underground' magazines such as the *East Village Other*, the *Berkeley Barb* and the *Los Angeles Free Press*. There is a particularly close resemblance to the work of Robert Crumb (b. 1943), creator of the anarchic beast-fable *Fritz the Cat*, and progenitor of the white-bearded Zen Master, Mr Natural, who has been everything from a bootlegger under Prohibition to a taxi-driver in Afghanistan. One curious detail which reinforces the comparison is the fact that both artists have a fascination with hobnailed boots at the end of spindly legs – these feature prominently in Guston's painting *The Rug* (1979). By working in this way, Guston seemed to reject his own generation in favour of a younger one; at the same time he turned his

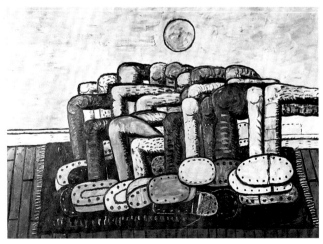

185. **Philip Guston**, *The Rug*, 1979

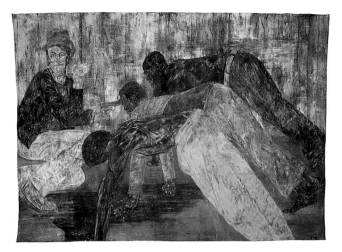

186. **Leon Golub**, *Mercenaries V*, 1984

work into an autobiographical vehicle for savage criticism of what was happening in American society. In a certain sense, he was returning to long-buried roots, since he had begun his career as an admirer of the Mexican muralists, visiting the studios of both Orozco and Siqueiros and producing a Mexican-style mural of his own (in collaboration with Reuben Kadish) for the Emperor Maximilian's summer palace in Morelia, Mexico.

The political paintings – the *Vietnam* series (1973) and the *Mercenaries* (1976–84) – produced by Leon Golub (b. 1922), usu- 186 ally categorized as a social realist, also reflect a deep distress about what was happening in the world, and to the American dream in particular. Like Kiefer in Germany, Golub made direct allusion to political and historical events that provided evidence of a sickness in their respective societies.

The Neo-Expressionist and painterly strains in American art produced somewhat less impressive work in the hands of younger artists. The most highly publicized of them was Julian Schnabel (b. 1951), who has never been slow to court public attention and who has been greatly praised and greatly abused in equal measure. Schnabel's signature works are those in which the surface is covered with fragments of broken crockery – an example is *Humanity Asleep* (1982). Schnabel originally borrowed the device 187 from some of the decoration in Gaudí's Parque Güell in Barcelona. He uses it not only as a way of producing a richly textured surface but of subverting his own fluency of drawing. This is another version of the search for awkwardness which one also finds in Baselitz's insistence on painting his images upside-down, and, earlier, in Dubuffet's use of what are generally considered

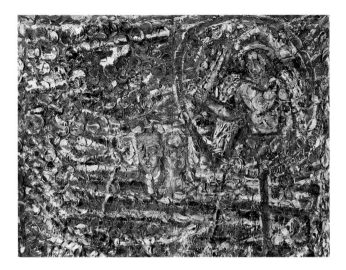

'inappropriate' materials, such as butterflies' wings or lumps of coal. Unlike Baselitz or Dubuffet, however, Schnabel uses the great humanist themes inherited from the pre-Modern epoch – *Humanity Asleep* is a good instance of this. If one strips away the technical trickery, one is left with a rather feeble allegorical composition, which might have been made in the nineteenth century.

Susan Rothenberg (b. 1945)'s work is not as varied as Schnabel's. She paints would-be archetypal images – a horse, a body, a part of a body (the arm in *Beggar*) – in simplified outline. These images are meant to be endowed with mysterious symbolic force. The more closely one examines her work, the more superficial it looks. *Horses*, her earliest and best work, are rather obviously derived from prehistoric cave-paintings.

189

Terry Winters (b. 1949) is technically a more accomplished painter than Rothenberg. His paintings often feature hugely enlarged mushrooms and other fungi – *Caps, Stems, Gills* (1982), for instance. His work, like Schnabel's but in a very different fashion, makes allusions to the past – in this case to the humble botanical drawings produced by eighteenth- and nineteenth-century naturalists. These representations are now blown up to an enormous scale – *Caps, Stems, Gills* is over two metres (well over six and a half feet long). The spectator gets the impression that it is the size of the picture that comes first, and that what is represented is simply a way of articulating the surface. The final result seems purely decorative.

188

It is perhaps a surprise to find a group of Neo-Expressionist painters from Italy, because Expressionism, from the time of

Edvard Munch (1863–1944) onwards, had always been considered a quintessentially northern or even Nordic style, the contrary impulse to southern classicism. The four Italian artists most closely associated with the tendency are the so-called 'three Cs' – Sandro Chia (b. 1946), Francesco Clemente (b. 1952) and Enzo Cucchi (b. 1949) – plus Mimmo Paladino (b. 1948). They are usually discussed as members of the so-called Trans-Avantgarde, a term invented by the Italian critic Achille Bonito Oliva and first used by him in an article which appeared in the periodical *Flash Art* in 1979. In the following year Bonito Oliva published a book, *La transavanguardia italiana*. The idea, according to him, was to find a means of escape from the shibboleths of

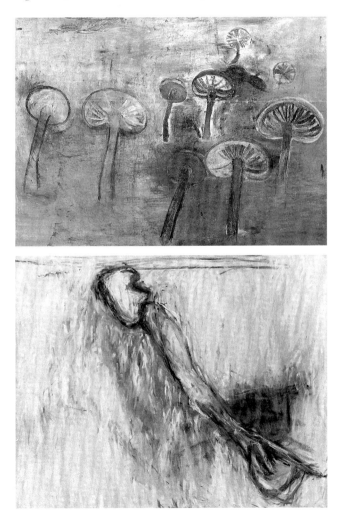

188. **Terry Winters**, *Caps, Stems, Gills*, 1982

189. **Susan Rothenberg**, *Beggar*, 1982

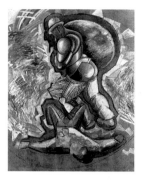

190. **Sandro Chia**, *Crocodile Tears*, 1982

avantgardism, and thus, by implication and in an Italian context, from some of the more puritanical aspects of Arte Povera.

It is not surprising, therefore, to find a strong element of parody in Italian Neo-Expressionist painting, which surfaces particularly in the work of Chia, with its mock-heroic figures – for example, in *Crocodile Tears* (1982), In certain respects, these look back to the work done by Giorgio de Chirico, at the time – from the mid-1920s onwards – when he attempted to lead a traditionalist revolt. There is also a resemblance, perhaps not fully intended, to the work of the Novecento group who flourished under Fascism, and especially to that of their leader, Mario Sironi (1885–1961). Chia's work has not worn well. Much of what he has produced in the past two decades is conspicuously empty.

Francesco Clemente, in contrast to the other members in the group, detached himself from the Italian art scene, and now commutes between New York and India. Clemente maintains a studio in Madras, and many images borrowed from Indian art, and in particular from Tantrism, appear in his work. The mystical element often seems a little suspect – but perhaps one is influenced in this judgment by Clemente's ardent pursuit of fashionability in the snobbish New York art world. Nevertheless many small-scale works, such as his series of watercolours illustrating mystical texts, have undoubted charm.

The most traditionally Expressionist of this group of Italians, and therefore the nearest to his German confrères, is Enzo Cucchi, whose *A Painting of Precious Fires* (1983) is reminiscent of very similar works produced by Anselm Kiefer. Cucchi's problem is that the fact Kiefer exists can make his own work seem redundant. Far more individual, and at the same time much more visibly Italian, is Mimmo Paladino. He comes from southern Italy; he was born near Benevento and spent his childhood in Naples. He has rooted much of his work in ancient but nonclassical sources. His imagery seems to owe much to Italian pre-Romanesque and Romanesque fresco painting, and also to types of sculpture – Sardinian and primitive Italic – on the very verges of the main classical tradition. In recent years he has worked almost as much with sculpture as he has with painting. In both media, his work has a distinctively hieratic, otherworldly quality, as can be seen from the painting *It's Always Evening* (1982) reproduced here. Of all the artists classified as part of the Neo-Expressionist movement, Paladino is the one who – apart from Guston – makes the most coherent and powerful impact. His work resonates with tradition, but is never overwhelmed by it.

190

191

193

192

191. **Francesco Clemente**, *Toothache*, 1981

192. **Mimmo Paladino**, *It's Always Evening*, 1982

193. **Enzo Cucchi**, *A Painting of Precious Fires*, 1983

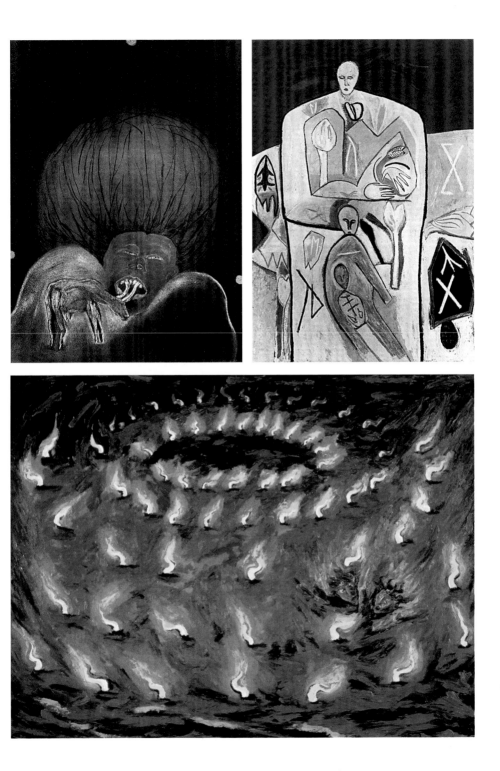

Chapter 8:   The USA – 1970s to 1990s

The most difficult art to come to terms with is neither that of the reasonably distant past, nor that of the immediate present, but art which lingers somewhere in the middle distance – art which is neither old enough to be established, nor entirely new. At the moment this is the situation with much American art of the last three decades. In retrospect, it offers what seems like a thoroughly confusing amalgam of situations and events. A large number of artistic reputations rose with the art-boom that dominated the 1980s, and some of these crumbled in the crash that followed, though others survived triumphantly into the following decade.

If Neo-Expressionism attracted a lot of attention during the late 1970s and the 1980s, so too did the now almost forgotten Graffiti movement. There were several reasons for the success of Graffiti. One was that Neo-Expressionism, despite the adherence of artists like Schnabel, seemed to many American critics to threaten the now-accustomed dominance of the New York art-scene, which had endured more or less unchallenged since the 1940s. Graffiti art, on the contrary, was an indigenous form of creative expression. Like Neo-Expressionism it first manifested itself in the 1970s (the first gallery show of Graffiti art was held in 1973), but did not burst into full bloom until the following decade. It transferred the signs and symbols which already adorned (or defaced, depending on one's point of view) New York subway trains to the walls of commercial art galleries, and thence to those of museums and opulent private homes. Graffiti seemed like a legitimate continuation of Pop art. At the same time, it was the favoured form of creative expression for the young artists who formed part of the new East Village art-scene – a proliferation of new galleries on New York's Lower East Side which suddenly arose to challenge the dominance which SoHo (South of Houston Street) had established in the previous decade.

Today only two reputations survive from the busy world of Graffiti art – those of Jean-Michel Basquiat (1960–88) and Keith Haring (1958–90). Both tragically short-lived, these two artists sum up many of the contradictions that then affected New York art. Basquiat, of mixed Haitian and Puerto Rican origin, is now sometimes presented as a standard bearer for a revival of interest in African-American art. In fact, he had few links with the main tradition of African-American culture as this had developed since the 1920s. While he made work that referred to certain aspects of African-American life (notably to its musical traditions) and to black hero figures, his interests were as widespread as his ambitions were unbounded. He was as likely to allude to Leonardo da Vinci or Homer as he was to turn to specifically 'ethnic' subject-matter. He did, however, enjoy challenging liberal values by using images and inscriptions which referred to his own racial origins in a fashion which in other hands would certainly have been perceived as racist. Basquiat's work is not an attempt to raise black consciousness or to assert specifically African-American values, but through it he often conducted an unsettling dialogue with his audience about what it meant to be a young black man in the American urban context.

Keith Haring was a very different figure – though one thing he shared with Basquiat was a middle-class background. He played no part in the working-class teen scene which spawned the original graffiti craze, and did not, in fact come to live in New York until he was twenty. He studied at the School for Visual Arts, where one of his teachers was the well-known Conceptual artist Joseph Kosuth. For Haring, taking art into the streets was a Conceptual gesture. In 1980, he began to make drawings in the subways, using the empty black panels where advertisements were due to make their appearance. The black background and the material Haring used on it – chalk, the quickest and cheapest means of drawing available – led him to evolve a large, uniform vocabulary of graphic signs quite unlike the playful, wilful style of home-grown New York Graffitists. When Haring began to

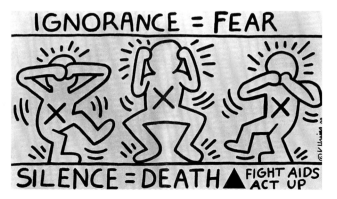

194. **Keith Haring**, *Ignorance = Fear*, 1989

work in a less ephemeral way, this vocabulary proved adaptable to any surface, from the traditional artist's canvas to T-shirts. For a while, until his illness and eventual death (from AIDS, of which he was one of the early victims), Haring became a symbolic figure in the East Village art-scene. However, adaptability of style in one sense mean a certain inflexibility in another. Oil paint or acrylics never seemed to be Haring's essential, primary means of expression. His graphic language was not truly painterly, and this, indeed, was one of the reasons why it could be used success-fully on so many different surfaces, employing a wide variety of media.

Another 'democratizing' New York artist who enjoyed an even more spectacular career than Basquiat or Haring was Jeff Koons (b. 1955). Koons began as a direct descendant of Marcel 196 Duchamp – his vacuum cleaners in Plexiglas cases, shown at the beginning of his career, are 'readymades' in the tradition of Duchamp's celebrated urinal. However, Koons is not an ironist, 86 like Duchamp. He regards his art as celebratory, and his declared aim is to 'communicate with as many people as possible'. It seems

195. Jean-Michel Basquiat and Andy Warhol, *Collaboration*, 1984

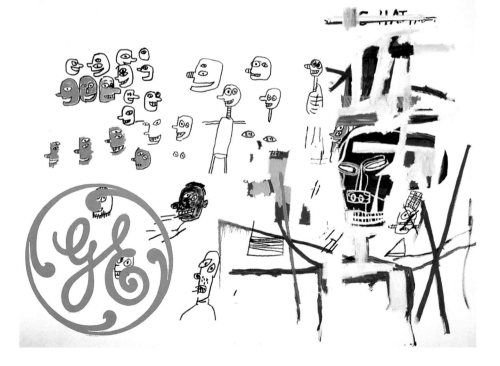

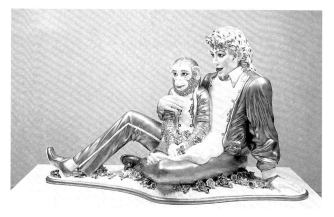

certain, however, that he communicates with different portions of his audience in very different ways. Sophisticated viewers take a certain pleasure in Koons's acts of aesthetic rape. The celebrated American critic and art historian Robert Rosenblum, for example, wrote as follows, when Koons's art was still relatively new:

In terms of first person experience, I still recall, the shock of my initial confrontation with Koons's lovingly hideous and accurate reconstructions of the lowest levels of three-dimensional kitsch, from porcelain Pink Panthers and Popples to painted wooden bears and angels. We have all, of course, been seeing this kind of stuff for years in every shopping centre and tourist trap, but never before have we been forced, as one is in a gallery setting, to look head on and up close at its mind-boggling ugliness and deliriously vapid expressions.[1]

Yet there is no reason to think that the less sophisticated part of Koons's audience reacted to his art with this mixture of fascination and horror. They simply enjoyed it for what it was – and saw it as something which gave them permission to like things which they secretly enjoyed already.

The same might be said, with even greater force, about a further series of works by Koons, modelled on images found in hardcore pornographic magazines. These are vastly enlarged photographs which show the artist and his then-wife Ilona Staller, a Hungarian-born professional pornographic actress and model who made her career in Italy, performing various sexual acts for the camera.

These photographs can be perceived in various ways – as an act of complicity with the mass audience, but also perhaps as an act of defiance directed against the 'political correctness' which was an increasing factor in the cultural climate of the 1980s. The

Conceptual element in Koons's work – its element of intellectual terrorism – is stressed by the fact that he is not the actual maker of the artworks associated with his name. The erotic images were produced by a professional photographer, commissioned for the purpose, and other tasks were assigned to qualified professionals in the same fashion. Koons's woodcarvings, for example, are made to his specifications by traditional Black Forest woodcarvers who generally produce sentimental tourist artifacts. Once the initial idea has been conceived, Koons's own role is organizational and supervisory.

The artists who were associated with Koons's rise to celebrity in the 1980s, such as Haim Steinbach (b. 1944), Peter Halley (b. 1953) and Philip Taaffe (b. 1955) all now look like essentially minor figures, busy recycling ideas which had already been around in the modern art world for a long time. More original is Robert Gober (b. 1954), who had already achieved a certain prominence at the end of the decade, and who became even better known in the 1990s. In many respects Gober seems like Koons replayed in a minor key. His creations are uniformly enigmatic – a Super Realist, fully clothed male leg sticking out of a wall; wallpaper with images of genitalia; a lay figure wearing a wedding dress. These creations are for the most part just as much 'appropriations' as Koons's gleanings from gift shops and the household

198
197
199

200

197. **Peter Halley**, *Yellow and Black Cells with Conduit*, 1985

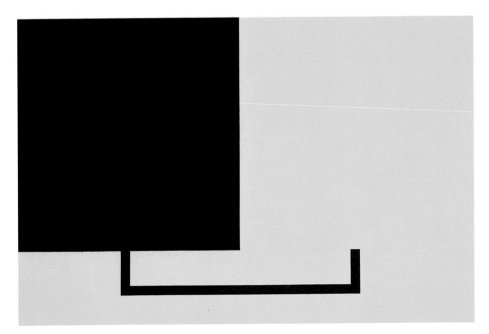

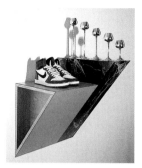

198. **Haim Steinbach**, *Related and Different*, 1985

199. **Philip Taaffe**, *Four Quad Cinema*, 1986

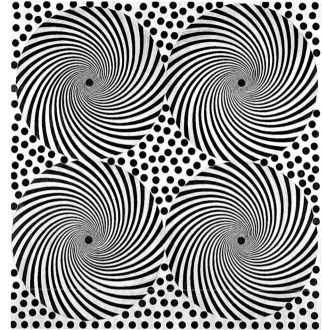

200. **Robert Gober**, *Untitled*, 1991

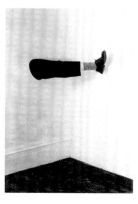

departments of department stores. But whereas Koons goes in for full disclosure – what you see is what you get – Gober's work always gives the impression that he is deliberately withholding information. There are signs of distress – a playpen built on a slant hints at some inner anguish – but a lack of anything really specific. Critics have put forward the idea that these are symbols devised by a gay man in the age of AIDS, but there is nothing one can really pin down. All explanations, including those occasionally offered by the artist himself, tend to spin out of control. Gober's images may indeed symbolize what they are said to symbolize, but there is no proof, no immediately apparent connection between the actual object and the meanings attributed to it.

Gober has said that he has been influenced by feminist art, and feminism was certainly an important theme in the art of the 1980s. The sequence begins with what is certainly the most ambitious feminist artwork of them all – Judy Chicago's *The Dinner Party*. This huge installation is one on the very few artworks made since the beginning of the 1970s which enjoys the kind of iconic status so readily given to Pollock's *Blue Poles*, Warhol's *Marilyns* or Roy Lichtenstein's *Whaam!*. 201

The Dinner Party, having occupied the artist since 1976, was first shown at the Museum of Modern Art in San Francisco in

1979. It then made an extensive tour, often, however, appearing in ad hoc, non-museum settings. Everywhere it was seen it drew large crowds, and it thus played an important part in the democratization of contemporary art – something which became an important theme in the 1980s and continued with unabated vigour in the 1990s. Response to it divided the American art world. When the piece was seen at the Brooklyn Museum in October 1980, the veteran art-critic Hilton Kramer assailed it in the *New York Times* as 'very bad art…failed art…art so mired in the pieties of political causes that it fails to acquire any independent life of its own.'[2]

The Dinner Party comprises a huge triangular table, with places set for thirty-nine women whom the artists wished to honour. Each woman is provided with a place setting, the most important feature of which is a ceramic plate, with decoration symbolizing the personality of the honoree. Chicago comments, in the book which accompanied the installation, that:

There is a strong narrative aspect to the piece that grew out of the history uncovered in our research and underlying the entire conception of 'The Dinner Party'… Beginning with prepatriarchal society, 'The Dinner Party' demonstrates the development of goddess worship, which represents a time when women had social and political control (clearly reflected in the goddess imagery common to the early stages of almost every society in the world). The piece then suggests the gradual destruction of these female-oriented societies and the eventual domination of women by men, tracing the institutionalizing of that repression and women's response to it.[3]

The feminist content of the piece has, however, served to divert attention from aspects of it which now, in historical perspective, seem almost equally important. Judy Chicago was not an artist who had made her career in New York – a fact which in part accounts for the extremely hostile reception her work tended to receive from critics based there. She was brought up in Chicago and afterwards studied and worked in Los Angeles, a city which, in the 1970s, was belatedly trying to establish an independent artistic identity. From the mid-West she took elements of its strong populist tradition. Despite the huge differences both in medium and in social attitudes, one of the artists whom she most closely resembles is the leader of the American Regionalists, Thomas Hart Benton. Both are didactic artists who are determined to address a mass audience in a language that the audience can sympathize with and understand.

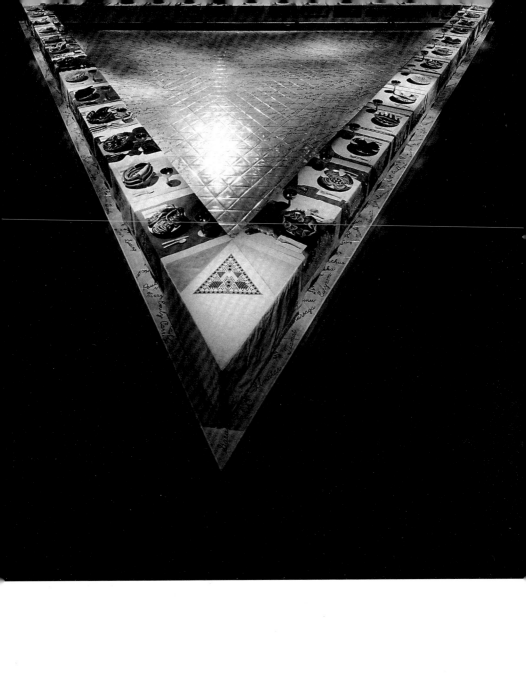

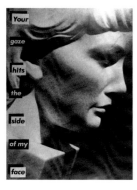

202. **Barbara Kruger**, *Untitled (Your Gaze Hits the Side of my Face)*, 1981

From California came a cavalier attitude towards the idea that there was a hierarchy of artistic media. Chicago chose china-painting and embroidery – two of the chief means of expression in *The Dinner Party* – because these were channel of creativity specifically associated with women, and often relegated to an inferior place by male commentators. But it was also important that California had long been a region where the so-called 'crafts' competed more successfully with the fine arts than they did on the East Coast of America. The fact that *The Dinner Party* was deliberately decorative was almost as important as its refusal to apologize for its didacticism.

Many feminist artworks followed in the wake of *The Dinner Party*, often using means very different from those which Judy Chicago herself had chosen. Barbara Kruger (b. 1945) made a name for herself in the 1980s with photopieces that reflected both her studies with the photographer Diane Arbus (1923–71) at the Parsons School of Design in New York and her later experience as head of design for *Mademoiselle*, a glossy women's magazine. Kruger appropriated old photographs of the 1940s and 1950s and overlaid them with brief accusatory texts, in a manner which owed much to Russian Constructivist poster designers, such as the Shterenberg brothers (1881–1948 and 1894–1979). Her work took many forms – it appeared on billboards and magazine covers and formed part of shop-window displays. She also made ambitious room-sized installations, once again in a manner derived from Russian Constructivist experiments, particularly those of El Lissitzky (1890–1941).

Reviewing a retrospective exhibition of Kruger's work held at the Whitney Museum in 2000, the chief art critic of the *New York Times*, Michael Kimmelman, commented tartly: 'Does it need to be said how victim credentials often came before aesthetic value? Or that choosing the art community as a context in which to denounce elitism always seemed strangely contradictory and unreflective?'[4] There was, however, an aspect of Kruger's work in the 1980s which now seems important historically. Though her photographic images were almost invariably appropriated, she was one of the artists of that period who was responsible for pulling photography into the mainstream of artistic activity. Or, as Kimmelman puts it in a more negative fashion, 'the already shaky hierarchy involving fine art, photography, graphic design, film and video was further disturbed.'[5]

Another artist, also sometimes classified as a feminist, who did even more to raise the standing of photographic imagery, was

202

Cindy Sherman (b. 1954). Sherman's *Untitled Film Stills*, a series of photographic self-portraits begun in 1977, show the artist in poses and situations borrowed from B-movies. The references are carefully unspecific, but Sherman presents herself, and American women of her generation in general, as the products of a culture saturated in Hollywood imagery and, through that imagery, victimized by the falsity of Hollywood's values. Sherman is more imaginative than Kruger in her approach. She pushed her analysis of female gender stereotypes still further in photographs which parodied celebrated Old Master paintings and in others which used medical prostheses to construct sexual tableaux.

If Sherman played a large part in raising the status of photography in the 1980s, so too did the most notorious American artist of the decade, Robert Mapplethorpe (1946–89). Mapplethorpe's reputation is now coloured by the fact that he was a victim of AIDS, and still more so by the censorship controversy that engulfed his work immediately after his death, when the Corcoran Gallery of Art in Washington DC cancelled a showing of a touring retrospective devoted to his work. The same exhibition was later the subject of a much publicized criminal prosecution when it was shown at the Cincinnati Contemporary Arts Center.

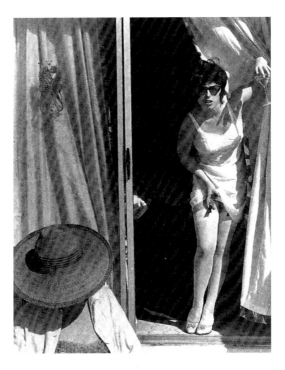

203. **Cindy Sherman**, *Untitled Film Still # 7*, 1978

Though Mapplethorpe never made any secret of his sexual orientation, he was not a militant supporter of homosexual liberation, and his work was an expression of preferences and tastes which he himself recognized as being purely personal. In a conversation held with his lover and memorialist Jack Fritscher in 1982, he expressed contempt for, but also complete indifference to the idea of censorship: 'He cared little really about sexual politics, racial equality, established religion or government grants.'[6]

Mapplethorpe's importance now seems to have comparatively little to do with his sexuality or his insistence on expressing it openly, and much more to do with his attitude to photography itself. His patron and lover Sam Wagstaff, a sometime museum curator who was wealthy in his own right, was one of the first people to collect photography systematically as an art form. Mapplethorpe had unrestricted access to this very rich collection and was thus perhaps the first photographer to have a complete photographic education, in aesthetic as well as in purely technical terms. His best images, such as those from the *Black Males* series *(Thomas*, 1986) show that he was part of the revival of Deco taste which took place during the 1980s, but his eye ranged more widely that this – he borrowed from the work of George Platt Lynes (1907–55), from the society portraits and images of flowers made early in the twentieth century by Adolph de Meyer (1868–1949), and from the works of his own somewhat older contemporary, the New Orleans-based painter and photographer George Dureau (b. 1930), such as *Wilbert Hines* (1972). Comparison with Dureau's work also tends to reveal Mapplethorpe's chief weakness – his lack of feeling. For Mapplethorpe his black men are beautiful objects, or, at best, beautiful male animals, representations of sexual power purged of almost any trace of human individuality. Dureau's photographs, on the other hand, show that he empathizes with his subjects. His interest in amputees and other physically disadvantaged people (particularly dwarfs) has led to his being placed with Diane Arbus. But he is superior to her, just as he is to Mapplethorpe, because he is always careful to present each of his subjects, however damaged physically, as a complete, complex personality, fully the equal of the photographer himself. The continuation of the story of the rise of photography to a central position in the world of contemporary art can be found in Chapter 11.

If the increasing emphasis on photography was one feature of the American art of the 1970s and 1980s, so too were an increasing number of challenges to the hegemony of New York. Judy

204

205

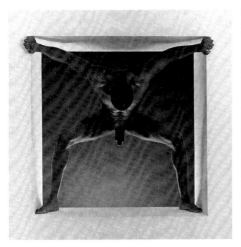

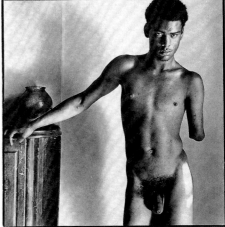

204. **Robert Mapplethorpe**, *Thomas*, 1986

205. **George Dureau**, *Wilbert Hines*, 1972

(overleaf)
206. **Roy de Forest**, *Untitled*, 1990

207. **William T. Wiley**, *Was It Ever Any Different From Now*, 1987

208. **Roger Brown**, *Randie's Donuts with Hollywood Junipers and Ranchhouses*, 1991

209. **David Bates**, *Sheepshead*, 1985

Chicago was by no means the only example. Throughout the post-World War II epoch attempts were made to create art worlds that were independent of the East Coast. The earliest of these was the rebellion staged in the 1950s, in and around San Francisco, against the then current New York obsession with non-figurative art. The 'Bay Area Figuration' of artists such as David Park (1911–60), Elmer Bischoff (1916–91) and the young Richard Diebenkorn (1922–93) was a conscious gesture of defiance directed against the orthodoxies of the dominant Abstract Expressionist school on the East Coast.[7] The return to figuration, partly under the influence of the Beat poets, who also flourished in San Francisco at that time, developed further into the kind of 'funk' art made by Bruce Conner (b.1933) and others, which has already been briefly mentioned in Chapter 4 (p. 102). From this in turn sprang the kind of narrative art, strongly influenced by personal fantasy, which is typical of much recent San Francisco painting.[8] Painters representative of the tendency are Roy De Forest (b. 1930) and William T. Wiley (b. 1937); the latter received most of his art education in northern California and his work remains very characteristic of the local sensibility, even though he no longer lives in the area.

206
207

As I have already noted when speaking of Judy Chicago, one major frontier that was often ignored by Bay Area artists was the then-accepted division between fine art and craft. Craft enjoyed a prestige, and also a seniority, in the structure of northern California culture which was denied it on the East Coast. San Francisco and its environs has been a major centre for the turn-of-the-century Arts and Crafts Movement. Especially typical

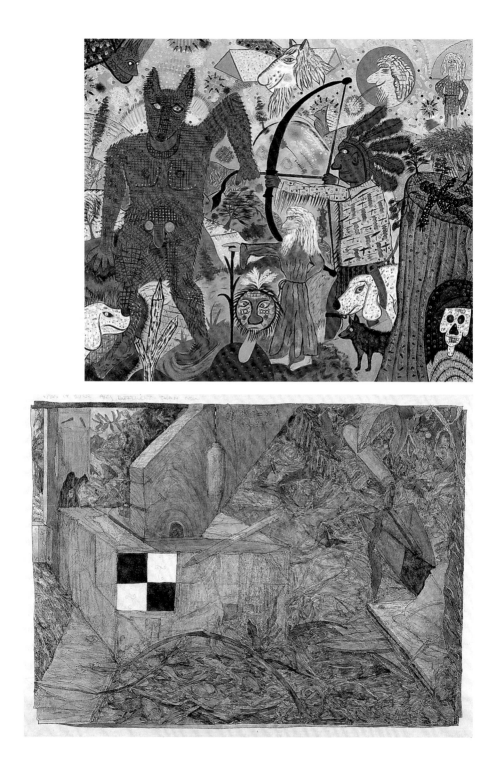

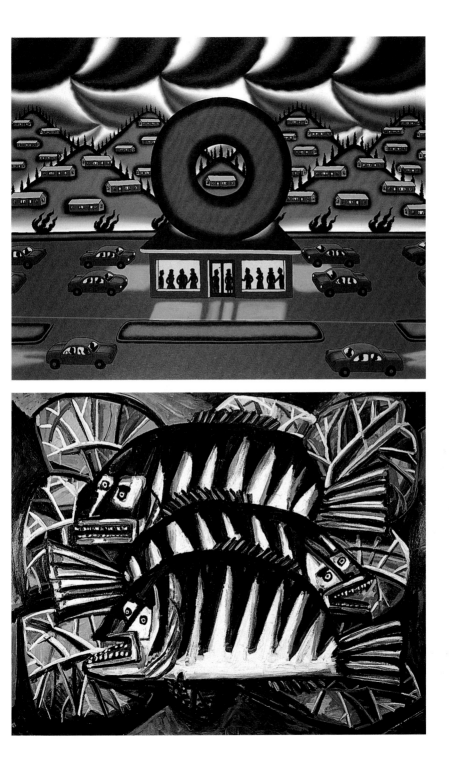

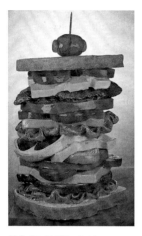

210. **David Gilhooly**, *An Excessive Dagwood Sandwich*, 1987

211. **Robert Arneson**, *Californian Artist*, 1982

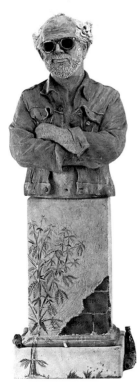

of the northern California arts scene in the 1960s, '70s and '80s was a group of ceramic sculptors whose members included Robert Arneson (1930–92), David Gilhooly (b. 1943) and Viola Frey (b. 1933). In the earlier part of their careers the first two of these had close links with the funk art movement. In some ways the craft-based art of northern California anticipated the post-medium situation which was to prevail in the art of the 1990s.

The art of southern California tended to take another direction from that typical of the area round San Francisco, but it remained visibly different from that produced in New York. From the late 1960s onwards, the painting of Californian Pop painters such as Billy Al Bengston (b. 1934) and Ed Ruscha (b. 1937) to some extent parallels that done by New York colleagues in the Pop movement. However, Ruscha's work shows a much more sophisticated understanding of the techniques of both still photography and film than that of New York-based painters mining the same aspect of popular culture. The most generically southern Californian art, however, is the work of artists deliberately manipulating the audience's perception of light and space, whose work has already been discussed in Chapter 5. Though

211
210
212

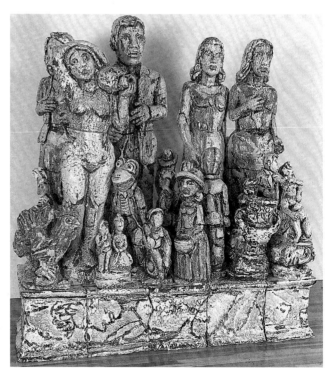

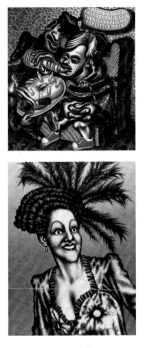

213. **Peter Saul**, *Jeffrey Dahmer*, 1993

214. **Ed Paschke**, *Minnie*, 1974

212. **Viola Frey**,
Artist/Mind/Studio/World Series I,
1993

many of the most important monuments of the Light and Space movement, chief among them Turrell's *Roden Crater* project, are not located within the boundaries of the state of California, the sensibility that informs them has long been recognized as typical of the region.

In Illinois, the breakaway from New York tastes and standards was led by the Chicago Imagists. These too were artists affiliated to Pop art yet approaching popular culture in a rather different spirit from that which inspired their East Coast confrères. Since the 1950s Chicago had had major private collections of classic European Surrealist art, including also work by the home-grown American Surrealist Joseph Cornell, and these exercised a major influence. Other, and very important influences were 'outsider' art – the product of untutored painters and sculptors, chief among them the black visionary Dwight Yoakum (1886/8–1976). a circus artist and hobo who at one point is his career had been personal valet to the circus tycoon John Ringling; and the work, simultaneously playful and threatening, of the sculptor H. C. Westermann (b. 1922), as well as the psychedelic images associated with rock music in the late 1960s. Among the best known Chicago Imagists are Ed Paschke (b. 1939) and Roger Brown (b. 1941). Their work, with its tinge of Expressionist intensity and (in Brown's case in particular) its frequent use of insistent repetitive patterning, has been widely influential. So too has the combination of Surrealist and Pop influence in the work of Chicago painters such as Jim Nutt (b. 1938) and Gladys Nilsson (b. 1940). The Chicago Imagists were, as a group, playful, sardonic and deeply involved in popular culture. The exuberance, energy and openness of their work, and its lack of heavy theoretical baggage made it easy to assimilate and widely influential in associated forms of visual expression, such as commercial graphic design.

Chicago art had an impact in other regions of America, but most notably in Texas. Evidence of can be found in the work of Texas artists such as David Bates (b. 1952) and Peter Saul (b. 1934). Bates's work also pays homage to an established tradition of folk-painting in Texas, paraphrasing and affectionately parodying typical aspects of its imagery. Peter Saul is a social and political commentator, whose work supports the Texan reputation for spinning tales while at the same time undermining the Lone Star state's reputation for rock-solid political conservatism.

152

214
208

209
213

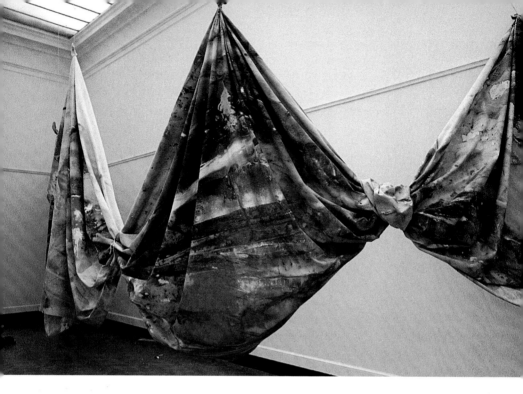

215. **Sam Gilliam**,
Horizontal Extension, 1969

216. **Martin Puryear**,
Noblesse O., 1987

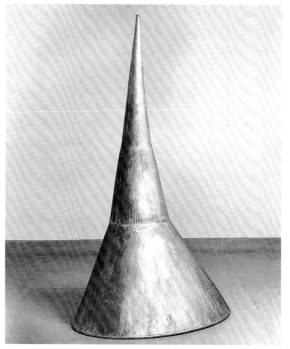

Chapter 9: Issue-based art and globalization

The ever-increasing emphasis on the importance of subject-matter in art, as opposed to individual expressive style, led in turn to the notion that one of the specific tasks of the contemporary artist was to give a voice to groups that in some way saw themselves as disadvantaged. This was not altogether a new idea – African-American art and its supporters and promoters had played at least an intermittent role in the history of American art almost from the beginning of the twentieth century. From at least the 1920s onwards, art by African-Americans was seen as one of the ways in which an oppressed minority could find a voice. Its development along this road can be traced through several stages – first the work of the painters of the Harlem Renaissance (Aaron Douglas 1899–1979, Palmer Hayden 1893–1973 and William Henry Johnson 1901–70), who made up the first coherent grouping of African-American artists. Then that of Jacob Lawrence (1917–2000) and Romare Bearden (1914–88). Then the African-American art of the 1960s and the Civil Rights Movement.

217

218

Exhibitions of African-American art were frequent in the early and mid-1970s, under a shifting array of titles. The most important were the following: 1971, 'Contemporary Black Artists in America', Whitney Museum of American Art, New York; 1975, 'Jubilee: Afro-American Artists in Afro-America', Museum of Fine Arts, Boston; 1976, 'Two Centuries of Black American Art', Los Angeles County Museum of Art. In contrast, there was only one major enterprise of this sort in the 1980s – 'Black Art: Ancestral Legacy – The African Impulse in African American Art', mounted by the Dallas Museum of Art in 1989.

The Dallas exhibition was somewhat coolly received, since by that time a reaction against direct ethnic identification had set in among leading African-American artists. Many of them – Sam Gilliam (b. 1933) or Martin Puryear (b. 1941), for example – preferred to emphasize the essentially personal nature of their art. Gilliam, the leading African-American abstract painter of his generation, made off-stretcher paintings which were a direct continuation of the tradition of Morris Louis. Martin Puryear, one of the very few African-American sculptors to have direct

215

216

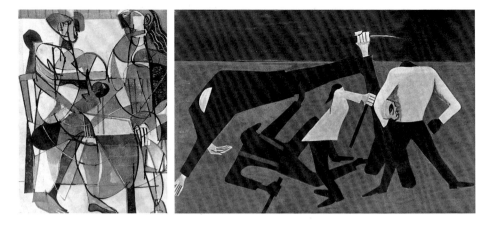

217. **Romare Bearden**, *The Family*, 1948

218. **Jacob Lawrence**, *One of the Largest Race Riots Occurred in East St Louis*, from the series *The Migration of the Negro*, 1940–1

experience of Africa – as a young man he served in Sierra Leone as a member of the Peace Corps – has always denied that either African art or the desire to assert African-American rights are motivations for his work, which falls within the tradition of Brancusi but has also been influenced by Minimalists such as Donald Judd. The wood-laminating technique he uses owes much more to his study of Swedish furniture-making methods during a period at the Royal Academy of Art in Stockholm that it does to anything identifiably African. African-American studies courses are nevertheless eager to claim him as one of their own, and point to similarities between some of his methods and African basket-making.

One area where African-American artists maintained a much more militant stance during the 1980s was in work done by women, where African self-identification and feminism proved a potent combination. One of the most politically committed figures on the American art scene during the period was Adrian Piper (b. 1948). Piper's installations and environments aimed to confront spectators with the true nature of their own attitudes. Some titles give the flavour of her work: *Aspect of the Liberal Dilemma* (1978), *Four Intruders Plus Alarm System* (1980), *Cornered* (1988) and *What It's Like, What It Is, No. 1* (1991). It is an important aspect of Piper's work that she is very light-skinned – this gives her performance work in particular a special edge. Other women working in this field, with somewhat similar attitudes, are Faith Ringgold (1930) and the mother and daughter Betye (b. 1929) and Alison Saar (b. 1956). In each case the work seems as much concerned with the special position of black women in American society as it does with African-American identity in general.

222

220

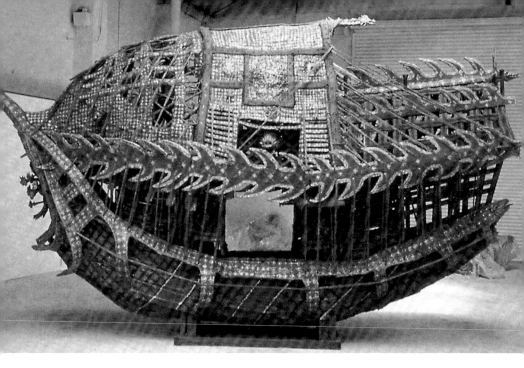

219. **Hew Locke**, *Ark*, 1992–4

220. **Betye Saar**, *The Liberation of Aunt Jemima*, 1972

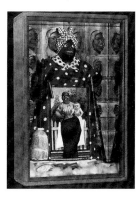

Afro-Caribbean art in Britain, has similar parameters and a somewhat similar relationship to the society that surrounds it as African-American art in the United States, but contrasts with it in that it has a much shorter history. Essentially it is the product of the great West Indian migration to Britain which took place in the years after World War II. Like African-American art it attempts to deal with issues such as slavery, racial discrimination and identification with an idealized Africa (a location in the mind which differs widely from its counterpart in everyday reality). Far more than African-American art, it is still in a state of formation. Some artists, such as Keith Piper (b. 1960) make paintings and environmental works with forthright political messages, thus resembling the more militant African-American artists of the 1970s. Others, such as the Guyanese sculptor Hew Locke (b. 1959) are experimenting with a self-invented 'folk' tradition. Locke's *Ark*, a large, richly decorated papier-mâché model of a boat, symbolizes both the transition from one culture to another and the brutal Middle Passage which brought the slaves from Africa.

221

219

The most conspicuous content-based art of the 1980s and 1990s was feminist. Examples of this have already been cited, such as Judy Chicago's *The Dinner Party* and the work of Barbara

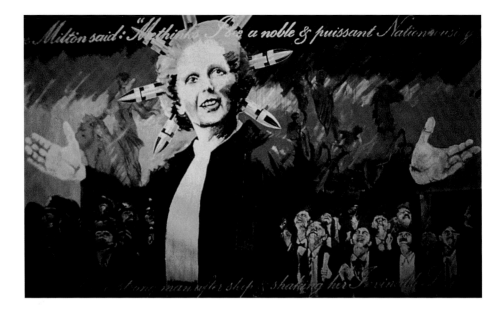

Milton said: "Me thi... ...e a noble & puissant Nation...

...man after sleep ...shaking her...

221. **Keith Piper**, *The Nanny of the Nation Gathers her Flock*, 1987

222. **Faith Ringgold**, *The Wedding: Lover's Quilt No. 1*, 1986

Kruger. By the time it was created in reality, feminist art already possessed quite a substantial history in terms of theory. In the early 1970s women artists and women art historians started to ask themselves a series of questions: why were women so undervalued as artists? (This was the question posed in Linda Nochlin's influential essay 'Why have there been no great women artists?', *Art News*, LXIX, January 1971)[1]. In what ways could women's art advance the feminist cause? Should women's art be fundamentally different from that produced by members of the opposite sex? In December 1976, just over two years before Judy Chicago unveiled *The Dinner Party*, Ann Sutherland Harris and Linda Nochlin were responsible for a major exhibition at the Los Angeles Country Museum of Art, 'Women Artists, 1550–1950'. This was a first step towards the rediscovery of role models such as Artemisia Gentileschi (1593–1651), Paula Modersohn-Becker (1876–1907) and Frida Kahlo (1910–54). Meanwhile feminist theoreticians elaborated new critical approaches to the artwork and its function within an aesthetic and social context. Many of these were derived from French structuralist and post-structuralist philosophy – that is, the work of art was not seen as an end in itself, nor as a complete, self-sufficient entity, but as something that modified the situation in which it was put, and that changed character and meaning as the situation itself changed. Feminist art theory, because it was

231

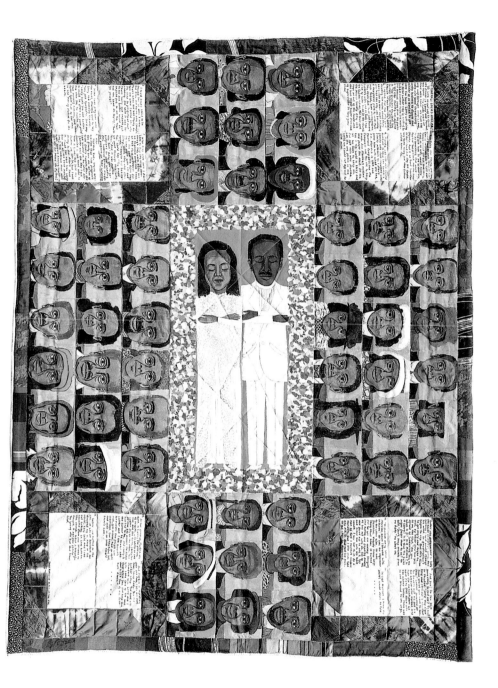

211

223. **Mary Kelly**, *Post Partum Document, Documentation VI*, 1978–9

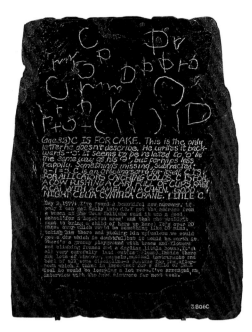

224. **Derek Jarman**, *Blood*, 1992

a coherent system, largely lacking in the contemporary art world since the decline of Marxism, had a profound impact on the development of art criticism in general: it seemed to offer a point of reference for all writers on contemporary art. A typical feminist work springing from this intellectual context is Mary Kelly's *Post Partum Document* (1973–79), an anthropological analysis of a mother's relationship with her son – their initial closeness and the inevitable separation imposed by society.

Feminist art developed in step with another kind of issue-based art: the art of gay liberation, which was soon transmuted into art that was a response to the AIDS crisis. Artists like David Wojnarowicz (1954–92) and Ross Bleckner (b. 1949) are cases in point. Bleckner's paintings are by no means all of them about AIDS – others play elaborate games with abstract and figurative conventions. There is, however, a long series of canvases featuring chalices and vases of flowers, often amid rays of light, which are commemorations of victims of the disease. Bleckner claims that in these, he is 'degrading the sublime. I want my paintings to attempt a belief and a sincerity which I, as an artist, don't necessarily feel, and certainly don't feel continuously.'[2]

Wojnarowicz, together with his fellow AIDS-victim, the British painter and film-maker Derek Jarman (1941–94), was one of the fiercest polemicists associated with the fight against AIDS.

Jarman's later paintings, for example those included in his exhibition 'QUEER', held in 1992, shortly before his death, and in the posthumous show 'EVIL QUEEN' in 1994, are made up of violent inscriptions and graffitoed emblems; Wojnarowicz's are more frequently complex personal narratives, often with overlapping systems of imagery which the spectator is forced to decode. However, they too spring from urban graffiti. Wojnarowicz began his career spray-painting emblematic designs on walls and in abandoned warehouses (notorious for clandestine homosexual encounters along the Hudson River waterfront). There is in fact no frontier between Wojnarowicz's work as a visual artist and his work as a writer, although (paradoxically enough) his fierce autobiographical book, *Close to the Knives* (New York, 1991) has little to say about art itself, though much to impart about the author's disturbed adulthood and damaged childhood. What the two artists have in common, besides their fate, is an urgency of utterance which has little or nothing to do with the idea of conscious stylistic gesture. In AIDS art, the actual subject-matter is primary.

Lesbian art has been slower to achieve public visibility than gay male art, but began to do so in the course of the 1990s. What is still currently the fullest account of the activity of 'out' lesbian

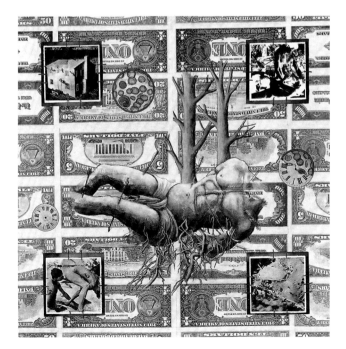

225. **David Wojnarowicz**,
Bad Moon Rising, 1989

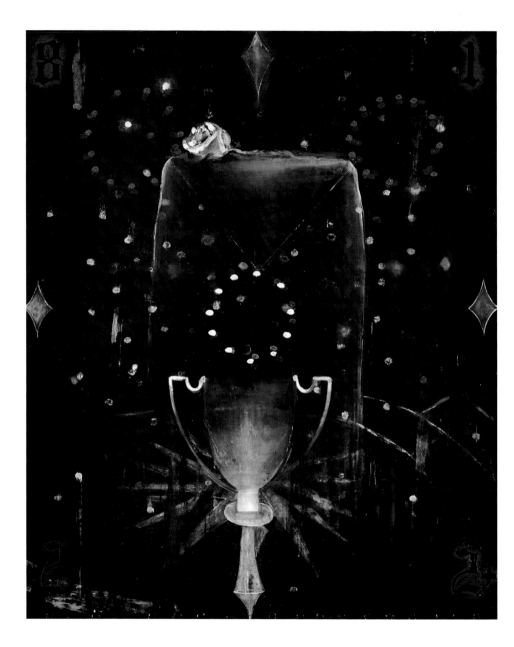

226. **Ross Bleckner**, *8,122+*
as of January 1986, 1986

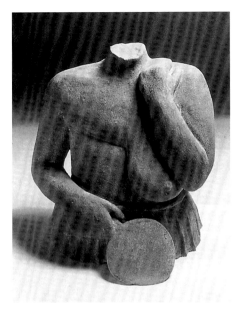

artists, the second edition of Emmanuel Cooper's *The Sexual Perspective: Homosexuality and Art in the Last 100 Years in the West* (London and New York, 1994 – first published in 1986) makes it clear that much of what he describes had to rely on 'alternative' spaces to achieve visibility and thus remained somewhat out of the mainstream.

There is also the fact that lesbian art has been divided between the wish to focus on women's issues and the desire to concern itself with purely lesbian ones. Nancy Fried's (b. 1945) 227 sculptured torsos in clay are about breast cancer and mastectomy – subjects that, in the circumstances, any woman artist might feel the need to tackle. Lesbian identity is often affirmed through appropriation, for example in Sadie Lee's (b. 1955) witty version of the *Mona Lisa,* showing Leonardo's iconic woman wearing a collar and tie. This image is an addition to the long series of *Mona Lisa* variants in twentieth-century art, beginning with Duchamp's *L.H.O.O.Q.*

One problem with a purely issue-based art is that it tends to devalue universal human emotions. Some of the most moving comments on the AIDS crisis, for example, have been made by the American performance artist Karen Finley who has lost many friends to the disease. Her installation piece *The Vacant Chair* 228 (1993), a throne-like seat covered with flowers, foliage and moss, confronting two plain chairs, is a comment on grief and loss. The

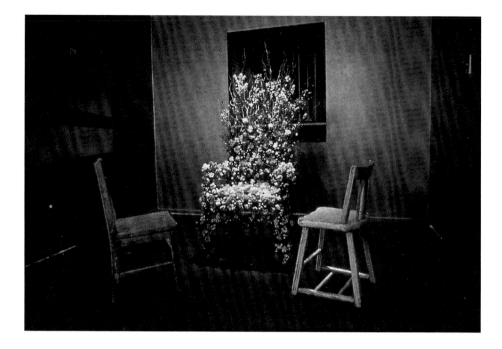

228. **Karen Finley**, *The Vacant Chair*, 1993

spectator takes one of the plain chairs and is asked to contemplate the fact of absence. Though triggered by a situation specific to the 1980s and 1990s, this looks at something much larger: our relationship as human beings to all those who have passed through our lives and are now departed from us. Finley points out that the symbolism of the chair or seat left vacant is in fact very old.

The rapid 'globalization' – as it came to be called – of contemporary art during the 1980s and 1990s was in part a consequence of increased concern with minority art at home. It was only natural, for example, that those who took an interest in African-American art forms should also interest themselves in the art of modern Africa. Similarly, those who saw art as one of the most effective ways in which African-Americans could express their minority status, were also attracted by the new art which began to be made by members of the Australian Aboriginal community. There were, however, other factors as well, such as the ever-increasing effectiveness of modern communications. Art books, art magazines, television and the Internet all had a part to play in familiarizing a wider and wider audience with artworks from all over the world. Even more effective in publicizing global diversity than the great museums were frequent international exhibitions. The old-established Venice and São Paulo biennales were joined by others, such as the Havana biennale and the biennale in Istanbul. Havana made a special point of emphasizing the work of artists from the Third World.

Havana itself belonged to a cultural nexus which had slipped in and out of European and North American consciousness from the 1920s onwards. The Mexican muralists – Diego Rivera, José Clemente Orozco (1883–1949) and David Alfaro Siqueiros (1896–1974) – made a considerable impact in the United States during the 1930s, but this interest diminished in the postwar years. Strangely enough, the artist who did most to bring the region back into the general consciousness was Rivera's wife, Frida Kahlo. Much of Kahlo's work was completed before this 231 book begins, and she was, in her own lifetime regarded somewhat condescendingly as the gifted but semi-amateur painter-wife of Diego Rivera, who was the most considerable figure in Mexican art. What changed responses to Kahlo's painting were, first, the rise of the feminist movement in the United States, and second, the publication of Hayden Herrera's brilliant biography in 1983. These brought into focus the extraordinarily vivid and personal nature of Kahlo's paintings, many of which were self-portraits. Though she possessed considerable powers of self-assertion, Kahlo would have been as surprised as anyone to find that her reputation now overshadows that of her husband.

Kahlo has had some successors in Latin America as a purveyor of intensely personal, autobiographical material. Examples are the pictorial meditations on the nature of memory made by the Venezuelan artist Jacobo Borges (b. 1932) and the best work of 229 the prolific Colombian painter Fernando Botero (b. 1932), whose 230 lively paintings of Medellín brothels, made in the 1970s, are like illustrations to an unwritten novel by his equally ironic fellow-countryman, Gabriel García Márquez.

In the 1970s and 1980s most Latin American art took a different track. Latin American artists became fascinated with Conceptual art and with installation. One of the leaders of this tendency in Argentina was Víctor Grippo (b. 1936). Interest in 232 Conceptual art of a rather hermetic kind was encouraged both by Argentine tradition – very advanced art of a near-Conceptual sort was produced by members of the Madí and Arte Concreto-Invencíon groups, both founded in Buenos Aires in 1945 – and by the political and economic situation in Argentina: there was a period of military rule from 1966 to 1970, Juan Perón's third, feeble presidency from 1973 to 1976, and a further period of military

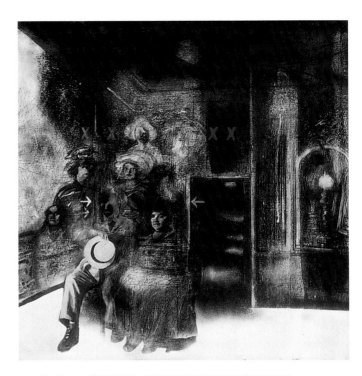

229. **Jacobo Borges**, *The Betrothed*, 1975

230. **Fernando Botero**, *The House of the Arias Sisters*, 1973

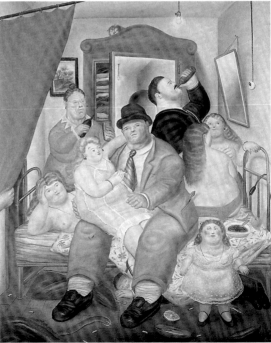

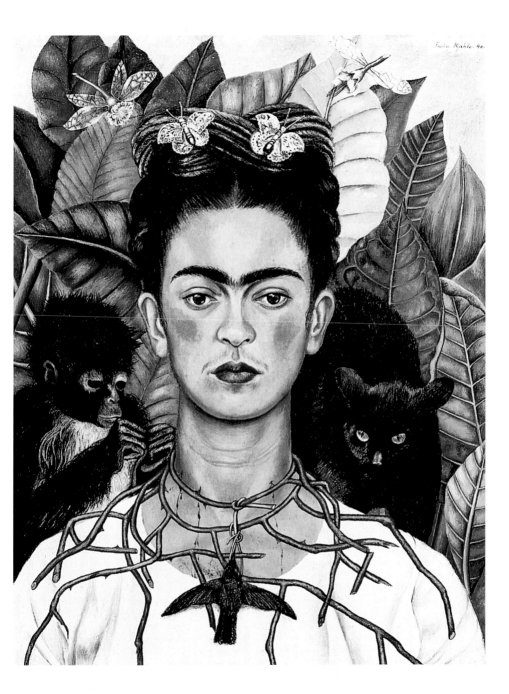

231. **Frida Kahlo**, *Self-portrait*,
1940

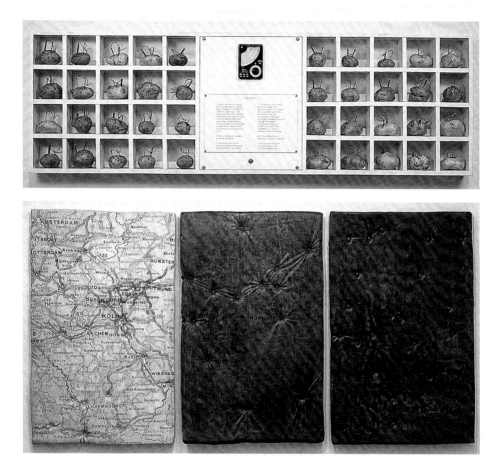

232. **Víctor Grippo**, *Analogía I*, 1971

233. **Guillermo Kuitca**, *Triptych of Mattresses*, 1989

rule from 1976 to 1984. During this time inflation rose as high as four hundred per cent, and from 1976 onwards the so-called 'dirty war' raged in the country, with many disappearances of supposed left-wing sympathizers. In these circumstances Conceptual art looked like the safest option. Even after the restoration of democracy, Conceptualist tendencies continued to be visible in the work of younger members of the Argentinian avant-garde. The work of Guillermo Kuitca shows not the slightest trace of indigenist or Pre-Columbian influence, but is instead an examination of the urban Argentina of the present day, and of Europe as the artist has come to know it through widespread travels.

In Brazil, there was also a rich production of Conceptual and site-specific work. This, with its disregard for conventional formats, and its liking for unexpected and often insubstantial

233

220

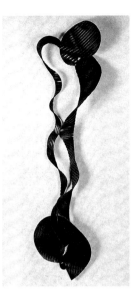

materials, has a kinship with Italian Arte Povera, but its deepest roots are in the work done in the 1960s by Brazilian Neo-Concretists such as Lygia Clark (1921–88) and Hélio Oiticica (1937–80), who had already anticipated many of Arte Povera's most typical ideas. The chief heirs of this way of working in Brazil today are such artists as Tunga (Antonio José de Mello Mourão, b. 1952), whose extraordinary environmental works, often filled with gargantuan locks of braided 'hair' (tresses made of lead wire) combine sexual fetishism with imagery reminiscent of Lewis Carroll's *Alice's Adventures in Wonderland*.

Chile has also seen the appearance of a new avant-garde. This began under the Pinochet dictatorship and continued after the restoration of democracy in 1989. Its chief members are Eugenio Dittborn, Gonzalo Díaz (b. 1947), Arturo Duclos (b. 1959) and the Australian-based Juan Davíla. The three participants who live in Chile all work in different ways – Dittborn became famous for his 'postal art', Díaz is known chiefly for installations, while

234. **Lygia Clark**, *Rubber Grub*, 1964 (remade 1986)

235. **Tunga**, *Lizart 5*, 1989

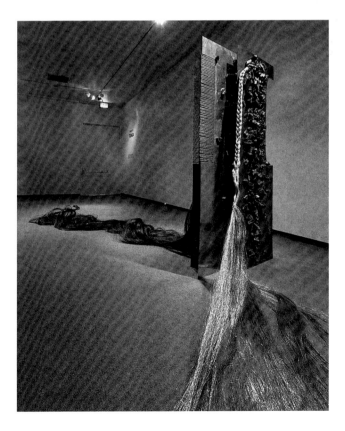

236. **Arturo Duclos**, *Black Mirror*, 1993

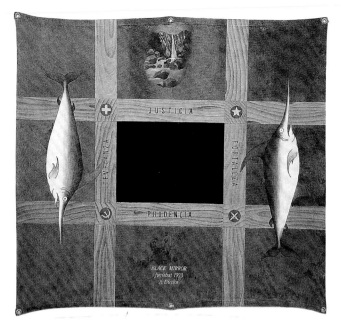

238. **Gonzalo Díaz**, *The Founding Father*, 1994

239. **Eugenio Dittborn**, *The Car of the Dead Spy*, 1994

237. **Juan Davíla**, *The Liberator Simon Bolívar*, 1994

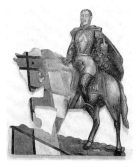

Duclos makes cryptic symbolic assemblages. What their work has in common is not a similarity of appearance – what would formerly have been called a style – but certain attitudes: an approach to the business of making art. The spectator's thought processes are directed down certain pathways, and across those pathways shadows are cast: those of the Catholicism of the colonial period; those of the fear and violence of Pinochet's seizure of power.

There are real, if elusive, resemblances between the Chilean art of the 1980s and 1990s and other kinds of Modernist art that made their appearance during the same epoch in parts of the globe away from traditional centres of innovation such as Paris and New York. For example, the *perestroika* art which appeared in Russia during the closing years of Soviet Communism looked, at first sight, like a revival of the old Russian avant-garde – the group of artistic experimentalists that had cast in its lot with the October Revolution, which had flourished until the mid-1920s, then lost much of its energy before being finally snuffed out by Stalin's imposition of the creed of Socialist Realism in the early 1930s. Some of the more prominent of these *perestroika* artists, among them Ilya Kabakov (b. 1933) and Eric Bulatov (b. 1933), had been associated with the shows of so-called 'unofficial art' from the Soviet Union which were seen in Western Europe during the late 1970s. Although these exhibitions

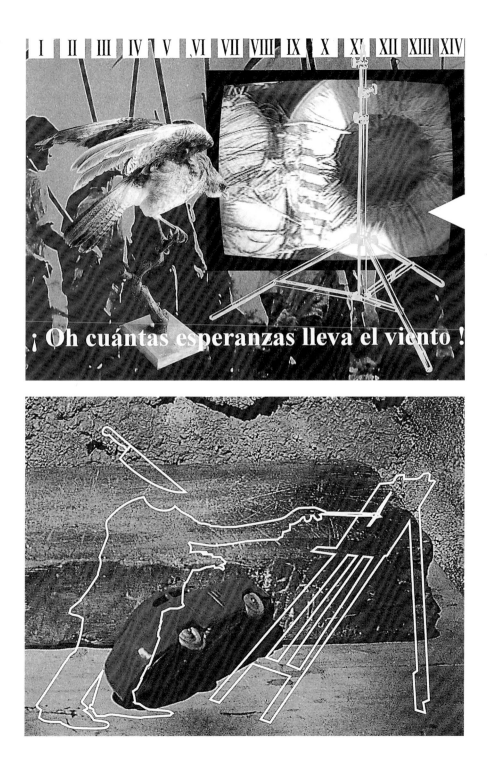

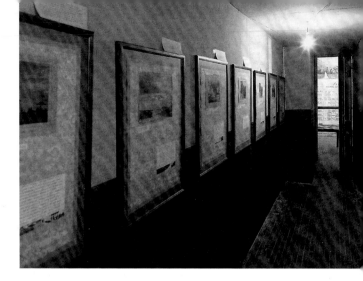

240. **Ilya Kabakov**, *My Mother's Life II*, detail from the installation *He Lost His Mind, Undressed, Ran Away Naked*, 1989

received a sympathetic reception from political journalists, Western art critics often dismissed the participants as feeble imitators of already outdated modes. In the 1980s, however, it became apparent that the more interesting of the new Russian artists were dependent, not on an imperfect knowledge of the development of the avant-garde in the West, but on their own intimate acquaintance with the codings of Soviet official art. That is, in order to 'read' the new Russian art correctly, the spectator had to understand its love-hate relationship with the more artistically degraded aspects of Socialist realism, and with the rhetoric of Soviet official art. The Soviet way of life was examined in detail by Ilya Kabakov, in a series of evocative installations. *He Lost His Mind, Undressed, Ran Away Naked* (1989) is an example – an autobiography in the form of a labyrinth. The detail shown here – *My Mother's Life II* – is a re-creation of a shabby 240 Soviet apartment block. The black-and-white landscape photographs hanging on the wall, taken by the artist's uncle, allude to the unquenchable Russian love of nature, which survives even in the direst conditions. Bulatov's painting *Perestroika* (1989) 241 alludes to the late-Communist situation in Russia in a more direct and much simpler way. The image has two sources – Constructivist poster-design, and the famous sculptural group of a heroic industrial worker and an equally heroic female collective-farm-worker made by Vera Mukhina (1889–1953) in 1936 and erected at the main entrance to the USSR Economic Achievement Exhibition in Moscow. This celebrated group became the Soviet equivalent of America's Statue of Liberty, and enjoyed the same iconic status in Soviet culture. Bulatov's transformation of the principal motif, the upheld hammer and sickle, into Cyrillic letters forming part of the word *perestroika* (the official slogan of the Gorbachev years) is savagely ironic.

The problem with this brief, final flowering of Soviet art is that, when the regime crumbled, the artists lost their subject. Most moved to the West in order to enjoy a better standard of living and maintain their contacts with the collectors and galleries who were now keenly interested in their work, and, doing so, they fell out of touch with the society that had originally nurtured them. Even Kabakov, the most talented artist in the group, seems strangely at sea since his move to New York, and his work has been increasingly nostalgic – an examination of something that no longer exists. In contemporary Russia, the heroes of *perestroika* art tend to be regarded as irrelevant.

The new Japanese avant-garde of the 1980s has also concerned itself with the idea of cultural coding. After Japan's defeat in World War II, the American occupation that followed brought with it many cultural influences from the United States which were assiduously fostered by the occupiers, and it seemed natural that contemporary Japanese art should seek to follow

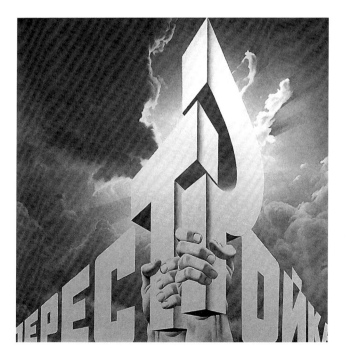

241. **Eric Bulatov**, *Perestroika*, 1989

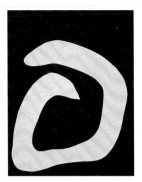

242. **Jiro Yoshihara**, *Untitled,*
1971

an American path. There were, nevertheless, also powerful influences from Europe. The first major postwar group in Japan showed the impact of both sets of influences. The Gutai Group was founded in December 1954 by the painter Jiro Yoshihara (1905–72), who had also made a substantial private fortune in the oil industry, and it was essentially his money that sustained the activities of the group. Early Gutai activities were directed at least as much towards creating artistic events, including groups of temporary outdoor sculptures, as they were towards making paintings which could be displayed in galleries. It was essentially the need to make money that drove the other members of the group into making work in more conventional formats. Their paintings, abstract and freely brushed, are a fusion of traditional oriental calligraphy and the dominant tendencies in abstract painting in the 1950s in New York and Paris. The revival of interest in Gutai in the 1990s, however, was based on the early environmental works which made the participants, like some of the Neo-Concrete artists in Brazil, look like precursors of Italian Arte Povera.

242

Japanese avant-garde art of the 1990s, for example the work of Yukinori Yanagi (b. 1959), takes a different tack. Basically conceptual, it presents ideas with a mocking irony directed in part against the Japanese tendency to run after Western fashions, but largely, too, against Western culture itself, and in particular Western pomposity in defending what are perceived as immutable cultural and moral values. Yanagi's *Flag Ant Farms*, such as the version shown at the Venice Biennale of 1993, are plastic boxes in which coloured sand has been arranged to form various national flags. As a colony of ants moves back and forth between the boxes through plastic tubing, they gradually blur the designs, so that one symbol of national identity crumbles into another. Yanagi presents this as an allegory of the futility of nationalism.

243

Yanagi's work displays exquisite craftsmanship. This quality is associated with much traditional Japanese art, but is viewed with disfavour by many Modernist artists and art critics as evidence of a lack of true creative spontaneity. The new generation of Japanese artists have found a way of making this refinement work within a Post-Modernist context.

Both contemporary Latin American and contemporary Japanese art show keen awareness of Modernist and Post-Modernist ideas, though a somewhat uneasy relationship with them. The situation is different with the art now emerging from modern Africa, although this has recently attracted attention from Western commentators, and has been made the subject of a number of survey exhibitions. African art of a 'classical' – that is to say traditional – kind, played a seminal role in the genesis of the Modern Movement and has been correspondingly idealized by Modernist art critics. This led to the idea that all African art that showed traces of reciprocal Western influence was ipso facto weak and corrupt, and unworthy of serious notice. Now attitudes have begun to change, though some Western commentators remain distressed by the lack of familiar institutional and social signposts. Jan Hoet, the Belgian-born curator of the 1992 Kassel Documenta (Documenta IX), gave a vivid, if also slightly naïve, description of his reactions when looking for art in contemporary Africa, lamenting that there was no trace of the familiar Western infrastructure that supports the work of contemporary artist: 'I did not find any houses of the well-to-do containing contemporary art. Nor any press providing artistic and cultural information.'[3] Yet he was constrained to add: 'And in spite of everything there is art. Isolated traces of expression, without any suggestion of academic references, or artisanal traditions and Western influences. Its basis consists of spontaneous commentaries and personal experiences, or else it is the product of adaptation mechanisms.'[4]

In fact, one of the characteristics of the art of modern Africa is that it is a reaction to the situation as it actually exists, not as we would like it to exist. Where it looks back to traditional forms,

243. **Yukinori Yanagi**, *Union Jack Ant Farm*, 1994

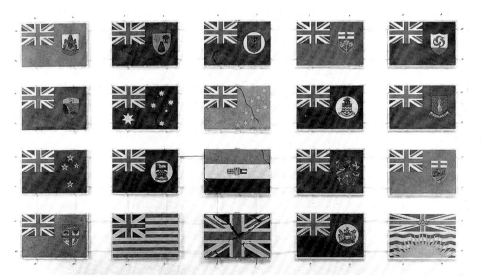

244. John Muafangejo, *Lonely Man, Man of Man*, 1974

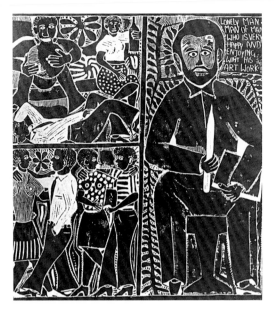

244. John Muafangejo, *Lonely Man, Man of Man*, 1974

more often than not it is because these find a profitable market with Western tourists. Where it is most itself, it owes much to things which enthusiasts for 'Africanism' prefer to overlook, such as the activity of Christian missionaries or the availability of new materials (linoleum for making prints, concrete for making sculptures), which are nevertheless very much part of the fabric of the new Africa. The Namibian printmaker John Muafangejo (1943–87) was born in a purely tribal context in Ovamboland, across the border in Angola, moved to Windhoek in what was then South West Africa as a result of political disturbances in the region, and came under the protection of the Anglican mission there. It was the members of the mission who discovered his talent as an artist and sent him to Rorke's Drift in South Africa, then the only school in South Africa where a black man could receive an artistic education. Muafangejo's prints deal with many themes: his tribal background, African proverbs, the political situation, his own Christian faith. There is one major underlying theme, and that is the process of detribalization. The catalogue raisonné of his prints, published in South Africa in 1992, bears the appropriate title *I Was Loneliness*. It is this concern with individuality, the shape of the self, which makes Muafangejo in a broad sense a modern artist. On the other hand, the fact that his linocuts often bear a startling resemblance to woodcut images produced by the first generation of German Expressionists is no more than

244

a coincidence – he cannot be aligned with the German Neo-Expressionists, such as Baselitz and Immendorf, who were his exact contemporaries.

Another African whose work has recently made a considerable impact in the West is Chéri Samba (b. 1956), from the Republic of the Congo, formerly Zaire. If Muafangejo's prints are sometimes anguished, Samba's work is satirical and often cheerfully cynical. It shows the strong narrative thrust typical of today's African culture, but bears little, if any, resemblance to traditional African art. It does, however, spring from a recognizable social background. Samba, who comes from a small village in the Lower Congo, left this for the capital, Kinshasa, and began his career in a studio making hand-painted advertising signs. From this he graduated to drawing strip cartoons for a newspaper. Eventually the two forms were integrated in his paintings.

Samba's work, which is a spontaneous expression of the new urban culture of Africa, makes a striking contrast with the paintings by Australian Aborigines, which have recently been co-opted into the universe of Western contemporary art, and which indeed look more at home there than anything now being made by an African artist living in Africa. The new Aboriginal art

245. **Chéri Samba**, *Pourquoi un contrat?* 1990

245

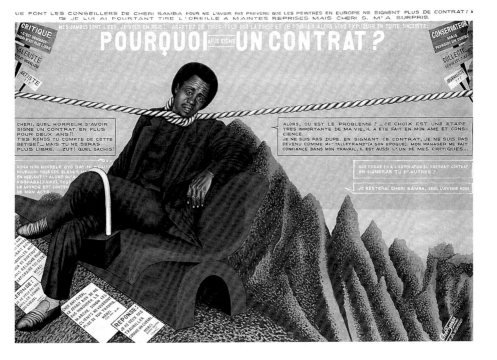

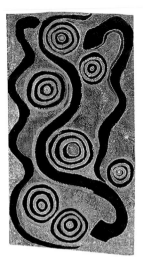

246. **Peter Blacksmith
Japanangka**, *Snake Dreaming,*
1986

was not absolutely spontaneous in origin. In the form in which they are now known, Aboriginal paintings originated in the promptings of a white art teacher, Geoffrey Bardon, who arrived to teach children at the outback settlement of Papunya in 1971. Bardon, having first encouraged adult members of the community to paint murals in his school, then provided them with the materials – synthetic paint and boards – to create independent works based on Dreamings, the images and symbols that formed part of a complex tribal network of ownership and interrelationship, and that had previously figured in ritual sand paintings and also in body decoration. The paintings, marketed through a Papunya Tula Artists' Collective, found a welcome with white Australians living in the great cities of the coast, and eventually became known outside Australia. As they became more popular they increased in size, and the artists began to work on canvas rather than on small boards, thus creating work that was directly comparable with the abstract paintings made in the West almost from the beginning of the Modern Movement.

The real question raised by Aboriginal painting, in the context of a general survey such as this, is not that of how the makers view it – they perceive it as an extension of traditional activities, one that simultaneously expresses and conceals tribal meanings and secrets, and at the same time makes a very welcome cash contribution to the depressed economy of the outback. It is how non-Aboriginal spectators view and assimilate the work. The problem was raised in acute form when a very senior and much respected white Australian landscape painter, Elizabeth Durack (1915–2000), revealed, just before her death, that she had made a series of pseudo-Aboriginal works under the pseudonym 'Eddie Burrup'. These were much acclaimed when they were exhibited as genuine products of Aboriginal culture. The incident suggests first, that Aboriginal paintings are essentially 'trade goods', produced in one community for consumption in another; and second, that these paintings owe their rapid success to a purely accidental resemblance to the abstract art long produced in the West. Aboriginal art has become Modernist not by design, but by default, just as African tribal sculpture did before it.

The different cultures dealt with in this chapter are obviously only a selection of the kinds of art from non-Western milieux that are now making an impact in the West and being absorbed, though sometimes with difficulty, into an international system of art-making and art-marketing. The kind of work these countries produce is affected by their own traditions, by their recent social,

246

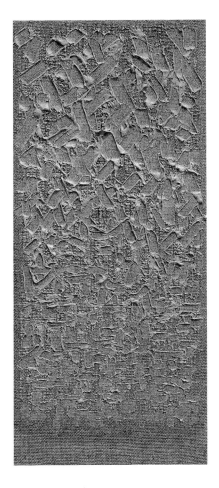

247. Ha, Chong-Hyun,
Conjunction 94–07, 1994

political and economic histories, and by the attitudes of the regimes in power. China and South Korea, for example, have much in common with one another culturally, but extremely different political regimes. South Korea, like Japan, but unlike China, has been exposed for a long period to Western, and specifically American, cultural ideas. There are, nevertheless, certain areas where modern Chinese and modern Korean art have much in common. Painting in traditional ink-and-brush style continues to be important in both. So-called 'Western-style' painting, however, tends to be very different in the two countries. Korean art has been largely abstract, and has tended to found itself, as the Gutai Group did, on the abstract painting made in Europe and the United States in the 1950s. The senior generation of Korean artists, such as Ha, Chong Hyun (b. 1935) have tended to produce

247

231

exquisitely refined monochromatic abstracts, with surface markings reminiscent of traditional calligraphy. It is only when one looks at Ha, Chong Hyun's work more closely that one realizes that it is created in a very different way from Western work superficially of the same sort. In his case, the foundation is a very coarse hemp cloth (a traditional Korean material), and the pigment is actually pushed through the hemp mesh from behind. Other Korean monochromists of the same generation layer the canvas with paint, then with Korean mulberry-bark paper, then with more paint. Their work rejects technology while that of the expatriate Korean, Nam June Paik (b. 1932), embraces it enthusiastically. Younger Korean artists have only gradually and rather tentatively moved towards making figurative work. 251

In China, Western ideas were theoretically banned during the period of the Cultural Revolution, though in fact one type of art favoured by Mao's regime was a realistic style of propaganda art which owed much to Soviet Socialist Realism. The other type was the cheerful, optimistic folk painting produced by peasant collectives. After 1979 a thaw began, and this accelerated rapidly after 1985. This took two forms – Environmental and Performance art, and a new variety of Pop. Associated with the first of these tendencies Wenda Gu (b. 1955, now resident in New York), who, after an education in traditional Chinese painting, began to make unconventional and subversive use of calligraphic signs. Often these were used on banners carrying unintelligible slogans, with the characters inverted or fragmented. An environmental piece, created for the Museum of Modern Art in Oxford in 1993, combined calligraphic banners, wooden children's cots, and dried placenta spread on the floor, and was a comment on China's population problem. Since he moved to the West, Wenda Gu has become a specialist in elaborate installations featuring human hair. It is easy to see that there might be no place for these within mainland China. Associated with the second Pop tendency in new Chinese art are Yu Youhan (b. 1943) and a group of young artists 248 surrounding him. Yu Youhan, a lecturer at the Shanghai College of Applied Arts since 1973, worked first as an abstract painter influenced by Constructivism, then fell under the influence of Cézanne, and finally began to make ironic analyses of the Chinese propaganda art devoted to the cult of Mao Zedong, as in *Chairman Mao in Discussion with the Peasants of Shao Shan* (1991). Art of this type was promptly dubbed 'Political Pop' for marketing purposes in Hong Kong and in the West, but actually has as much to do with Russian *perestroika* art as it does with Andy Warhol

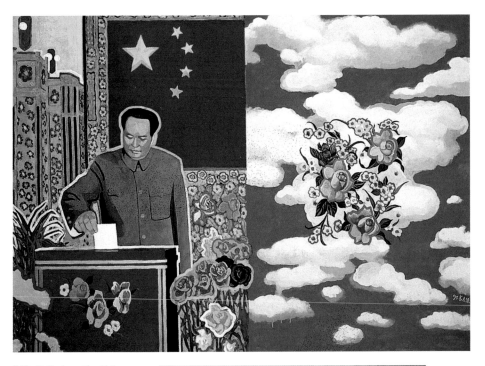

248. **Yu Youhan**, *Mao Voting*, 1993

249. **Ralph Hotere**, *The Black over the Gold*, 1993

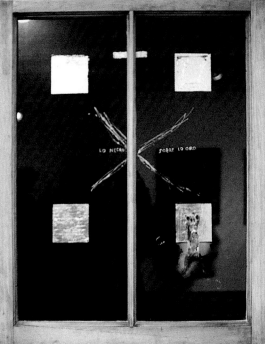

(despite the precedent offered by the latter's own images of Mao, which date from 1972–74). The spectator is asked to deconstruct the visual coding associated with a totalitarian regime.

In New Zealand, forms familiar from art made in Europe and the United States are similarly appropriated and made the vehicle for imagery specific to the region and for themes of pressing local interest. The preoccupation of recent art has been the relationship between Maori culture and the *pakeha* or non-Maori community. Another preoccupation is the defence of the New Zealand ecology. Maori art is split into two quite separate camps. The Maori Councils encourage traditional activities, such as carving, but tend to feel that painting in Western style is non-Maori. Official government agencies, the Arts Council of New Zealand, for example, support Maori artists, such as Robyn Kahukiwa (b. 1940), who use ethnic imagery but work in Western formats. Many of these Westernizing Maori artists are women. Fully traditional Maori art, specifically carving, has tended to be regarded by the Maori Councils as men's business. Meanwhile the senior artist of Maori descent, Ralph Hotere (b. 1931) wishes 249 to be perceived as an artist without ethnic trappings – in this resembling Sam Gilliam and Martin Puryear in the United States – and has devoted much of his work to a consideration of ecological perils to the New Zealand environment, most strikingly in his *Aramoana* series (1983) which makes use of 'typical' New Zealand building materials, such as corrugated iron. Another artist, this time of *pakeha* background, also concerned with the defence of the ecology, is the sculptor Chris Booth (b. 1948), perhaps best known for his *Rainbow Warrior Memorial* (1988–90), erected on a headland overlooking Matarui Bay in New Zealand's North Island, where the Greenpeace ship of that name was eventually scuttled, after damage inflicted by French saboteurs.

This by no means exhausts the list of countries where something resembling contemporary art as it is known in the West either exists fully or is just beginning to emerge. In India, for example, Modernist art has existed since the time of Amrita Sher-Gil (1913–41), the daughter of a Sikh father and a Hungarian mother, who studied in Paris before returning to live and work in India. Her chief models were Gauguin and Modigliani, and it was through their eyes that she interpreted what she saw on her extensive travels around the subcontinent. Nevertheless Indian Modernist artists have had an uphill struggle for survival because of the lack of local patronage, and many of the best known, such as Francis Newton Souza (b. 1924) and the late

Avinash Chandra (1931–92) were forced to make their careers outside the country. Bhupen Kakhar (b. 1934), probably the best known Indian artist now living in India itself, and the leading figure in the so-called School of Baroda, was not free to paint full-time till he was in his fifties. After training in a Western-style art school, he spent many years working part-time as a bookkeeper in a small factory. His work is a blend of Eastern and Western elements: among his influences are the Douanier Rousseau, Sienese painting of the fourteenth and fifteenth centuries, and David Hockney; but also Indian bazaar oleographs, Nathwadara paintings devoted to celebrating the cult of Krishna, and the work of late eighteenth- and nineteenth-century Company School painters – Indian artists working for British patrons. Kakhar's work is significant for more than one reason: amongst other things it demonstrates the immense range of visual information available even to a painter of comparatively low income, living and working in what is, from a European or American perspective, a remote region.

The Islamic countries have had the greatest difficulty in making a place for themselves in the new universe of contemporary art. This is not surprising, since the Islamic revival has now established itself as the great opponent of contemporary Western culture in general. In the West, the best known artist of Islamic origin is undoubtedly Mona Hatoum, born in the Lebanon (in 1952) of a Palestinian Arab family and now domiciled in Britain. Some of Hatoum's early work refers to her situation as an exile, but her main theme is gender – the business of being female. Her most direct and spectacular exploration of this is the environmental and video work *Corps Etranger* (1994). To make this, Hatoum introduced an endoscope into her own body, and the images thus recorded were projected on to the floor of an enclosure. All the most secret recesses of the female body thus became public, and were, as the title of the piece suggests – subtly 'estranged' from their owner by this act of public disclosure. It is, however, difficult to imagine this piece being put on display in any strictly Islamic country.

Chapter 10:   The rise of video

'New media' have been a much debated issue in contemporary art since the 1960s. It is generally held that a key date in this story is 14 October 1966, when Robert Rauschenberg, in conjunction with the electronic engineer Billy Klüver, organized the series *Nine Evenings: Theater and Engineering* at the Ninth Regiment Armory in New York. This in turn led the next year to the foundation of an organization called EAT (Experiments in Art and Technology), with the same collaborators in charge. Yet it is immediately necessary, when talking of this beginning, to sound a note of caution. Those who were actually present at *Nine Evenings* remember them, not as a technological triumph, but as being disorganized because of technical glitches. And the kind of things Rauschenberg and Klüver experimented with – for example, tennis players playing with rackets fitted with radio-transmitters – do not now seem to represent the main line of development in the contemporary technological arts.

These arts are, however, fascinating for several reasons. One is the way technology itself is defined in the world of the avant-garde arts. The alliance between Rauschenberg and Klüver was in fact one of the very few occasions during the past forty years when progressive artists have had direct access to cutting-edge technology. For the most part, when we speak of 'new media' we mean the use which artists have been able to make of technologies that were already fully available to the commercial sphere – to design and advertising studios, for example. Usually, in fact, artists have had to wait until such technologies are marketed to the general public, for domestic and hobbyist purposes. What is spoken of as high-tech by commentators on contemporary art is seen as middle- or even low-tech by the engineering and scientific community. In this sense, the supposed sophistication of new media is a convenient fiction. The appearance on the market, in the late 1960s, of the portable video-camera was a much more significant event for artists than the experiments made by Rauschenberg and his allies.

Handheld video had a major social impact in more than one field of human activity. It transformed television news reporting, making it much quicker to respond to major news events and much more informal in style. It also had an impact on television advertising, which also became more experimental and informal, following the example set by news programmes. Finally it had an impact on private life. It has been noted that many of the techno-logical innovations characteristic of the second half of the twentieth century have owed their initial acceptance to sex – this is especially true of polaroid photographs and of video, both of which enabled people to act out sexual fantasies in a new way, because the images created were immediately available, and did not require the participation of outside agencies, such as photo-graphic laboratories.

Video precisely suited the climate of sexual liberation and political protest that was typical of the late 1960s and early 1970s, and it is not surprising that much of the early video made by art-ists concentrated on these twin themes. One video collective, Top Value Television (TTV) provided provocative 'alternative' cover-age of the Republican and Democratic conventions of 1972. In the following year, the experienced provocateur Vito Acconci (b. 1940) made a video called *Theme Song* based on the conven-tions of the peepshow. In it he lies on the floor and, in extreme close up, pleads with the anonymousviewer to pass through the screen and join him, 'I want you inside me,' he pleads.

One reason why video originally attracted the world of contemporary art was that it provided an effective means of pre-serving the improvised 'Happenings' and 'Actions' which already played an important part in the artistic discourse of the avant-garde. Suddenly what was ephemeral became permanent and easily repeatable. The disadvantages of early video did not count for so much in comparison with this. They were that video required much greater skill to edit than it did to shoot, and that editing at this early stage required repeated copying from one tape to another. With each generation of copies, the quality of the image degenerated.

The art world this new medium penetrated tended to be strictly that of the Western democracies, with an extension of influence to Japan. There were several reasons for this. One was that governments in countries with authoritarian regimes were afraid, with good reason, of the power of the moving image, and were determined to see that its use was always controlled from above. There was little experimentation with video in the Soviet Union, or in the countries of the Eastern bloc, despite the fact that these regions had a particularly rich tradition of documentary film-making. The same reticence prevailed in China, and even now, despite a considerable liberalization of the political climate since the days of Mao's Cultural Revolution, the Chinese authorities are more worried by artists' video than by any other manifestation of Westernizing avant-garde art. The only part of China where video has become an important means of artistic expression is Hong Kong, not only because Hong Kong is still a 'special economic zone', which to some extent follows its own rules, but because of the lack of gallery space due to very high property values. Hong Kong Chinese artists can show videos, even when they have no walls for exhibitions of a more conventional kind.

Another reason for video's lack of currency outside the capitalist West was economic. In Third World terms, it was from its beginnings, and still remains, an expensive medium. Third World artists can make ambitious environments from scavenged materials – this has, for example, become the prevailing form of artistic expression in Cuba, thanks to the constraints of the American economic blockade. What they cannot do is gain easy access to high-value electronic equipment, manufactured outside their own borders.

The financial gap has led to some curious distortions. Artists exiled from their own societies for whatever reason – one thinks of Ana Mendieta (1948–85, Cuba), Mona Hatoum (Lebanon and Palestine) and Shirin Neshat (b. 1957, Iran) have frequently used video both to analyse their own feelings about their situation and to offer a critique of what is taking place 'at home'. But the audience they address is the audience that surrounds them in exile, not that of their country of origin, which remains largely ignorant of their activity.

Another irony is the fact that, while much artists' video is bitterly hostile to the prevailing consumer culture, it remains dependent on consumerism for each major leap forward in technical development. New and improved ways of creating video are elicited, not by demand from the art world but from an insatiable market composed partly of the advertising and television industries, and partly of amateurs and home hobbyists. If all the artists in the world who now make videos suddenly decided to renounce the medium, the suppliers of video cameras and related products would never feel their loss.

This is not to say that there has been an absence of creative interchange between the art world on the one hand, and mainstream television plus the advertising industry on the other.

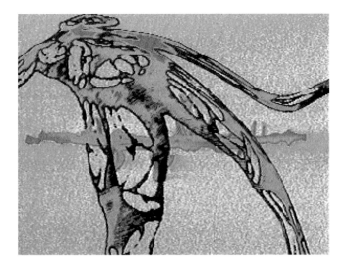

In the early days of artists' video, Ed Emshwiller (1925–90) developed forms of computer animation which were later to be used both in films and for music videos on television. His video *Thermogenesis* (1972) linked computer animation to music gener- 250 ated by a Moog Audio Synthesizer. Emshwiller's use of computer manipulation was at that time very unusual and only became common currency with the advent of personal computers as universally accepted office and household tools – a development that was not fully established until the 1990s.

One problem for the visually creative aspect of artists' video was the fact that any innovations were swiftly taken over for commercial use. There is a particularly close link between videos made simply as works of art and others made as promotional tools for the music industry. A number of leading contemporary artists, among them Damien Hirst (b. 1965), have crossed over into the commercial sphere and directed or designed videos for the music industry. The much more generous budgets available for this kind of activity has often meant that the commercial product seemed superior in many respects to what they created independently. Now, rather belatedly, videos made by people whose background is in commercial and music videos, not in fine art, are beginning to find their way into art exhibitions. A striking example is the work of Chris Cunningham (b. 1970), whose reputation is based on music videos made in collaboration with performers like the Icelandic-born singer Björk. Cunningham's video *flex* (2000), included in the 'Apocalypse' exhibition at the 1 Royal Academy in London, is a technically brilliant layering of sounds and images, much superior in this respect to ninety-nine per cent of the work done by videographers with a purely fine art background – their efforts tend to look extraordinarily naïve in comparison. *flex* has a story line which runs as follows: slightly built nude woman hits powerfully built nude man. Powerfully built nude man beats up woman, then copulates with her. Woman crawls to embrace man. The scene then dissolves into abstract white swirls – smoke or sperm, according to taste. This kind of simplistic message survives in popular culture, which continues to thrive on misogyny – it is endemic, for instance in rap music – but has in the past few decades usually been banished from other manifestations which describe themselves as 'art'.

There has also been cross-fertilization between artists' video and film. This is not surprising, since the artists come from a culture saturated with cinematic images, and where images and lines of dialogue from celebrated films form part of a common frame of reference. A number of the most discussed videos of the 1990s were acts of appropriation. The most celebrated was Douglas Gordon's (b. 1966) immensely slowed down version of Alfred Hitchcock's film *Psycho* – it lasts for twenty-four hours – in which all sorts of profound meanings were discovered, though few people could claim to have seen it complete. Another was Steve McQueen's (b. 1966) mercifully much shorter *Deadpan* (1997 – four-and-a-half-minutes), which reconstructs a stunt from the Buster Keaton silent comedy *Steamboat Bill, Jr.* (1928) in which a house falls on the protagonist and miraculously fails to injure him. McQueen's version has been described, in what seem to me extravagant terms, as 'a paean to black determination and resolve'.[1] If this can be said about McQueen, what should we now say about Keaton himself, who actually invented the image? Even when there is no direct appropriation, the border between artists' video and film becomes very blurred the more elaborate the flow of images becomes and the nearer things get to some kind of continuous narrative. Matthew Barney's (b. 1967) *Cremaster* series, for example, has a dream-like, quasi-surrealist quality which is strongly reminiscent of Alejandro Jodorowski's (b. 1929) cult movie *El Topo* (1970), which enthralled art-world audiences soon after Barney's own birth.

As its technical resources have increased, video as an art-form has increasingly tried to find ways of justifying its presence in an art gallery rather than in a cinema, or even on the small screen at home. It has been assisted in this endeavour by changes in museums themselves, which have more and more become places of popular entertainment. From the curatorial point of view, video, as opposed to other forms of artistic expression, has much to recommend it. It is inexpensive to tour, and can offer spectacular images for little financial outlay. In addition to this, the mass audience, which museums must now attract, find art videos more accessible than most other forms of avant-garde expression, since they can relate them to their own previous experience of cinema and television. One problem is, however, that even relatively new museum buildings are not always well adapted to showing videos which, instead of requiring large spaces flooded with light (which is what museums traditionally provide), call for relatively small ones which can be darkened. Called upon to show a large number of art videos at one time, a museum building, filled with a labyrinth of adhoc partitions, can come to resemble the video arcades that are sometimes attached to pornographic bookstores.

One solution has been to turn the video-monitor itself into a component part of a larger work of art. The most celebrated exponent of this strategy is the Korean-born Nam June Paik. Paik was originally associated with the Fluxus Group in Germany, later moving to New York, where he was a participant in the *Nine Evenings* organized by Rauschenberg and Klüver. Paik both changed the image on the television screen – for example, by distorting it with the help of powerful magnets – and used television sets as elements in increasingly massive assemblages. Sometimes he put them together to form crude anthropomorphic figures, emblematic of the increasingly dominant part television plays in people's lives. Sometimes he filled an entire space with winking monitors. His most ambitious effort of this kind was his retrospective exhibition held in 2000 at the Guggenheim Museum in New York. Frank Lloyd Wright's soaring spiral space was filled with moving images, while in the centre there was a waterfall the entire height of the building, pierced by a laser beam. The show looked like an apotheosis of technological art. Unfortunately, it also looked very much like an expensive night-club out of hours – the monitors became mere decorations for a festivity which was already over, or which had not yet taken place.

A more sophisticated use of television monitors as components in larger art works has been made by the American artist Gary Hill (b. 1951). Hill began his career as a sculptor, but also spent part of the 1970s working in community video. He has been interested in two things – first, the video image as a thing in itself, an electronically generated shape or sequence of shapes,

251

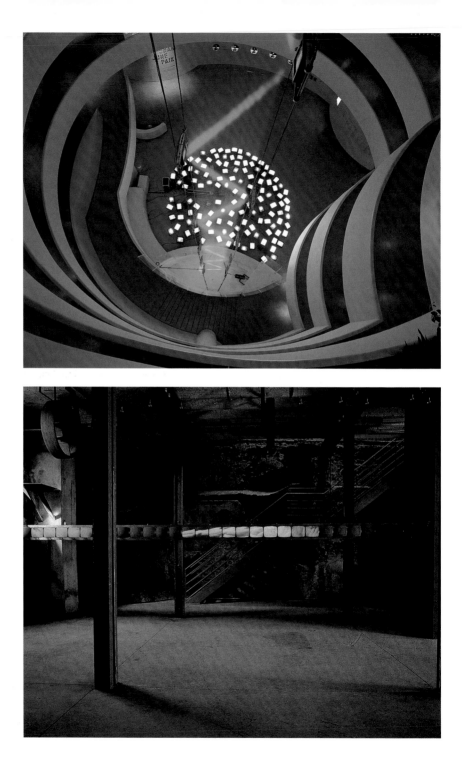

251. **Nam June Paik**, installation, Solomon R. Guggenheim Museum, New York, 2000

and second in its function as part of some larger concept. In his *Suspension of Disbelief (for Marine)* (1992) a row of thirty video monitors are mounted on a beam which is two metres (over six feet) above the floor. These images represent the fragmented bodies of a man and a woman, moving across the screens, meeting, sometimes overlapping, then breaking apart. It has been rightly said that 'this seductive montage of swiftly sequencing images at once conjures up a notion of togetherness and simultaneously withholds it.'[2] Hill has also been one of the pioneers of interactive video, which seems to be the direction that video art must inevitably take as it becomes more and more central to museum practice. In his installation *Tall Ships* (1992) there are multiple projection surfaces, and the images that appear on them are triggered by the entrance of a viewer. As the spectator moves, figures appear, approach him, murmur barely audible sentences and then vanish again. This work by Hill is directly comparable to some interactive videos by Bill Viola (b. 1951), whose work in this medium made him one of the most discussed video artists of the 1990s. For example, it is close to Viola's *Hall of Whispers* (1995), where viewers pass through a long, narrow, dark room, between ten video projections arranged in two rows – life-sized heads with closed eyes, gagged, but straining to speak. In both these works the visitors enters a magical, slightly sinister realm of ghosts.

252. **Gary Hill**, *Suspension of Disbelief (for Marine)*, 1992

252

253

A major reason for Viola's popularity has been his ability to evoke religious or quasi-religious states of mind. His best known video is probably *The Messenger* (1996), first shown in Durham Cathedral. In this a nude man rises slowly to the surface of a body of water, then sinks back into it again. Viola intends this to be emblematic of the endlessly repeated cycle of life and death:

It reminds you of where you came from. When you see the man emerge out of the water and take a breath, there is a birth every time he comes back into our world. And everyone in the room watching this has come into the world that way; whether they consciously recognize that or not at the moment they're seeing it doesn't matter.[3]

His ideas have been attacked as being naïve, but the impact of his best work is undoubted.

Though ambitious interactive videos of the kind made by Hill and Viola are usually thought of as primarily an American phenomenon, even more brilliant examples have been made in Italy, by a group of artists, actors and technicians called Studio Azzurro. Studio Azzurro creates 'ambienti sensibili' – 'sensitive environments'. In one of these, *Chorus* (1996), the visitor enters

254

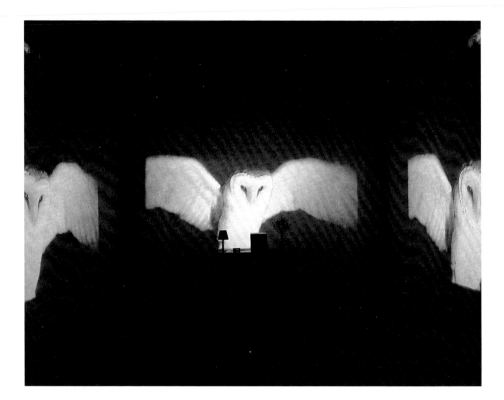

253. **Bill Viola**, *The Sleep of Reason*, 1988

a darkened space and is invited to walk on a large 'carpet' – an image projected on felt of entangled semi-nude figures, male and female. As he or she walks, the figures who are trodden on become angry and begin to shout: 'The visitors' steps stimulate the characters' reactions, trigger a series of alternating voices, make the mass of bodies move and begin their chanting.'[4] In *Total of the Battle* (1996), inspired by Uccello's paintings of the *Rout of San Romano*, the idea was to make a heap of images which the spectator is forced to organize for himself or herself. Some of these images are projected on to loose heaps of earth, which increases the effect of physical fragmentation. The *Prelude* section, sometimes shown separately, is the most easily grasped aspect of the piece. It consists of four illusory 'pits' in the floor, each seemingly filled with a different material – water, sand, dead leaves, chopped up stalks of bamboo. When the visitor stands on the edge of one of these pits and makes a sound – shouting, or loudly clapping – struggling nude figures rise to the surface, then slowly sink back into it again, till they are summoned by another burst of noise.

Studio Azzurro collaborates with the Arrocco theatre company and uses a large number of carefully choreographed actors, but the participants recognize that what they do is subtly different from theatre: 'The actions must not have an absolute, incontrovertible, dramatic character; they have to be more similar to a river rather than to the stone falling into it; they have to support the *interactor's* response without attacking him, without ignoring him.'[5] The narrative element in their work prompts a comparison with yet another video artist, very different in most respects from the others whose work has been described here – Tony Oursler (b. 1957). Oursler might, in a previous epoch, have been called not an artist but a puppeteer. He projects faces, and sometimes just a single eyeball, on to spheres and ovoids of different dimensions – some very small, some quite large – which thus become the heads (or eyes) of eerie personages who rant obsessively, sigh and gibber and moan. The resemblance between some of these personages to the theatrical characters invented by Samuel Beckett has often been noted. In fact, these are players in Beckett-derived dramas which can, unlike live performers in a theatre, be turned on and off at will.

255

Hill, Viola, Studio Azzurro and Oursler have important things in common, despite their equally obvious differences. They cater to the contemporary taste for the uncanny and the

254. **Studio Azzurro**, *Chorus,* 1996

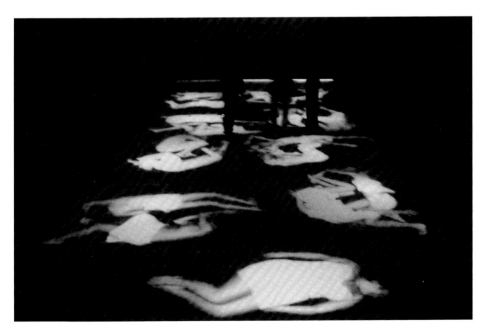

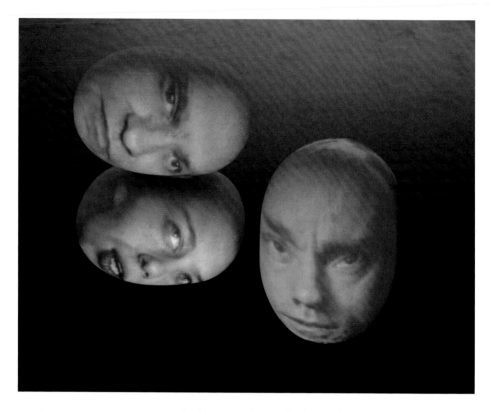

255. **Tony Oursler**, *Mansheshe*, 1997

magical in a way that marks them off from the first generation of artist-videographers. They are also much more obviously classifiable as entertainers. When their work is shown in a museum context – and it hardly has a place elsewhere – the museum or gallery concerned is redefined, pulled nearer to the sphere of popular entertainment and further from that of visual or intellectual analysis. The paradox is that the most purely technological art is now very often the art that stimulates emotion rather than reflection. Those who go to museums of contemporary art to search for magic are most likely to find it in works of this kind.

Chapter 11: The photographic medium

At first sight it is tempting to place still photography with video, treating them as essentially two different aspects of the same subject. Closer investigation, however, indicates that the two forms of expression are often very different from one another, both in their intentions and in their results. This holds good even in those cases where they are produced by the same artist.

Contemporary photography is much more various stylistically than contemporary video, and it has a wider technical range. As I have already suggested, what artists can do with video depends very much on the kind of equipment that is readily available, and this, in turn, depends on the needs and demands of the consumer market, which caters for the most part for amateurs rather than professionals. The one area of real technical originality in the field of artist's video is where video becomes part of an enveloping environment and is interactive, as in some recent work by Bill Viola and Studio Azzurro, described in the last chapter.

Photography, on the contrary, both capitalizes on its position as the primary image-maker of our society, familiar to everyone and familiar to everyone, and exploits a great variety of different technical possibilities. One reason why it is able to this is because it has now established its own tradition and is no longer regarded as being merely the client of older methods of image-making, such as drawing and painting. The last quarter of the twentieth century witnessed a rapid growth of what one can only call photographic self-consciousness. The first really thorough history of early photography was the large book by Helmut and Alison Gernsheim published in 1969. This took the story from its beginnings in the 1840s to 1914. This was followed, in the 1970s and 1980s by a rapid growth of photographic collecting, exemplified, for example, by the activities of Robert Mapplethorpe's lover and patron Sam Wagstaff, who has already been mentioned in Chapter 9. Wagstaff's vast holdings are now in the hands of the Getty Museum. When photography rediscovered its past, it also acquired a unique power to diversify.

One aspect of recent photographic practice has been the re-exploration of photographic techniques that were once thought

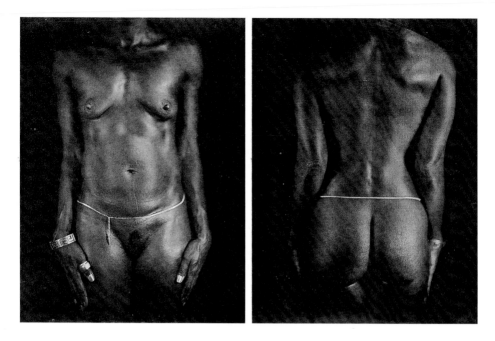

256. **Chuck Close**, *Untitled Torso Diptych*, 2000

of as having been lost forever. Chuck Close (b. 1940), who has intelligently analysed photographic effects in his painting, has, for example, recently made a series of daguerreotypes, thus reviving the oldest of all photographic technologies. The images he makes, however, are of a candour which would probably have been impossible in Victorian times – for example, the nude female torsos illustrated here. 256

These nudes do, however, immediately remind the viewer of celebrated images from the history of European art, notably the nude figures of Eve produced in the early sixteenth century by Dürer and Cranach. One important aspect of recent photography has been its affection for elaborate staged tableaux, often linked together to create narrative sequences. Two fascinating examples are the *Memoirs of an African Dandy* by the British 259 domiciled Nigerian-born artist Yinka Shonibare (b. 1962) and the *Ecce Homo* series by the Swedish photographer Elisabeth Ohlson (b. 1961). Both these sequences have a polemical intent, which is reinforced by the use of deliberate incongruity. Shonibare shows himself genially at ease in Victorian society, which would certainly have rejected a black man. Ohlson, working with members of the Stockholm gay community, portrays a 260 *Last Supper* which borrows from Leonardo's celebrated version of the subject, but where all Christ's disciples are drag queens in full regalia. Her series caused enormous controversy in Sweden – one of the venues where it was shown was Uppsala Cathedral, the nation's premier church.

Staged tableaux of this kind were often, in Victorian times, created by using a number of different negatives. The contemporary equivalent for this is the use of computer digitization, which enables different photographic images to be blended seamlessly together. This technique has attracted a number of the younger artists now working in Russia, among them Olga Tobreluts (b. 1970), who has used it to illustrate classical myths and has 258 endowed a *St Sebastian* by Perugino with the features of film-star Leonardo di Caprio. Another Swedish artist, Per Wizén (b. 1966), 257 disassembles Old Master compositions – for example the work of Piero della Francesca and Caravaggio – and then uses the elements he has borrowed to create new works. His paraphrases of Caravaggio make pointed comments about the artist's supposedly homosexual inclinations.

The most celebrated artists now making use of digital manipulation are the Canadian Jeff Wall (b. 1946) and the German photographer Andreas Gursky (b. 1955). Wall presents his images as large transparencies mounted in light-boxes, a technique familiar from the world of advertising. While some of these images are deceptively naturalistic, others, such as *The Giant* (1992) stray into the world of fantasy. Gursky's reconstructions of architectural spaces subtly distort perceived reality and seem to transport the viewer into an alternative, parallel universe.

Many different photographic techniques are being pressed into service by younger artists. Working in Britain, Alexander de 261 Cadenet (b. 1974), perhaps borrowing a hint from Meret Oppenheim's (1913–85) celebrated self-portrait, has made a series of

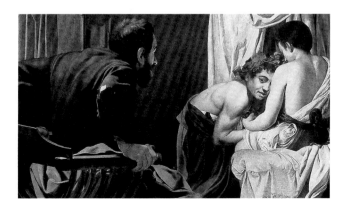

257. **Per Wizén**, *Untitled* (from the series *Reworkings*), 1998

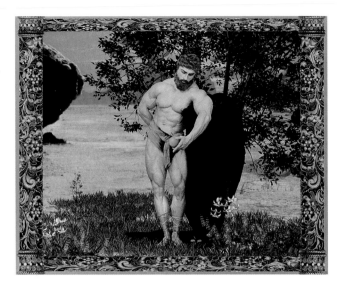

258. Olga Tobreluts, *Hercules in the Garden of the Hesperides,* from the series *The Feats of Hercules,* 1996

celebrity portraits which are X-rays of the heads of his subjects, showing, not the fleshly envelope, but the bony structure of the skull. De Cadenet enlarges these X-rays and presents them in vivid pastel colours, chosen to suit the personality of the subject, against a dazzling white ground. He says that our skulls are, after all, the most immutable things about our physical appearance – the flesh may age and change, but the skull does not change with it.

One technique which has remained curiously isolated is holography, which was once hailed as representing the future of photography in general. The theoretical basis for this was discovered as long ago as 1948, by the Hungarian-born scientist Dennis Gabor, and finally made practicable by the introduction of laser technology in the 1960s. Holography uses a laser beam split into two parts to create a complex interference pattern on a photographic negative, without the use of a lens. This pattern forms the record of the three-dimensional appearance of the object or objects towards which one part of the beam has been directed. When the pattern is illuminated in its turn, using either reflected or transmitted light, the image of the original object re-appears. Though a number of artists, such as Salvador Dalí and (once again) Chuck Close, have experimented at different times with holography as an artistic medium, it has never fully entered the mainstream, largely due to the difficulty and expense of the process. Living beings, for instance, cannot be turned into holograms directly, not only because they do not remain completely inert for the long exposure period required, but also because the

259. Yinka Shonibare, *Diary of a Victorian Dandy: 14.00 hours,* 1998

260. Elisabeth Ohlson, *Last Supper,* from *Ecce Homo,* 1998

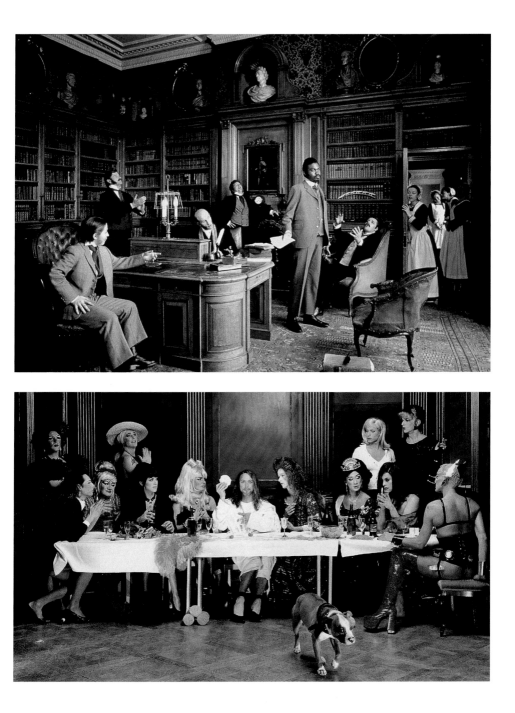

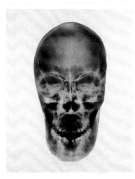

261. **Alexander de Cadenet**,
Skull Portrait, 1999

laser beam is dangerous to tissue, and can do particular damage to eyes. Holographic portraits can only be made using cine-film as an intermediary process. Using film, the holographer can, however, incorporate apparent motion into his work. Very large holograms are especially difficult and expensive to produce. Some of the most spectacular work in this genre has been created by the British, but now American-domiciled, sculptor Alexander (b. 1927), who has made holograms of up to two metres by one metre (over six by three feet) in size.

262

Much contemporary photography has taken a completely different route from the directions so far described in this chapter. It takes its cue from the informality of the snapshot. This direction was already indicated in the 1970s, in the work of American photographers such as William Eggleston (b. 1939). When the then director of the photographic programme at the Modern Museum of Art, John Szarkowski, gave Eggleston a solo show in 1976, the event aroused huge controversy, not only because of the informality of Eggleston's compositions but because of the photographer's uninhibited use of colour. Today what seems most innovative about Eggleston is not so much the technical aspect of his work, but its attitudes towards society. Though figures appear rather rarely in his photographs, the images, when assembled, make up a self-portrait – they are the subjective record of a bohemian life-style. At the same period Larry Clark (b. 1943) was making some of the images that appear in his book *Tulsa* (1971). This is a candid portrait of a group of bored, violent, drug-taking teenagers whom the photographer seems to idolize rather than condemn. Though they had of course been preceded by Robert Frank's (b. 1924) seminal book of photographs *The*

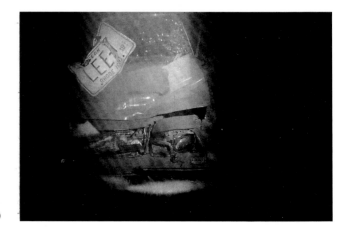

262. **Alexander**, *Car Crash,* 1989

Americans (1959), it was essentially Eggleston and Clark who set the terms for a new approach to photography. That approach has been described as follows by Ilse Kotz, in her essay 'Aesthetics of "Intimacy"':

As anyone who has spent any time in the visual art world in recent years well knows, a certain kind of work is everywhere: gritty, quasi-documentary color images of individuals, families or groupings, presented in an apparently intimate, unposed manner, shot in an off-kilter snapshot style, often a bit grainy, unfocussed or off-color. The subjects are outside the apparent 'mainstream' (though they are almost always white); gay people, transvestites, the drug culture and punk rock, urban bohemians, club kids, an occasional maladroit family. Some are in distress, but not all.[1]

Among the chief exponents of the style are Nan Goldin in the 263 United States and Richard Billingham in Britain. Goldin records the lives of her immediate circle of friends, most of them bohemians living on New York's Lower East Side. Billingham records the doings of his own dysfunctional family, cooped up in a tower-block in Sheffield. Kotz specifically connects the photography of Goldin and others who resemble her with the idea of class: 'As critics and artists such as Martha Rosler, Allan Sekula and others have long insisted, documentary photography has always been premised on looking either down the social scale (Strand, Stieglitz, *et al.*) or, more rarely, up (Weegee).'[2] She concludes rather brutally: 'In the work of subcultural photographers such as Clark and Goldin, the claim to inside-ness, to belonging to the group which is being surveilled, seems to have two principal functions: it allows us greater access, and, as insiders, the photographers' voyeurism authorizes own own.'[3]

This seems to me rather harsh, but it is undoubtedly true that photography, perhaps even more than artists' video, has become a directly autobiographical medium, in which the maker of the photographs is the hero in his or her own play, and the ongoing theme is undoubtedly voyeurism, that of the spectator as well as that of the artist. This aspect has recently been acted out in candid fashion by the young Chinese performance artist Ma Liuming (b. 1965). There is one event which he has now done in a number of different locations – in Geneva, at Munster in Germany and in Nagoya. For this he drugs himself into a state of insensibility and is then carried naked on to a stage, where he is propped up while various audience members are asked to disport themselves around him, improvising as they please. Ma

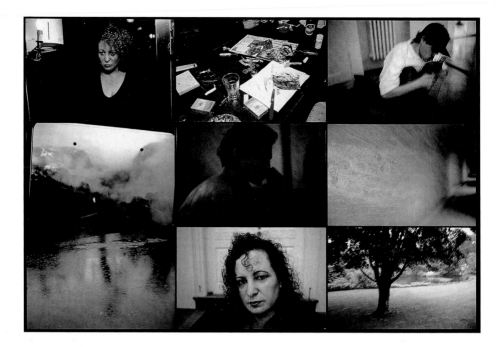

263. **Nan Goldin**, *Relapse/Detox*, 1998

Liuming remains unaware of what has happened until he sees the photographic record later – the pictures take on an additional importance as the surviving residue of an event which he has not in fact experienced directly.

Ma Liuming also makes use of photography to challenge sexual stereotyping. He makes transgender self-portraits – pictures, as he says, of a being with 'a woman's head and a man's body', some of which show him cavorting naked on top of the Great Wall of China. These belong to a well established genre. There are, for instance, very similar role-playing images by the Japanese artist Yasumasa Morimura (b. 1951). In *Black Marilyn* he contrives a parody of the famous image of the star standing over a subway grating with her skirt blowing up around her. In this case the fluttering skirt reveals an erect, though obviously artificial, penis.

Works of this kind lead one towards another piece of territory that photography has increasingly tended to make its own. The psychological force of photographs, as opposed to that of paintings or drawings, often lies in what we still tend to think of as their credibility, though by this time most people have become at least intellectually aware of the ease with which photographs can be altered by processes such as computer digitization . One of the first photographers who consciously exploited the camera's

264

265

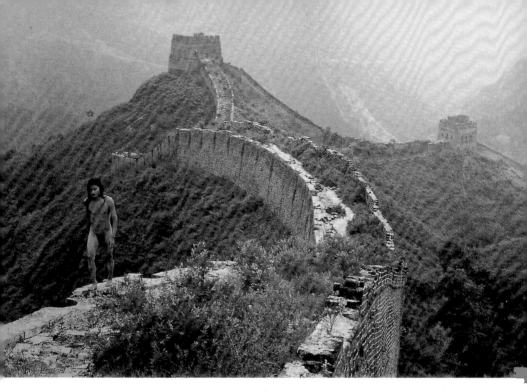

264. **Ma Liuming**, *Fen-Ma Liuming Walks the Great Wall*, 1998

265. **Yasumasa Morimura**, *Playing with the Gods, No. 1 Twilight*, 1991

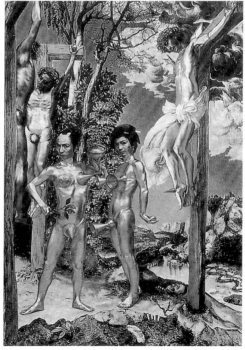

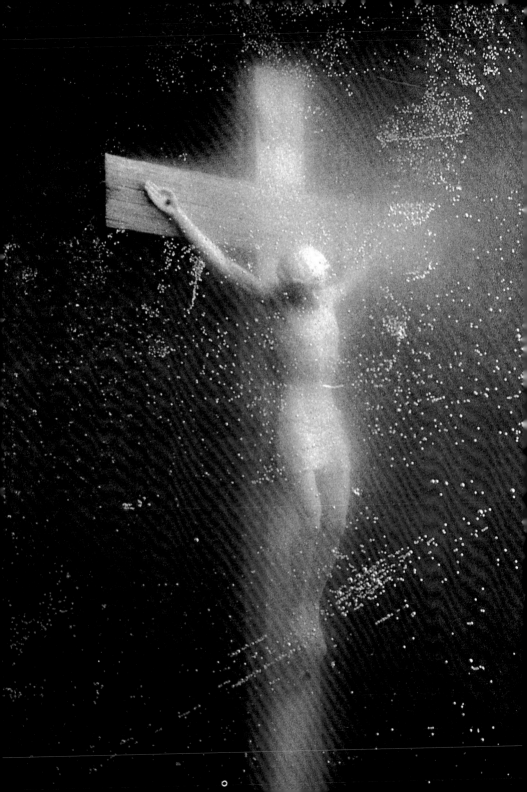

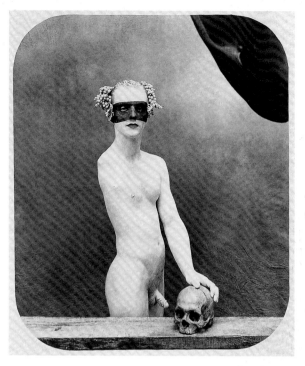

267. **Joel-Peter Witkin**, *Portrait as a Vanité, New Mexico,* 1994

affinity for what was exceptional and grotesque was probably Diane Arbus with work done in the 1960s – though one can find at least traces of the same attitude in the photographs of street people made much earlier by Paul Strand (1890–1976). Since that time, the grotesque and the bizarre have become major topics for the camera. Leading exponents of this approach have been Andres Serrano (b. 1950) and Joel-Peter Witkin (b. 1939), both of whom are as much fascinated with death as they are with physical deformity and with images of sexual acts and gestures. Witkin is especially interesting because he combines the nineteenth-century influences cited at the beginning of this chapter – his photographs, like those of Shonibare and Ohlson, are elaborately staged tableaux – with an entirely contemporary boldness in his choice of subject-matter.

266
267

The fascination with what is psychologically outré has led to much recent interest in the work of photographers who seem to be entirely the prisoners of their own obsessions. The most striking of these are the Frenchman Pierre Molinier (1900–76) who acted out narcissistic and androgynous fantasies for the camera, making images which only became widely known after his death, and the Spanish schizophrenic David Nebreda (b. 1952) whose

266. **Andres Serrano**, *Piss Christ,* 1987

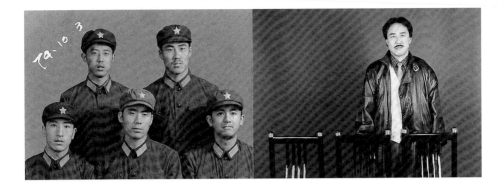

268. **Hai Bo**, *They – 3*, 1999

long series of self-portraits, made in the 1980s and 1990s, is a striking record of the course of his illness and the fantasies to which it gives rise. The memorable nature of these photographs is due quite largely to their ambiguity. Nebreda is sufficiently detached from his situation to create them, yet on another plane he remains completely the prisoner of his malady.

Much closer to the mainstream is the work of the Dutch photographer Rineke Dijkstra (b. 1959), whose pictures of gangling adolescents on North European beaches, and of new mothers holding their babies sometimes radiate a feeling of unease but nevertheless have a touching directness and humanity that makes one feel that the photographer has achieved a high level of empathy with her subjects.

Another example of this directness – a very striking one but much more impersonal – is a series of diptychs by the Chinese artist Hai Bo (b. 1962). Made in 1999, they look at the changes which have taken place in China in the course of a quarter of a century, In each case the left-hand image is a group photograph taken in 1974, when Mao Zedong was still alive and the Cultural Revolution still controlled Chinese society. In the right-hand image, the photographer has posed the same people – those who are still alive – in exactly the same grouping, with each person in his or her previous place. In the example illustrated, *They – 3*, 268 only one man, of the five shown in the original group, is still living. He looks very different, not only because he is now middle-aged, but because he is wearing fashionable Western clothes. The true father of a photographic project of this kind is the German, August Sander (1876–1964). The link to Sander demonstrates the way in which photography leaps over both geographical and cultural differences. This form of contemporary expression is essentially universal.

Chapter 12:   Post-Pop blues

When one looks at the kinds of art that have been most fashionable in the 1990s, one sees the still all-pervasive influence of Pop art. It is, however, Pop which has undergone a sea-change – it no longer uses popular forms with the upbeat enthusiasm that characterized much of the art of the 1960s, even when this was, supposedly at its most transgressive, but, instead, approaches the imagery of modern urban society with a sourness combined with melancholy frivolity. This has been linked partly to a fusion between Pop and other kinds of art – Arte Povera, for example. The influential West Coast artist Mike Kelley (b. 1954) offers an 269 example. Kelley's installations made with stained, dirty, second-hand toys have sometimes been compared to the popular shrines created by members of the public following some violent, newsworthy death – most conspicuously that of Princess Diana. However, their creator does not see them in this quasi-religious light. In a document placed on the Internet in connection with its Kelley exhibition of 1997, the Van Abbemuseum in Eindhoven, Holland, commented, quoting the artist himself:

Kelley does not want to produce his work from the rational position of an adult artist who presents a problem and then solves that problem in

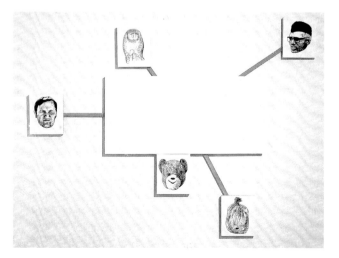

269. **Mike Kelley**, *Center and Peripheries #5*, 1990

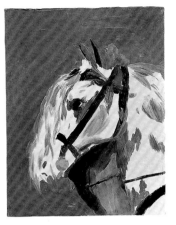

his work. For him the most productive starting point for his work is the attitude of an adolescent someone who is not yet an adult and attacks adulthood. 'I think an adolescent attitude is the attitude of the humorist, like somebody who knows the rules but doesn't see any reason to be involved in them. The adolescent period interests the most. Modernism usually valorizes childhood, childishness, or insanity – something that is supposedly pre-adult. But then adult art has to get involved in questions of faith and belief, and I don't have any faith or belief, so I don't want to make adult art. I'd rather make adolescent art.'

This deliberate abandonment of adult responsibility can be observed in the work of a number of artists who have been fashionable in the 1990s. Karen Kilimnik (b. 1955), another American, became one of the most discussed artists of the decade in the New York art press, despite her lack of any very highly recognizable signature style. Her success was due to her embrace of what critics described as 'abjection' – her programmatic unwillingness to strive for any kind of moral or aesthetic value. 'By consuming the shreds of glamour, by setting them up as dumb props for her own fantasies with the most minimal intervention, Kilimnik is tapping into the same hot line to power as Andy Warhol and Jeff Koons, who, also, refuse to reassure us by providing a free moral judgement with every art product.'[1] Kilimnik's concentration on the utterly ephemeral was what seemed to fascinate her admirers. Or, as another critic put it, 'Kilimnik's pose swings wildly between unadulterated abjection and the omniscience of a whimsically infantile deity rearranging reality like a child on a carpeted floor.'[2]

270

Different as they seem at first sight, it is possible to see a link between Kilimnik's nihilism and the attitudes of the prominent post-*perestroika* Russian artist Oleg Kulik (b. 1961), though Kulik substitutes other qualities for Kilimnik's petulant wispiness, making violent and aggressive performance works – in one he stripped naked and pretended to be a savage and uncontrollable dog. He also makes photo and video pieces that toy with ideas about unacceptability. In a series of photographs, *Deep into Russia* 271 (1993), he seems to commit acts of bestiality with various animals. His wife, the critic Mila Bredikhina, provides a justificatory text to support what he does:

Kulik's activities simultaneously reveal two vectors in contrast with one another, both equally topical in today's Russia. His aggressive external unpredictability today coexists with the deep, tormented contemplation of one's obscure, stifling unmetaphysical profundities. The madly energetic explorer of the profundities of the cow reveals the two co-existing codes of two Russian realities: anxiety and aggressiveness.
By barking and snapping, the aggressive crawling naked man is in fact completely defenceless in the face of all types of social establishments. Kulik's aggressiveness is not unlike the desperate moralizing by a human being disappointed by the values of modern anthropocentric culture with its prospects and verbal communication. For Kulik the great moralist and writer Leo Tolstoi and his critique of the social establishment and the literary language, remains a figure of strong principles.[3]

Nevertheless, the references to morality and principle, however seemingly bizarre, also mark Kulik's distance from the territory

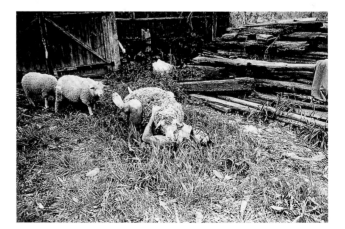

271. **Oleg Kulik,**
Deep into Russia, 1993

which American artists like Kelley and Kilimnik seem to inhabit, and perhaps help to explain the current decline in the international reputation of American art.

Kulik is very typical of his period in his almost frantic search for topics and indeed for actual imagery that his audience is likely to find unacceptable, or, at the very least, disturbing and threatening. One can perhaps connect this with the increasingly ambiguous position of the artistic avant-garde within Western society. On the one hand, the avant-garde bases its rights to that title on its transgressive and oppositional attitude to received ideas and to ordinary social norms – this being the way in which 'advanced' artists have identified themselves ever since the rise of Romanticism. On the other hand, what is still labelled avant-garde art has moved into the situation once occupied by the Salon artists of the late nineteenth century. It is in receipt of state patronage, often lavish, and is housed and made available to the public in official institutions.

The rush to find unacceptable subjects and images accelerated throughout the 1990s. Artists experimented with references to excrement – as in the much-publicized *Naked Shit Pictures* by Gilbert and George, and the works making use of actual balls of elephant dung created by Chris Ofili (b. 1968), a British-born artist of African descent. Despite the fact that the theme had already been used by the Italian artist Piero Manzoni (1933–63), who as long ago as 1961 offered tins of his own shit as artworks, it retained much of its potency. One of Ofili's paintings – an image of the Virgin Mary with a lump of elephant dung substituted for one of her breasts and elements cut from pornographic magazines taking the place of cherubs in the background, offended, on a purely hearsay basis, the mayor of New York, Rudolph Giuliani, who was at that time thinking of running for the Senate and who needed the support of the city's Catholic voters. He threatened to deprive the Brooklyn Museum of the subsidies it received from the city if it persisted with the 'Sensation!' show in which it was included, and the ensuing row ensured long queues for the exhibition when it opened to the public, as inevitably it did, despite Giuliani's best efforts.

Artists also exploited one of the deepest modern fears – the terror of paedophilia. The British artist Marcus Harvey (b. 1963) aroused a satisfactory uproar with a large portrait of Britain's most notorious murderess, Myra Hindley, based on the police mug-shot taken at the time of her arrest in 1966, and created by applying paint using moulds made from children's hands.[4] Subtler

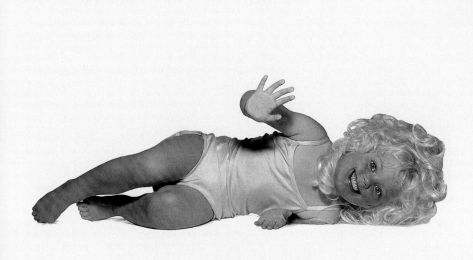

272. **Inez van Lamsweerde,** *Final Fantasy, Ursula,* 1993

allusions to this fear were made by the Dutch photographer Inez van Lamsweerde (b. 1963) whose *Final Fantasy* series, named after a video-game, uses three-year old models, and poses them as if they were sexually knowing adults. The girls' lips are then replaced, by means of computer manipulation, with the leering mouths of adults. As one commentator remarked, 'These toddlers, with their enormous teeth and coy poses, catch us between our need to recognize children's sexuality and our fear of getting too close to it.'[5] Another version of this kind of imagery, less immediately transgressive because translated into more traditional terms, can be found in the work of the young South African-born painter Nicky Hoberman (b. 1967). Her children, too, radiate the kind of knowingness one associates with photographs of pre-pubescent American beauty queens, like the mysteriously murdered JonBennet Ramsey.

Both Ofili and Harvey belonged to a group of British artists who were amongst the most potent newsmakers of the decade. Their attitudes can be traced fairly far back in the history of British culture after World War II. The starting point seems to have been the British Punk Rock movement of the 1970s. The Sex

Pistols, the most important Punk Rock group, gave their first public performance in 1975. Punk was a response to profound upheavals taking place in British society. It came into being hot on the heels of the Arab oil embargo of 1973 and the 'winter of discontent' presided over by the short-lived Conservative government of Edward Heath, and marked a new and far more militant stage in the development of British youth culture, which had started with the Beatles, ten or more years earlier. The new art of the 1990s was the product of a later bout of economic misfortune. It was born at the end of the 1980s, in the midst of the most prolonged economic downturn endured by the British for fifty years. This economic collapse decimated the commercial gallery system, and left artists to fend for themselves at a time when teaching jobs, their other traditional source of financial support, were increasingly hard to find. Their reaction was to create their own self-help system, based on London's East End, an event marked by the revival of the self-confident aggression that had characterized Punk.

The chief figure in the art movement which sprang up as a result was Damien Hirst. In the late 1980s Hirst attended Goldsmiths' College, which was to be a nursery for the new art, and, while still a student there he organized an exhibition called 'Freeze' (1988) in a disused Docklands warehouse space. At first he was chiefly thought of as a prodigiously energetic young entrepreneur, but he soon made a mark as an independent creative artist with signature works which consisted of dead animals and fish floating in tanks of formaldehyde solution. The most celebrated of these is his fourteen-foot long tiger shark, entitled *The Physical Impossibility of Death in the Mind of Someone Living* (1991), which was commissioned by the collector and advertising magnate Charles Saatchi. This piece caught the public imagination to such an extent that it was even the subject of caricatures in British newspapers. The chief theme of Hirst's work is one familiar from some of the greatest works of British literature – for example, Donne's religious poetry, Milton's 'Lycidas', Shelley's 'Hyperion' and Alfred, Lord Tennyson's 'In Memoriam'. It is the terror of death and the exploration of ideas and feelings about human mortality. His most characteristic works appropriate their forms from displays in old-fashioned museums of natural history.

Another prominent British artist of more or less the same generation is Rachel Whiteread (b. 1963). Where Hirst preserves things in glass tanks, Whiteread makes sculpture by filling up

273

and thus solidifying negative spaces. Her most celebrated work to date is *House* (1993) which preserved the spaces of an ordinary East London council house, scheduled for demolition, as a kind of temporary memorial to the lives that had been lived there.

Whiteread and Hirst differ from most of the other artists who have been lumped together with them as so-called YBAs or Young British Artists – an appellation that will inevitably become obsolete – because they tackle large and serious themes such as death and memory. Hirst also has a considerable output of much more trivial works which seem chiefly designed to turn his celebrity to commercial account – for example, large editions of prints offered for sale on the Internet. The problem they both share is an inflexibility of method – for example, once Whiteread has cast every negative space she can think of, from the under-sides of chairs and stools to the inside of a hotwater bottle, where will she go then? Hirst's most recent major work at the time of writing is *Hymn* (2000), a literal six-metre, twenty-foot-high enlargement of an anatomical model made for children.

273. **Damien Hirst**, *Away from the Flock*, 1994

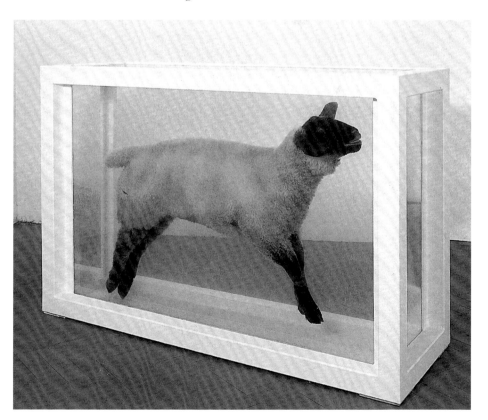

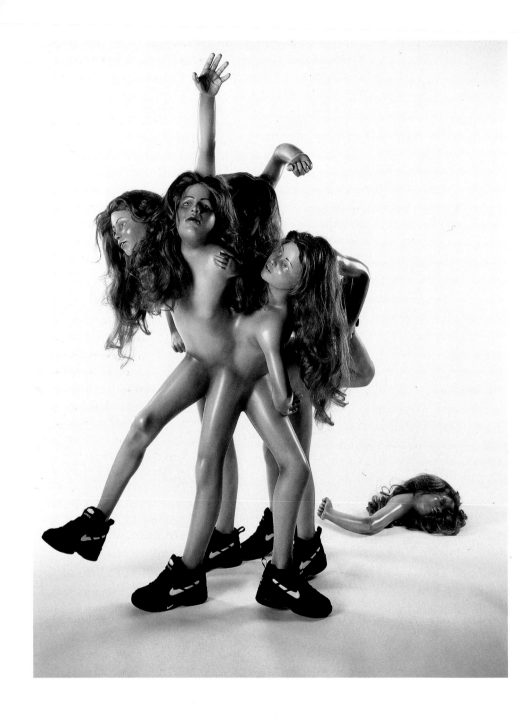

Other artists of the YBA group have concentrated on trying to communicate the squalor of bohemian lifestyles. Sarah Lucas (b. 1962) pokes fun at the raucous British tabloid newspapers and at sexist attitudes towards women, Tracey Emin garnered enormous publicity for *My Bed* (1999), an installation which was a reconstruction of the scruffy disorder of her own bedroom. It failed to win her the Turner Prize, now Britain's most prestigious award for an avant-garde artist but stole all the headlines connected with the event.

The artists from this group who, in addition to Hirst and Whiteread, seem most likely to make lasting reputations are the brothers Jake (b. 1966) and Dinos Chapman (b. 1962). The Chapmans originally made an impact, like others mentioned above, by playing on fears about paedophilia. Their signature works were sculptures of nude female children with misplaced sexual organs – erect penises instead of noses for example. It is interesting to note that the brothers have now gone on to a yet more controversial subject – the Holocaust. Their route has been via their fascination with Goya's *Disasters of War*. They reconstructed one of the most notorious of Goya's images as a life-sized sculpture (*Great Deeds Against the Dead*, 1994), then made their own series of prints based on Goya. This, in turn, led to what is at the time of writing their most ambitious artistic project, *Hell* (1997–2000), which consists of a multitude of miniature figures, with appropriate landscape and architectural backgrounds, placed in large glass cases which, in turn, are arranged in the form of a swastika. As with Damien Hirst's tiger shark, there seem to be references to the kind of museum display which has now completely gone out of fashion – if Hirst alludes to old-fashioned natural history museums, the Chapman brothers seem to have been inspired by the battlefield panoramas which were once a popular feature of military museums of the same vintage.

Hell is not simply a literal illustration of the Holocaust. Nazis are often represented as the tortured, paying for their crimes in some other world, condemned to suffer what they made others suffer. The Chapmans differ from most recent avant-garde artists by making use of a wide range of artistic and historical allusions – to the prints of Goya and Callot, and to scenes of Christian martyrdom – in particular to Mannerist and Baroque representations of *The Martyrdom of the Ten Thousand*. There are also references to the demonic imagery invented by Hieronymus Bosch and Pieter Bruegel the Elder. This gives their enterprise a much larger dimension than the work of other artists who have

274

recently tackled the same theme. The connection to these artists is nevertheless clear.

The best known of them is probably Christian Boltanski (b. 1944), who has been making use of the Holocaust theme since the mid 1980s, usually presenting it through anonymous, and often somewhat doctored, mugshots borrowed from sources such as school yearbooks, presented under strong lights which suggest an interrogation chamber. His use of this imagery is, however, unspecific and deliberately ambiguous. That is, while his work is usually perceived as being Holocaust-inspired, or Holocaust-related, Boltanski is careful to point of that he sets himself certain limits:

I have never used images that came from the camps, it would be impossible for me, it would be something shameful to use, too sacred. My work is not about the camps, it is after the camps. The reality of the Occident was changed by the Holocaust. We can no longer see anything without seeing that. But my work is not about the Holocaust, it's about death in general, about all our deaths.[6]

In turning to the Holocaust as their new theme, the Chapmans are also following the lead of a number of other artists, not British, who have recently done the same thing. These artists include the American David Levinthal (b. 1949), the Pole Zbigniew Libera (b. 1959) and the Israeli Roee Rosen (b. 1963). Like the Chapmans in their new work, all three seem intent on distancing the story by representing it in miniature. Unlike them, they tend to do so in deliberately kitsch terms, thus giving yet another twist to the aesthetics of shock already described in earlier sections of this chapter. Levinthal, for example, recreates the events of 1940–45 by photographing toy figures, often basing himself on concentration camp and ghetto photographs taken by the Nazis themselves. Libera has gone a step further by creating a series of boxed sets based on Lego construction kits from which one can build one's own miniature concentration camp – the inmates become robotic toy skeletons. Roee Rosen proposed a 'virtual reality scenario' called *Live and Die as Eva Braun* (1997) which was shown at the Israel Museum, Jerusalem, and caused a predictable uproar. The illustrations to his text are cut paper silhouettes of a deliberately sentimental kind.

In all these works, as in so many of the others cited in this chapter, one is aware of the lingering influence of Pop, in that they make use of means of representation which are associated with mass culture rather than high culture. The prevailing atmos-

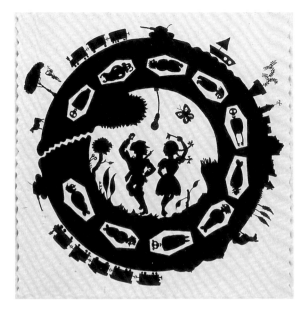

275. **Roee Rosen**, *Live and Die as Eva Braun # 34*, 1994–97

phere nevertheless is one of sourness and disillusion. Underlying the repeated acts of provocation, there is a nihilism which can plausibly be described as *fin-de-siècle*. The assaults on convention of the officially sanctioned avant-garde have become subject to the law of diminishing returns.

The few exceptions to this, in the Post-Pop era, seem to come from the Far East. One of the most conspicuous is the Japanese Mariko Mori (b. 1967). Mori's sources are a mixture of Japanese popular culture and Buddhist doctrine, especially the beliefs of the so-called Pure Land sect, whose adherents are confident that after death they will be reborn in the Western Paradise or Pure Land and attain Nirvana. Mori's most ambitious and successful work is the video *Nirvana* (1997), in which the artist herself appears as the goddess Kichijōten, surrounded by six Disneyesque multicoloured musicians called 'Tunes'. The video incorporates startling 3-D effects which require the spectator to wear special glasses. The video forms part of an installation which also incorporates four mural-sized digitally manipulated photographic images which symbolically represent the four elements of Buddhist cosmology – wind, fire, water and earth – and, notionally, a clear plastic teardrop 'Enlightenment Capsule' containing a plastic lotus flower suspended in mid-air by magnets. In this the spectator will be invited to sit, once the technology has been perfected.

276

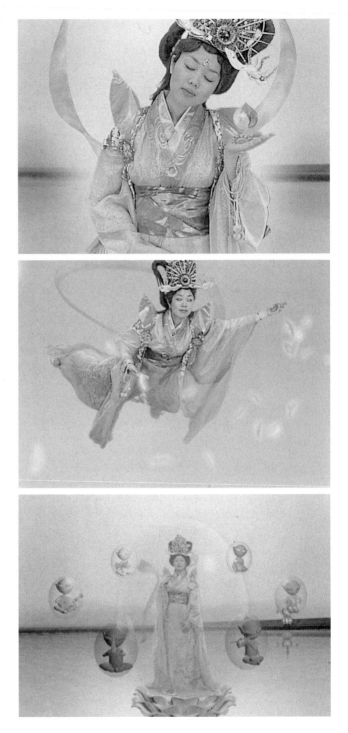

Mori skilfully mingles the sugary whimsicality and self-conscious coyness of much contemporary urban Japanese culture with references to eternal verities that have won her a large number of Western admirers. Her approach is, however, disconcertingly simplistic. As one critic remarked: 'Mori visualizes the body as a set of radiant energies that sublimate the thing-of-flesh into a spirit made of (celluloid) light.'[7] The more one considers this description, the less complimentary it becomes. Mori's work makes an interesting comparison with that of the much older Japanese woman artist, Yayoi Kusama. Kusama lived in New York from 1958 to 1972 and made a considerable reputation for herself there with paintings and environmental works based on obsessive pattern-making, which seemed to combine ideas taken from Pop with others linked to Minimal art. In the 1970s, after her return to Japan, she retired into a psychiatric institution, which still remains her place of residence, and was largely forgotten in the West. In 1998 her reputation was revived by a survey of her early work staged by the Museum of Modern Art in New York, and another at the Serpentine Gallery in London in 2000. She is concerned with cultural identity, but in a much rawer, more genuinely confrontational fashion than Mori. Kusama's insistent patterns affect the spectator in a visceral way; their effective simplicity makes Mori's high-tech visual effects look flimsy and superficial by contrast.

Recent Chinese art has also made occasional allusions to traditional religious customs and beliefs, but usually does so in a way which seems intended to disconcert rather than reassure, which is Mori's essential purpose. A good example is the work of the Beijing artist Sun Yuan (b. 1972). A graduate of the Beijing Academy, Sun Yuan began his career as a painter, but moved, at the end of the 1990s, into making installations, often collaborating with his partner Pen Yu (b. 1974). Though his view is that 'there is no explicit border between Chinese and Western culture,'[8] these installations often cross boundaries which are still tenuously maintained in Western art. For example, a number of them make use of foetuses – children carried nearly to full term, or else born dead. These little corpses are easily procured in China, where there are stringent limitations on the number of children a couple may have. Sun Yuan says he purchases them, quite legitimately, from hospitals[9]. *Soul Killing* (February 2000) was a collaboration between Sun Yuan and Pen Yu. It featured, not a dead child but a dead, skinned dog, perhaps bought in a Beijing food market, which was used to to illustrate the Chinese

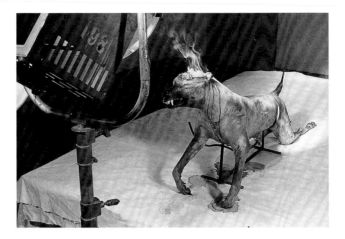

277. **Sun Yuan and Pen Yu**, *Soul Killing*, 2000

folk belief that the spirit may linger in a mischief-making fashion within or close to a dead body, and needs to be driven out by violent means. The dog's brain was burned away with a powerful light projector. The manifestation lasted just an hour, but only narrowly escaped being banned, and aroused violent debate within the Beijing art world.

The shock element in this case was not simply the image presented by the installation itself, but the realization that the much vaunted globalization of contemporary art which took place in the 1980s and 1990s still left room for huge differences of cultural attitude. However, this realization seems to have been felt at least as strongly in Beijing itself as among those who come to know the work in the West through illustration and description rather than through direct experience. This example, while in one sense demonstrating cultural difference, also exemplifies the degree to which the aesthetics and politics of shock became the common currency of the art world of the 1990s. Karen Kilimnik's scatty frivolity and Mariko Mori's over-sweetened optimism were the exceptions, not the rule.

Chapter 13:   New classicism

Efforts to revive classicism were, perhaps paradoxically, a recurrent feature in the history of twentieth-century art. They took a number of different forms – initially that of a conservative recoil from the supposed excesses of Modernism (the so-called 'return to order' inspired by the horrors of World War I). In the first half of the century classical forms and allusions in art also became associated with the efforts made by various dictatorships – Fascist, Nazi and Soviet – to provide themselves with an imperial identity. In later decades, classicism re-appeared and took on a surprising number of different and apparently contradictory guises. In the eyes of architectural historians like Charles Jencks, the revival of classical forms and ornaments meant the rejection of the International Modern style, till then triumphant in the hands of architects such as Le Corbusier and Mies van der Rohe. Revived classicism thus became, in terms of architectural discourse, almost identical with what Jencks was one of the first to call Post-Modernism. His book, *The Language of Post-Modern Architecture*, first published in 1977, and frequently reprinted since, is the standard text on the subject.

Classicism did not, however, establish itself nearly as firmly in painting and sculpture, or in related forms of visual expression, such as video and photography, as it did in architecture. A number of classicizing painters appeared, both in the United States and in Britain, but they never succeeded in organizing themselves into anything resembling a coherent artistic movement. In Britain, Michael Leonard (b. 1933), an immensely skilful painter of nudes, remained an isolated figure, better known for the portrait drawings which transposed his sitters into different historical epochs, than for his more important work on a larger scale. In America, painters of classical compositions fared a little better. Among them were Edward Schmidt (b. 1946), Alan Feltus (b. 1943) and David Ligare (b. 1945). A certain number of exhibitions highlighting classical tendencies in art were organized in the United States, but while the painters found an audience through these, and also patrons, they were never perceived as forming a tendency which might dare to challenge the ruling

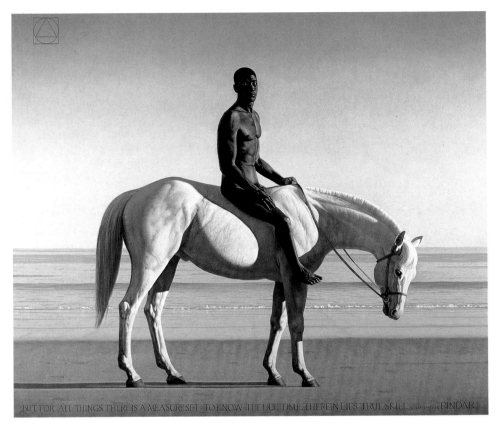

BUT FOR ALL THINGS THERE IS A MEASURE SET : TO KNOW THE DUE TIME, THEREIN LIES TRUE SKILL COMPILED IN PINDAR

278. **David Ligare**, *Areta (Black Figure on White Horse),* 2000

279. **Michael Leonard**, *Nectarine Man,* 1997

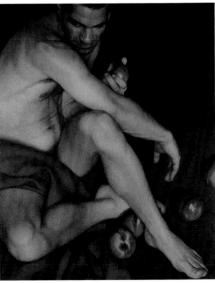

hierarchy. Often they used classicism as a means of signalling difference. A good example of this is the work of the homosexual activist painter Delmas Howe (b. 1935), based, like Elisabeth Ohlson's work, on the idea of the 'Stations of the Cross' as metaphors for gay oppression. 280

A younger and more fashionable American artist, John Currin (b. 1962) has found ingenious ways of reconciling classical, or at least traditional, elements with the prevailing taste for kitsch. Currin, who says that he has been influenced by Northern Renaissance painters such as Lucas Cranach and Hans Baldung Grien, and also by early Mannerists such as Parmigianino, synthesizes ideas taken from them with others borrowed from today's fashion magazines. When Currin was included in the 1999 Carnegie International, the internet website for the exhibition proclaimed: 'While Currin's nudes carry seemingly recognizable faces and modern hairstyles, their bodies are often elongated and distorted. *This uneasy juxtaposition* precludes 281

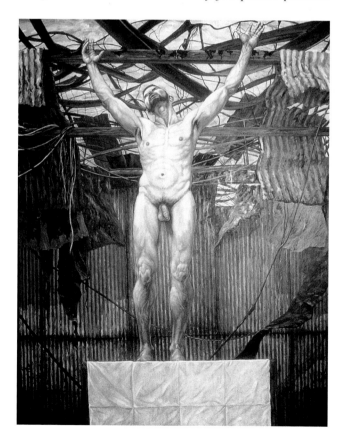

280. **Delmas Howe**, *Stations,*
The Triumphs, 1999

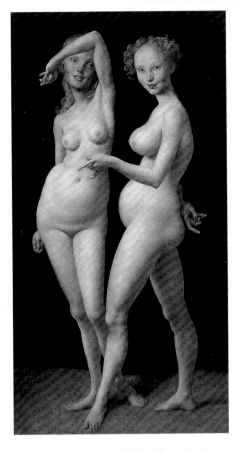

[italics mine] what might otherwise be perceived as an erotic image.' If Chris Cunningham's video *flex* (see Chapter 10) turns a deliberately blind eye to what is politically correct, this museum pronouncement runs to the opposite extreme. Currin's Cranach paraphrases in fact have a flaunting, challenging sexuality which serves as a reminder that classical values in art are linked, more often that not, to a candid worship of the human body, whatever its gender.

Feltus lives and works in Italy, and Ligare exhibits his work there. This is significant, since Italy is, despite the international success of the Trans-Avantgarde in the 1980s, one of the few countries where a classical sensibility remains dominant.

Looking at the Italian art which was produced from 1979 onwards – that is from the year when Giorgio de Chirico died – one can now see two opposing tendencies which nevertheless have concealed links with one another. The first of these is Arte Povera, which has already been discussed. The second is the influence of de Chirico himself. A number of the artists who were at least loosely part of the Arte Povera impulse in the 1970s made use of classical images. The best known is Giulio Paolini (b. 1940), who included classical heads and other classical plaster casts in his installations. Another was Carlo-Maria Mariani 282 (b. 1931). Mariani is an especially complex and interesting artistic personality. A very accomplished painter and draughtsman, equipped with skills which many of his contemporaries had mislaid, he took over the personality of the Italian neo-classicist Vincenzo Camuccini (1771–1844), and also became a devoted student of Anton Raphael Mengs (1728–79), the painter who was Winckelmann's instrument in the invention of Neo-Classicism. For Mariani, the works he produced in this vein were essentially efforts of intellectual analysis, and he therefore aligned himself with the development of Conceptual art. Similar attitudes are expressed in the environment sculptures of Ian Hamilton Finlay (b. 1926), and in the installations using classical models and fragments created by Anne and Patrick Poirier (both b. 1942). Nevertheless Mariani's paintings have a seductiveness which has often led to a misreading of his intentions.

The situation with most of his Italian contemporaries was somewhat different. An exhibition entitled 'La Pittura Ritrovata' ('Painting Refound'), held in Rome in 1999, highlighted the work of many of the painters who had lived and work in Rome during

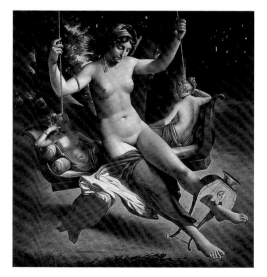

282. **Carlo Maria Mariani**,
Monument to Poetry, 1994–95

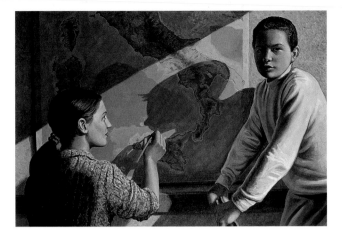

283. **Carlo Bertocci**, *The Origin of Painting*, 2000

the two preceding decades. The exhibition demonstrated their debt to Giorgio de Chirico, but also their differences from him. De Chirico, having been one of the pioneer figures in the Modernist avant-garde, rebelled against Modernism in the mid-1920s and spent the rest of his career trying to re-establish himself as a rival of the Old Masters. This enterprise, however, was continually undermined by the artist's own sense of irony – he mocked his own enterprise; he seemed to succumb to banality, yet made it clear that the banal elements in his work were intended to be subversive. Since his death, he and Francis Picabia, who pursued a somewhat similar path, have increasingly often been described as the first true Post-Modernists.

The agenda of the Italian classical painters who followed in his wake is less complex, but their work does represent a conscious rebellion against the Modernist ethos. This rebellion is openly expressed in some of their subject matter – for example in Carlo Bertocci's (b. 1946) *The Origin of Drawing* (2000), which refers to a Greek legend about the birth of figurative art. One notes that the profile which the young artist traces is thrown, not on a blank wall, as the original legend states, but against a map of Italy. Other leading figures in the new Italian classical school are Stefano di Stasio (b. 1948), Ubaldo Bartolini (b. 1944), Alberto Abate (b. 1946), Massimo Livadiotti (b. 1959) and Paola Gandolfi. Each articulates the idea of 'classicism' in a slightly different way. Bartolini, for example, is purely a landscape painter, who refers himself back, not to Poussin and Claude, but to the tradition of northern landscape painters working in Italy such as Paul Brill (1554–1626) and Adam Elsheimer (1578–1610). Abate

283

284. **Ricardo Cinalli**, *Homenaje Humanista Para el Nuevo Milenio* (Humanistic Homage for the New Millennium), detail, 1999–2000

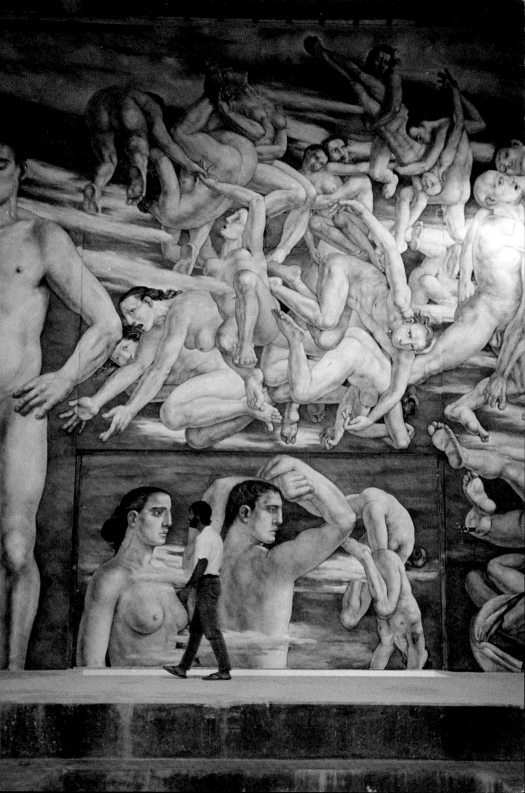

is interested in the Symbolist Movement that preceded Modernism, often painting allegorical female figures (*The Language of Birds*, 1993) which are in direct line of descent from painters such as Frans von Stuck (1863–1928), a German academic-Symbolist painter who also influenced de Chirico when the latter was a young man studying in Munich. Paola Gandolfi combines a use of classical forms with erotic and surrealist elements.

This rebirth of classicism has also manifested itself among Spanish-speaking artists – for example in the work of Ricardo Cinalli (b. 1948) from Argentina, Roberto Marquez (b. 1959) from Mexico, and Carlos Forns Bada (b. 1956) and Guillermo Perez Villata (b. 1948) from Spain. Cinalli has recently undertaken a very ambitious mural cycle, in a style and on a scale to rival leading Italian Mannerists such as Jacopo Pontormo (1494–1557) and Agnolo Bronzino (1503–72), in a cultural centre at Punta del Este in Uruguay. If these murals were more accessible geographically they would have greater impact, as they are undoubtedly one of the more ambitious enterprises

285

284

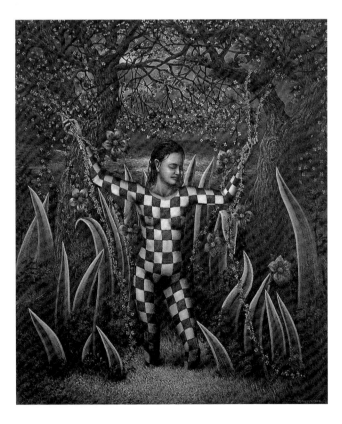

285. **Roberto Marquez**, *La otra primavera* (The Other Spring), 2000

of this sort undertaken since the heyday of the Mexican muralists in the 1930s – though they are also very different in spirit.

The other major centre for a revival of classical art, in addition to Rome, has, however, been St Petersburg in Russia. This revival is intimately linked with the political and cultural turmoil that has prevailed in Russia since the fall of Communism, and journalists have sometimes perceived the new Petersburg classicism as an ally of 'dangerous and potent political ideologies'[1] – in other words, conservative Russian nationalism. Essentially what has happened is that the new generation of Russian artists have rejected the late-Modernist experiments of the artists of the *perestroika* epoch, most of whom are in any case now living outside Russia. The only artists of this type for whom they preserve a degree of respect are the SOTS Art duo Vitaly Komar (b. 1943) and Alexander Melamid (b. 1945), whom they admire for their accomplished parodies of the Stalinist classical style. In addition to rejecting the *perestroika* artists, they condemn the whole of the Russian Modern Movement of the early years of the twentieth century as a misguided aberration.

The new St Petersburg classicism has a dominant theoretician, the artist and critic Timor Novikov (b. 1948), who began his career as a comparatively minor '*perestroika* Modernist' – a follower of the folkloric doctrines of Mikhail Larionov (1881–1962), a member of the early twentieth-century Russian avantgarde which he later came to despise. After travels to Western Europe and the United States in the 1980s, where he met leading vanguard artists, such as Robert Rauschenberg and John Cage, whom he still refers to as his 'teachers', Novikov returned to Russia to exhibit his first neo-academic works in 1988 and 1989 and to found the Novia Akademia or New Academy of Arts in 1993. As he declared then: 'continuity will become a symbol of the 1990s among us.'[2] 286

Novikov bases his support of 'traditional values' on the history of St Petersburg itself, a classical city conserving the architectural forms of the eighteenth and nineteenth century. In the first two decades of the twentieth century it was the seat of two Hellenizing art movements, both focused on luxuriously produced literary periodicals. The first of these surrounded Serge Diaghilev's early venture *Mir Iskusstva* (*World of Art*, 1899–1904); the second was the Acmeist review *Apollon* (1906–17), one of whose founders was the poet Nicolai Gumilyov, shot as a counter-revolutionary in 1921. To these purely local elements other more international ones are added – a cult, for example, of

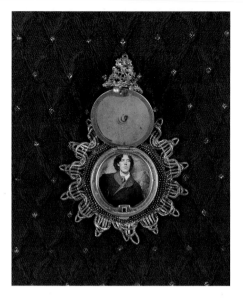

the photographic work of Wilhem von Gloeden (1856–1931), an aristocratic Baltic German who spent the greater part of his life in Sicily, photographing the local peasants and fishermen as reincarnations of the Ancient Greeks. For Novikov, the idea of Beauty, banished from contemporary art, has taken refuge in related forms of visual representation, notably in advertising. He cites, in particular, the Gloeden-esque images used to advertise the products of the great Italian fashion house Versace, whose products are immensely popular with the new elites of modern Russia. The Novia Akademia prides itself on being not only classical but deliberately academic. It offers an elaborate parody of the way such institutions operated in the past, with its own bureaucracy – professors, students, honorary diplomas awarded at an annual awards ceremony, an academic secretary, a press secretary, publishing and research departments. It now enjoys the hospitality of the State Russian Museum, which has assigned it a suite of rooms in the Mikhailovsky Castle, next door to the Museum itself. Novikov, despite the recent onset of blindness, remains the dominant figure. He continues to publish, and to create artworks – collages of fabric and old photographs– with his wife as intermediary.

More typical of its production are the consciously camp classical scenes produced, both as paintings and as photographs, by the duo Oleg Maslov (1965) and Viktor Kuznetsov (1960), and the heroic canvases of Georgii Guryanov (b. 1961), which echo

287

classical elements in Soviet Socialist Realism. Olga Tobreluts, who has already been cited in Chapter 11, is a member of the Academy., and the Novia Akademia also has members in good standing who live and work abroad. The most active of these are Genia Chef (b. 1954) and Julia Strausova (b. 1966), who both live in Berlin. In 2000, Strausova created a major environmental work in the context of the city's Pergamon Museum.

Far more than with the Italian classicists, the spectator is conscious of the stylistic instability of most of these works, the way in which they hover between reverence for the past and a mischievous determination to parody it. The effect is intensified by the wide variety of technical means used by the Russians – by their interest in digitized photographic images, for example.

This element of parody also manifests itself in new Chinese art. It is at first sight surprising to find that the Chinese have recently been fascinated by classical themes, but the situation explains itself more clearly if one considers the situation in China at the time of the Cultural Revolution. It has already been said, one of the permitted kinds of art during this period was a collective folk expression produced by peasant communes, but another

287. **Oleg Maslov/Viktor Kuznetsov**, *After the Shipwreck*, 1997

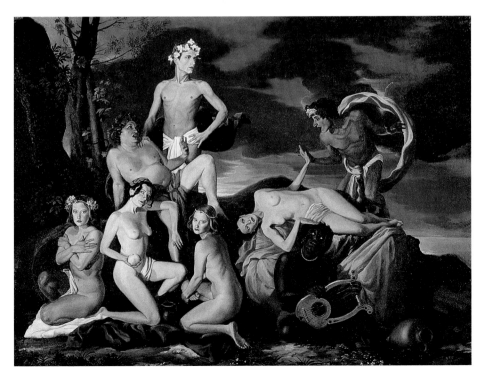

283

kind derived directly from Soviet Socialist Realism and was made by highly skilled artists trained in academic methods. There is still quite a strong emphasis on academic training in China – the street outside the entrance to the Hangzhou Academy, generally considered one of the two most important art schools in the country, is lined with shops selling classical plaster casts. In addition, European classicism retains an element of commercial prestige in Chinese society, just as it does in St Petersburg, though the results of this enthusiasm are sometimes bizarre. A large supermarket which was just nearing completion in the centre of Shanghai in 1999 was equipped with a cantilevered entrance canopy with same-size casts of Michelangelo's 'Day' and 'Night' from the Medici tombs in Florence perched on top of it.

Two Chinese artists who have made use of classical imagery are Wang Xingwei (b. 1969) and Sui Jianguo (b. 1956). Wang Xingwei became famous in the 1990s for a version of Poussin's *Et in Arcadia Ego*, where it is a young man in shirt and jeans, 288 rather than the traditional shepherd's tunic, who gazes at the classical tomb with its mournful inscription. The meaning is much the same as it is in Hai Bo's photographic diptych *They – 3*, 268

288. **Wang Xingwei**, *Arcadia*, 1996

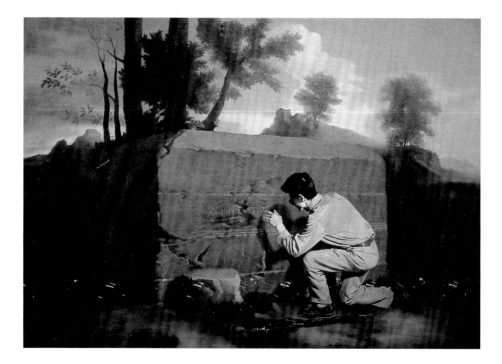

on p. 258, even though the imagery is superficially different. For a certain generation in China the Cultural Revolution has paradoxically come to seem like a golden age, a time of promise and certainty. In Beijing today, in restaurants that offer popular entertainment, a singer will sing songs from once-popular Cultural Revolution operas and invite the audience to join in. In Sui Jianguo's *Creases in Clothes – the Discobolus* (1998), where the classical statue is shown in a bulky modern suit, the approach is different, critical not nostalgic. The reference is not to the Chinese past, to things shared, but to the intellectual discomfort of forced Westernization.

The examples offered in this chapter show several things. The first is the increasing prevalence of classical forms in contemporary art, despite official hostility. It is often some form of Post-Pop art which commands the official citadels of culture, and the classical artists who are outside conducting an assault. Whichever way one chooses to look at it, this represents a strange reversal of once-traditional values. On the other hand, the classicists themselves often display uncertainty – classicism is often allied with kitsch. Striking examples are the work of John Currin in the United States and that of some members of the St Petersburg-based Novia Akademia. Indeed, what classical imagery very often does is to build bridges between intellectual theorizing and popular life – the life of commerce and the street. Works that employ classical imagery can be approached in many ways, unlike their depressive Post-Pop rivals. In the context of today's fragmented culture, they are inevitably ambiguous, and this ambiguity gives them energy.

Text References

Sources with short-title references can also be found in the Select Bibliography

Chapter 1

1 Breton, *Manifestes du Surréalisme*, p. 40.
2 Nadeau, *History of Surrealism*, p. 202.
3 Rose, *American Art Since 1900*, pp. 127 *et seq.*
4 Harold Rosenberg, 'Arshile Gorky: The Man, the Time, the Idea', *Horizon*, New York, 1962, p. 106.
5 *Arshile Gorky*, 1962 exhibition catalogue, p. 45.
6 Talcott B. Clapp. 'A painter in a glass house', quoted in *Arshile Gorky* exhibition catalogue, 1962, p. 43.
7 Jackson Pollock, 'My Painting', *Possibilities*, 1, New York, winter 1947–8.
8 Breton, *Manifestes du Surréalisme*, p. 44.
9 Rosenberg, *The Tradition of the New*, p. 31.
10 Ibid., p. 30.
11 O'Hara, *Jackson Pollock*, p. 116.
12 Patrick Heron, 'The Ascendancy of London', *Studio International*, London, December 1966.

Chapter 2

1 From interviews with Francis Bacon by David Sylvester, recorded and filmed in London for BBC TV, in *Francis Bacon: Recent Paintings*, catalogue of an exhibition at the Marlborough New London Gallery, March–April 1967, p. 26.
2 Selz and Dubuffet, *The Work of Jean Dubuffet*, pp. 81–2.
3 Jean Dubuffet, *Prospectus et tous écrits suivants II*, Paris, 1967, p. 74.

Chapter 3

1 Rose, *American Art Since 1900*, p. 234.
2 Max Kozloff, 'The New American Painting' in Kostelanetz (ed.), *The New American Arts*, p. 102.
3 Clement Greenberg, 'Louis and Noland', *Art International*, vol. 4, No. 5, Zurich 1960.
4 Fried, introduction to *Morris Louis 1912–1962*, p. 21.
5 Fried, *Three American Artists*, p. 27.

Chapter 4

1 Seitz, *Art of Assemblage*, p. 87.
2 John Cage, *Silence*, Middletown, Conn., 1961, p. 10.
3 Quoted by Pierre Descargues in *Yves Klein*, 1967 catalogue, p. 18.
4 Amaya, *Pop as Art*, p. 33.
5 Ibid., p. 33.
6 Rosenberg, *The Anxious Object*, pp. 27–8.
7 Quoted by Gene Baro in 'Claes Oldenburg, or the things of this world', *Art International*, New York, November 1966.

8 From replies to questions put by G. R. Swenson, *Art News*, New York, November 1963.
9 Quoted by Amaya, *Pop as Art*, p. 95.
10 *Andy Warhol*, catalogue of the 1965 exhibition at the Institute of Contemporary Art, University of Pennsylvania (8 October–21 November).
11 Quoted by Henri, *Environments and Happenings*, p. 168.

Chapter 5

1 O'Hara, in *David Smith*, pp. 9–10.
2 'Anthony Caro interviewed by Andrew Forge', *Studio International*, London, 1968.
3 Statement in *Tony Smith*, catalogue of two exhibitions, 1966–67.
4 Ibid., note on *Black Box*.
5 Donald Judd, 'Specific Objects', *Contemporary Sculptors*, New York, *The Art Digest (Arts Yearbook 8)*, 1965, p. 79.
6 Robert Morris, 'Notes on Sculpture', *Artforum*, New York, February 1966, p. 44.
7 Dan Flavin '. . . In Daylight or Cool White', *Artforum*, December 1965, p. 24.

Chapter 6

1 Meneguzzo, in *Verso l'arte povera*, p. 17.
2 Ibid., p. 19.
3 Celant, *Arte Povera: storie e protagonisti*, p. 27.
4 Charles Hall in *Damien Hirst*, catalogue of an exhibition held at the Institute of Contemporary Arts, London, 1991, no pagination.

Chapter 8

1 Rosenblum in *The Jeff Koons Handbook*, p. 15.
2 Hilton Kramer, 'Judy Chicago's "Dinner Party" opens at the Brooklyn Museum', *New York Times*, 1980, October 17, Section C1.
3 Chicago, *The Dinner Party*, p. 53.
4 Michael Kimmelman, 'Barbara Kruger: Familiar Icons With a Bold Face', *New York Times*, 14 July 2000.
5 Ibid.
6 See Fritscher, *Mapplethorpe*, p. 65 and passim.
7 The movement has been chronicled by Caroline E. Jones in her excellent book, *Bay Area Figurative Art*, which contains a year-by-year chronology of its development.
8 This impulse has been authoritatively discussed by Professor Whitney Chadwick in her essay 'Narrative Imagism and the Figurative Tradition in Northern California Painting', *Art Journal*, XLV, winter 1985, pp. 309–14.

Chapter 9

1 Reprinted in Hess and Baker (eds), *Art and Sexual Politics*; and in Nochlin, *Women, Art, and Power*.
2 Ross Bleckner, in *Ross Bleckner*, catalogue of an exhibition held at the Kunsthalle, Zurich, 1990, no pagination.

3 Jan Hoet, in *Africa Now: The Jean Pigozzi Collection*, Groninger Museum, Groningen 1991, p. 29.
4 Ibid., p. 30.
5 See, for example, *Peasant Paintings from the Hu Country, Shensi Province, China*, which illustrates a full range of these images.

Chapter 10

1 Rush, *New Media in Late 20th-century Art*, p. 164.
2 Lynn Cooke, 'Gary Hill: Beyond Babel', *Gary Hill*, exhibition catalogue, 1993.
3 Bill Viola in conversation with Lewis Hyde, in *Bill Viola*, exhibition catalogue, p. 164.
4 *Studio Azzurro*, pp. 129–30.
5 Ibid., p.49.

Chapter 11

1 Ilse Kotz, 'Aesthetics of "Intimacy" ', in Bright, *The Passionate Camera*, p. 204.
2 Ibid., p. 208.
3 Ibid. p. 208.

Chapter 12

1 Rhonda Lieberman, 'Revenge of the Mouse Diva', *Art Forum*, February 1994, p. 78.
2 Jack Bankowsky, 'Openings: Karen Kilimnik', *Art Forum*, May 1991, p. 138.
3 Mila Bredikhina in *Flesh and Fell / Tout Cru / Met Huid en Haar*, portfolio issued by ArtKiosk, Brussels, n.d. [*c.* 1997], no pagination.
4 Hindley was convicted, together with her lover Ian Brady, for the so-called Moors Murders in 1966. The murders, which involved the torture and sexual molestation of children, have made her a prominent figure in British popular demonology.
5 Collier Schoor, 'Openings: Inez van Lamsweerde', *Art Forum*, October 1994, p. 96.
6 Interview with Georgia Marsh, quoted by Andrea Liss, *Trespassing Through Shadows*, 1998, pp. 50–1.
7 Norman Bryson, 'Cute Futures: Mariko Mori's Techno-Enlightenment', *Parkett*, 54, 1998–9, p. 80.
8 Artist's statement on the Internet website 'Artscene China'.
9 Interview in Beijing with ELS, August 2000.

Chapter 13

1 John O'Mahony, 'Embracing the Ghosts of Nationalism', *St Petersburg Times*, reproduced on the Internet at http://www.friends-parners.org/ oldfriends/spweb/228/esp-cent.html
2 Quoted by Victor Mazin in 'The New Academy's Defence: Olseya Turkina', in the catalogue of Manifesta 3, Ljubljana, 1999, http://manifesta.org/catalogue7.htm

Select Bibliography

General

Ades, Dawn, et al. *Art in Latin America: The Modern Era, 1820–1980* (exh. cat.), Hayward Gallery, London, 1989.

Archer, Michael, *Art Since 1960*, London and New York, 1997.

Battcock, G., *The New Art: A Critical Anthology*, New York, 1966.

Bois, Yve-Alain, and Rosalind Krauss, *Formless: A User's Guide*, New York, 1997.

Bonito Oliva, Achille, *Europe/America: The Different Avant-gardes*, Milan, 1976.

Bowlt, John E., *The Quest for Self-Expression: Painting in Moscow and Leningrad 1965–1990* (exh. cat.), Columbus Museum of Art, OH, 1990.

British Art in the 20th Century: The Modern Movement (exh. cat.), Royal Academy of Arts, London, 1987.

Celant, Germano, *Unexpressionism: Art Beyond the Contemporary*, New York, 1988.

Chipp, Herschel B., *Theories of Modern Art*, Berkeley, Los Angeles and London, 1973.

Cohen, Jean Lebold, *The New Chinese Painting 1949–1986*, New York, 1987.

Crow, Thomas, *Modern Art in the Common Culture*, London and New Haven, 1996.

Day, Holliday T., and Hollister Sturges, *Art of the Fantastic: Latin America, 1920–1987* (exh. cat.), Indianapolis Museum of Art, 1987.

Doubletake: Collective Memory and Current Art (exh. cat.), Hayward Gallery, London, 1992.

Fer, Briony, *On Abstract Art*, New Haven and London, 1997.

Fox, Howard N., Miranda McClintic and Phyllis Rosenzweig, *Content: A Contemporary Focus 1974–1984* (exh. cat.), Hirshhorn Museum and Sculpture Garden, Washington DC, 1984.

Gablik, Suzi, *Has Modernism Failed?*, London and New York, 1985.

German Art in the 20th Century: Painting and Sculpture, 1905–1985 (exh. cat.), Royal Academy of Arts, London, 1985.

Goldstein, Ann, and Anne Rorimer, *Reconsidering the Object of Art*, Los Angeles, 1995.

Harrison, Charles, and Paul Wood (eds), *Art and Theory 1900–1990*, Oxford, 1992.

Hertz, Richard, (ed.), *Theories of Contemporary Art*, Englewood Cliffs, NJ, 1985.

Italian Art in the 20th Century: Painting and Sculpture 1900–1988 (exh. cat.), Royal Academy of Arts, London, 1989.

Jencks, Charles, *Post-Modernism: Neo-Classicism in Art and Architecture*, New York, 1987.

Joachimides, Christos M., and Norman Rosenthal (eds), *American Art in the 20th Century* (exh. cat.), Royal Academy of Arts, London, 1993.

Krauss, Rosalind, *The Originality of the Avant-Garde and Other Modernist Myths*, Cambridge, MA, 1986.

Kuspit, D., *Signs of Psyche in Modern and Postmodern Art*, New York, 1996.

Kuspit, D., *The Cult of the Avant-Garde Artist*, New York, 1996.

Levin, Kim, *Beyond Modernism: Essays on Art from the '70s and '80s*, New York, 1988.

Lucie-Smith, Edward, *Latin American Art of the 20th Century*, London, 1993.

Modernidade: art brésilien du 20e siècle (exh. cat.), Musée d'Art Moderne de la Ville de Paris, 1987.

Munroe, Alexandra, *Japanese Art after 1945: Scream Against the Sky* (exh. cat.), Guggenheim Museum, New York, 1994.

Moszynska, A., *Abstract Art*, London and New York, 1990.

Nuevos Momentos del Arte Mexicano/New Moments in Mexican Art (exh. cat.), Parallel Project, New York, 1990.

Pacific Rim Diaspora (exh. cat.), Long Beach Museum of Art, CA, 1990.

Rasmussen, Waldo, *Artistas Latinoamericanos del siglo XX: Latin American Artists of the Twentieth Century* (exh. cat.), MOMA, New York, 1993.

Rosenberg, Harold, *The De-Definition of Art*, New York, 1972.

Rosenberg, Harold, *Art on the Edge*, New York, 1975.

Rosenberg, Harold, *Art and Other Serious Matters*, Chicago, 1985.

Russell, John, *The Meanings of Modern Art*, New York, 1981; London, 1991.

The Spiritual in Art: Abstract Painting 1890–1985 (exh. cat.), Los Angeles County Museum of Art, 1986.

Stiles, Christine, and Peter Selz (eds), *Theories and Documents of Contemporary Art: A Sourcebook of Artists' Writings*, Berkeley and Los Angeles, CA, and London, 1996.

Sylvester, David, *About Modern Art: Critical Essays, 1948–96*, London, 1996.

Taylor, Brandon, *The Art of Today*, London, 1995.

Vogel, Susan, *Africa Explores: 20th Century African Art* (exh. cat.), Center for African Arts, New York, 1991.

Wheeler, Daniel, *Art Since Mid-Century: 1945 to the Present*, New York, 1991.

Wood, Paul, et al., *Modernism in Dispute: Art Since the Forties*, London and New York, 1993.

Chapter 1
Abstract Expressionism

Arshile Gorky: Paintings, Drawings, Studies (exh. cat.), Museum of Modern Art, New York, with Washington Gallery of Modern Art, 1962.

Bois, Yve-Alain, *Painting as Model*, Cambridge, MA, and London, 1990.

Breton, André, *Manifestes du Surréalisme*, Paris, 1962.

Golding, John, *Paths to the Absolute*, London, 2000.

Greenberg, Clement, *Art and Culture*, Boston, 1961; London, 1973.

Guilbaut, Serge, *How New York Stole the Idea of Modern Art* (trans. A. Goldhammer), Chicago and London, 1983.

Leja, Michael, *Reframing Abstract Expressionism*, London and New Haven, 1993.

Nadeau, Maurice, *The History of Surrealism*, New York, 1967, and London, 1968

O'Hara, Frank, *Jackson Pollock*, New York, 1959.

Rose, Barbara, *American Art Since 1900*, London and New York, 1967.

Rosenberg, Harold, *Arshile Gorky: The Man, the Time, the Idea*, New York, 1962.

Rosenberg, Harold, *The Tradition of the New*, New York, 1959; London, 1962.

Rosenberg, Harold, *Willem de Kooning*, New York, 1974.

Sandler, Irving, *The Triumph of American Painting: A History of Abstract Expressionism*, New York, 1970.

Chapter 2
The European scene

Bandini, Mirella, *L'Estetico, il politico: Da Cobra all'Internazionale Situazionista 1948–1957*, Rome, 1977.

Haftmann, W., et al., *Abstract Art since 1945*, London, 1971.

Hughes, Robert, *Frank Auerbach*, London and New York, 1990.

Klossowski de Rola, Stanislas, *Balthus*, revised edn, London 1996.

Paulhan, Jean, *L'Art informel*, Paris, 1962.

Russell, John, *Francis Bacon*, revised edn, London and New York, 1993.

Schiff, G., (ed.), *Picasso: The Last Years 1963–1973* (exh. cat.), New York, 1983.

Selz, Peter, and Jean Dubuffet, *The Work of Jean Dubuffet* (exh. cat.), Museum of Modern Art, New York, 1962.

Spalding, F., *British Art since 1900*, London, 1986.

Sylvester, David, *The Brutality of Fact: Interviews with Francis Bacon*, 3rd enlarged edn, London and New York, 1987.

Tapié, Michel, *Un Art autre*, Paris, 1952.

Vallier, Dora, *La peinture en France: début et fin d'un système visuel 1870–1970*, Milan, 1976.

Chapter 3
Post-painterly abstraction

Elderfield, John, *Morris Louis* (exh. cat.) Museum of Modern Art, New York, 1986.

Fried, Michael, *Three American Artists* (exh. cat.), Fogg Art Museum, Boston, MA, 1965.

Helen Frankenthaler (exh. cat.) Museum of Modern Art, New York, 1989.

Hess, Thomas, *Barnett Newman* (exh. cat.), Museum of Modern Art, New York, 1971.

Josef Albers: A Retrospective (exh. cat.), Guggenheim, New York, 1988.

Kostelanetz, Richard, (ed.), *The New American Arts*, New York, 1967.

Morris Louis 1912–1962 (exh. cat.), introd. by Michael Fried, Museum of Fine Arts, Boston, MA, 1967.

Rubin, William S., *Frank Stella* (exh. cat.) Museum of Modern Art, New York, 1970.

Staber, M., *Max Bill*, London, 1964.

Chapter 4
Pop, Environments and Happenings

Alloway, Lawrence, *American Pop Art*, London and New York, 1974.

Amaya, Mario, *Pop as Art*, London, 1965.

Andy Warhol (exh. cat.), Institute of Contemporary Art, University of Pennsylvania, 1965.

Battcock, Gregory, (ed.), *Super-Realism*, New York, 1975.

Battcock, Gregory and Robert Nickas, *The Art of Performance: A Critical Anthology*, New York, 1984.

Chase, Linda, *Hyperrealism*, New York, 1975.

Crow, Thomas, *The Rise of the Sixties*, London and New York, 1996.

English Art Today 1960–76 (exh. cat.), 2 vols., Palazzo Reale, Milan, 1976.

Goldberg, RoseLee, *Performance Art, from Futurism to the Present*, 3rd revised edn, London and New York, 2001.

Henri, Adrian, *Environments and Happenings*, London, 1974.

Kellein, Thomas, *Fluxus*, London, 1995.

Lippard, Lucy, (ed.), *Pop Art*, London, 1990.

Livingstone, Marco, *Pop Art*, London, 1990.

Mahsun, Carol Anne Runyon, (ed.), *Pop Art: The Critical Dialogue*, Ann Arbor, MI, 1989.

Mamiya, Christin J., *Pop Art and Consumer Culture: American Super Market*, Austin, 1992.

Meisel, Louis K., *Photo-Realism*, New York, 1980.

Rosenberg, Harold, *The Anxious Object: Art Today and its Audience*, London, 1965.

Russell, John, and Suzi Gablik, *Pop Art Redefined*, London, 1969.

Schimmel, Paul, et al., *Out of Actions: Between Performance and Object, 1949–79*, London and New York, 1998.

Seitz, William C., *The Art of Assemblage*, New York, 1961.

Vergine, Lea, *The Body as Language*, Milan, 1974.

Yves Klein (exh. cat.), Jewish Museum, New York, 1967.

Chapter 5
Abstract sculpture, Minimal art, Conceptual art

Andersen, Wayne, *American Sculpture in Process: 1930–1970*, Boston and New York, 1975.

Armstrong, Richard, *Mind over Matter: Concept and Object* (exh. cat.), Whitney Museum of American Art, New York, 1990.

Armstrong, Richard, *The New Sculpture, 1965–1975* (exh. cat.), Whitney Museum of American Art, New York, 1990.

Ashton, Dore, *American Art Since 1945*, New York and London, 1982.

Batchelor, David, *Minimalism*, London, 1997.

Battcock, Gregory, (ed.), *Idea Art*, New York, 1973.

Battcock, Gregory, (ed.), *Minimal Art: A Critical Anthology*, New York, 1968, reprinted Berkeley, CA, and London, 1995.

Bird, Jon, *Rewriting Conceptual Art*, London, 1999.

Colpitt, Francis, *Minimal Art: The Critical Perspective*, Ann Arbor, MI, 1990.

Geldzahler, Henry, *New York Painting and Sculpture: 1940–1970* (exh. cat.), Metropolitan Museum of Art, New York, 1969.

Harrison, Charles, *Essays on Art and Language*, Oxford, 1991.

Karshan, Donald, (ed.), *Conceptual Art and Conceptual Aspects*, New York, 1970.

Krauss, Rosalind, *Passages in Modern Sculpture*, London and New York, 1977.

Lippard, Lucy R., *Six Years: The Dematerialization of the Art Object from 1966 to 1972*, New York, 1973.

Lucie-Smith, Edward, *Art in the Seventies*, Oxford, 1980.

McShine, Kynaston, (ed.), *Information*, New York, 1970.

Meyer, Ursula, (ed.), *Conceptual Art*, New York, 1972.

Muller, Grégoire, *The New Avant-Garde: Issues for the Art of the Seventies*, London, 1972.

O'Hara, Frank, *David Smith 1906–1965* (exh. cat.), Tate Gallery, London, 1966.

Tony Smith: Two Exhibitions of Sculpture (exh. cat.) Wadsworth Atheneum, Hartford, Conn., and Institute of Contemporary Art, University of Pennsylvania, 1966–67.

Szeeman, Harald, (ed.), *Live in Your Head: When Attitudes Become Form*, Berne, 1969.

Chapter 6
An age of pluralism

Celant, Germano, *Arte Povera: Conceptual, Actual or Impossible Art?*, Milan and London, 1969.

Celant, Germano, *Arte Povera: storie e protagonisti*, Milan, 1985.

Lippard, Lucy, *Overlay: Contemporary Art and the Art of Prehistory*, New York, 1983.

McShine, Kynaston, (ed.), *Berlin Art 1961–1987*, Museum of Modern Art, New York, 1987.

Meneguzzo, Marco, *Verso l'arte povera* (exh. cat.), Padiglione d'arte contemporanea, Milan, 1989.

De Oliveira, Nicolas, Nicola Oxley, Michael Petry, *Installation Art*, London, 1994.

Pincus-Witten, Robert, *Postminimalism*, London, 1977.

Tisdall, Caroline, *Joseph Beuys*, Solomon R. Guggenheim Museum, New York, 1979.

Seymour, Anne, *The New Art* (exh. cat.), Hayward Gallery, London, 1972.

Walker, John A., *Art Since Pop*, London, 1975.

Chapter 7
Neo-Expressionistic tendencies

Bonito Oliva, Achille, *The Italian Transavantgarde*, Milan, 1980.

Bonito Oliva, Achille, *La Transavanguardia Internazionale*, Milan, 1982.

Godfrey, Tony, *The New Image: Painting in the 1980s*, London, 1986.

Hughes, Robert, *Lucian Freud Paintings*, London and New York, 1989.

Joachimides, Christos, (ed.), *A New Spirit in Painting* (exh. cat.), Royal Academy of Arts, London, 1981.

Joachimides, Christos M., and Norman Rosenthal (eds.), *Metropolis* (exh. cat.), Martin-Gropius-Bau, Berlin, 1991; English-language version, New York, 1991.

Kuspit, D., *The New Subjectivism: Art in the 1980s*, New York, 1988.

López-Pedraza, Rafael, *Anselm Kiefer*, London 1997.

Lucie-Smith, Edward, *Art in the Eighties*, Oxford, 1990.

Lucie-Smith, Edward, Carolyn Cohen and Judith Higgins, *The New British Painting*, Oxford, 1988.

Richter, Gerhard, (trans. David Britt), *The Daily Practice of Painting: Writings and Interviews 1962–1993*, London 1995.

Siegel, Jeanne, (ed.), *Art Talk: The Early 80s*, Ann Arbor, MI, 1988.

Tomkins, Calvin, *Post- to Neo-: The Art World of the 1980s*, New York, 1988.

Chapter 8
The USA – 1970s to 1990s

Allbright, Thomas, *Art in the San Francisco Bay Area, 1945–1980: An Illustrated History*, Berkeley, 1985.

Beardsley, John, *Earthworks and Beyond: Contemporary Art in the Landscape*, New York, 1984.

Butterfield, Jan, *The Art of Light and Space*, New York, 1993.

Carlozzi, Annette, *50 Texas Artists*, San Francisco, 1986.

Chicago, Judy, *The Dinner Party: A Symbol of our Heritage*, Garden City, 1979.

Foster, Hal, *Recodings*, Seattle, 1985.

Hispanic Art in the United States: Thirty Contemporary Painters and Sculptors (exh. cat.), Museum of Fine Arts, Houston, 1987.

Jones, Caroline E., *Bay Area Figurative Art*, Berkeley, 1990.

Lucie-Smith, Edward, *American Art Now*, Oxford, 1985.

Lucie-Smith, Edward, *American Realism*, London and New York, 1994.

Lucie-Smith, Edward, *Judy Chicago: An American Vision*, New York, 1999.

Plagens, Peter, *Sunshine Muse: Contemporary Art on the West Coast*, New York, 1974.

Rosenblum, Robert, *The Jeff Koons Handbook*, London, 1992.

Wallis, Brian, (ed.), *Art After Modernism: Rethinking Representation*, New Museum of Contemporary Art, New York, 1984.

Who Chicago? (exh. cat.), Ceolfrith Gallery, Sunderland Arts Centre, Sunderland, 1981.

Chapter 9
Issue-based art and globalization

Against Nature: Japanese Art in the Eighties (exh. cat.), Grey Art Gallery and Study Center, New York University, New York, 1989.

Araeen, Rasheed, *The Other Story: Afro-Asian Artists in Post-War Britain* (exh. cat.), Hayward Gallery, London, 1989.

Archer Shaw, Petrine, and Kim Robinson, *Jamaican Art: An Overview*, Kingston, Jamaica, 1990.

Beckett, Wendy, *Contemporary Women Artists*, New York, 1988.

Black Art: Ancestral Legacy – the African Impulse in African American Art (exh. cat.), Dallas Museum of Art, 1989.

Broude, Norma, and Mary D. Garrard (eds.), *The Power of Feminist Art*, New York and London, 1994.

Caruana, Wally, *Aboriginal Art*, London, 1993.

Chadwick, Whitney, *Women, Art and Society*, London, revised edn, 1996.

Contemporary Indian Art (exh. cat.), Royal Academy of Arts, London, 1982.

Cooper, Emmanuel, *The Sexual Perspective: Homosexuality and Art in the Last 100 Years in the West*, 2nd revised edn, London, 1994.

Crimp, D., and A. Rolston, *AIDS Demo Graphics*, Seattle, 1990.

Difference: On Representation and Sexuality (exh. cat.), New Museum of Contemporary Art, New York, 1985.

Dunn, Michael, *A Concise History of New Zealand Painting*, Auckland, 1991.

Fine, Elsa Honig, *The Afro-American Artist: A Search for Identity*, New York, 1982.

Glusberg, Jorge, *Art in Argentina*, Milan, 1986.

Gutai – Japanische Avantgarde / Japanese Avant-Garde, 1954–1965 (exh. cat.), Mathildenhohe, Darmstadt, 1991.

Hammond, Harmony, *Lesbian Art in America*, New York, 2000.

India, Myth & Reality: Aspects of Modern Indian Art (exh. cat.), Museum of Modern Art, Oxford, 1982.

Lewis, Samella, *Art: African-American*, 2nd revised edn, Los Angeles, 1990.

Lippard, Lucy, *From the Center: Feminist Essays on Women's Art*, New York, 1976.

Lippard, Lucy R., *Mixed Blessings: New Art in a Multi-Cultural America*, New York, 1990.

Lucie-Smith, Edward, *Race, Sex and Gender in Contemporary Art*, London, 1994.

Magiciens de la Terre, Centre Georges Pompidou, Paris, 1989.

Mistaken Identities (exh. cat.), University of California Art Museum, 1993.

Mount, Marshall W., *African Art – the Years since 1920*, 2nd revised edn, New York, 1989.

Nochlin, Linda, *Women, Art and Power and Other Essays*, London and New York, 1989.

Owens, Craig, *Beyond Recognition: Representation, Power and Culture*, Berkeley, 1992.

Parker, Roszika, and Griselda Pollock, *Old Mistresses*, London, 1981.

Pollock, Griselda, *Vision and Difference: Femininity, Feminism and the Histories of Art*, London, 1988.

Peasant Paintings from the Hu Country, Shensi Province, China (exh. cat), Arts Council of Great Britain, 1976.

Powell, R. E., *Black Art and Culture in the Twentieth Century*, London and New York, 1997.

Raven, Arlene, (ed.), *Art in the Public Interest*, Ann Arbor, MI, 1989.

Raven, Arlene, Cassandra Langer and Joanna Frueh (eds.), *Feminist Art Criticism: An Anthology*, New York, 1988.

Rose, Jacqueline, *Sexuality in the Field of Vision*, London, 1986.

Ross, David A., *Between Spring and Summer: Soviet Conceptual Art in the Era of Late Communism*, Cambridge, MA, 1990.

Shone, Richard, *Some Went Mad, Some Ran Away . . .* (exh. cat.), Serpentine Gallery, London, 1994.

The New Culture: Women Artists of the Seventies (exh. cat.), Turman Gallery, Indiana State University, 1984.

Unbound: Possibilities in Painting (exh. cat.), Hayward Gallery, London, 1994.

Working with Nature: Traditional Thought in Contemporary Art from Korea (exh. cat.), Tate Gallery, Liverpool, 1992.

Chapter 10
The rise of video

Battcock, Gregory, (ed.), *New Artists Video: A Critical Anthology*. New York, 1978.

Bill Viola, Whitney Museum of American Art, New York, and Paris, 1998.

Gary Hill (exh. cat.), Stedelijk Museum Amsterdam, and Kunsthalle, Vienna, 1993.

Lovejoy, Margaret, *Art and Artists in the Age of Electronic Media*, Ann Arbor, 1989.

Popper, Frank, *Art of the Electronic Age*, London, 1993.

Rush, Michael, *New Media in Late 20th-Century Art*, London and New York, 1999.

Studio Azzurro: ambienti sensibili, Milan, 1996.

Chapter 11
The photographic medium

Bright, Deborah, (ed.), *The Passionate Camera: Photography and the Bodies of Desire*, London and New York, 1998.

Celant, Germano, *Joel-Peter Witkin*, Berlin, New York, Zurich, 1995.

Davis, Melody D., *The Male Nude in Contemporary Photography*, Philadelphia, 1991.

Doswald, Christopher, (ed.), *Missing Link: The Image of Man in Contemporary Photography* (exh. cat.), Kunstmuseum Bern, New York and Zurich, 2000.

Fritscher, Jack, *Mapplethorpe: Assault with a Deadly Camera*, Marmaroneck, New York, 1994.

Krauss, Rosalind, *Cindy Sherman 1975–1993*, New York, 1993.

Ohlson, Elisabeth, *Ecce Homo*, Stockholm, privately published, 1997.

Chapter 12
Post-Pop blues

Abject Art: Repulsion and Desire in American Art, Whitney Museum, New York, 1993.

Apocalypse: Beauty and Horror in Comtemporary Art, (exh. cat.), Royal Academy of Arts, London, 2000.

Art of Our Time: The Saatchi Collection, 4 vols., London and New York, 1984.

Cameron, D., *NY Art Now: The Saatchi Collection*, London, 1988.

Collings, Matthew, *Blimey! The London Artworld from Bohemia to Britpop*, London, 1997.

Collings, Matthew, *It Hurts: New York Art from Warhol to Now*, London, 1998.

Danto, Arthur, *After the End of Art*, Princeton, 1997.

Deitch, Jeffrey, and Dan Friedman (eds.), *Artificial Nature* (exh. cat.), Deste Foundation for Contemporary Art, Athens, Geneva, New York, 1990.

Deitch, Jeffrey, and Peter Halley, *Cultural Geometry* (exh. cat.), Deste Foundation for Contemporary Art, Athens, 1988.

Deitch, Jeffrey, *Post Human* (exh. cat.), FAE Musée d'Art Contemporain, Pully/Lausanne, 1992.

Deitch, Jeffrey, *Strange Abstraction* (exh. cat.), Touko Museum of Contemporary Art, Japan, 1991.

Foster, Hal, *The Return of the Real: The Avant-Garde at the End of the Century*, London and Cambridge, MA, 1996.

Foster, Hal, *Postmodern Culture*, New York, 1995.

Hicks, Alistair, *New British Art in the Saatchi Collection*, London, 1989.

Hughes, Robert, *Culture of Complaint*, New York and London, 1993.

Kent Sarah, *Shark Infested Waters: The Saatchi Collection in British Art in the 1990s*, London, 1994.

Liss, Andrea, *Trespassing Through Shadows*, London and Minneapolis, 1998.

Millet, Catherine, *L'art contemporain en France*, Paris, 1987.

Morphet, Richard, *The Hard-Won Image: Traditional Method and Subject in Recent British Art* (exh. cat.), Tate Gallery, London, 1984.

Risatti, Howard, (ed.), *Postmodern Perspectives: Issues in Contemporary Art*, Englewood Cliffs, NJ, 1990.

Sandler, Irving, *Art of the Postmodern Era*, New York, 1996

Sensation! Young British Artists from the Saatchi Collection, (exh. cat.), Royal Academy of Arts, London, 1997.

Stallabrass, Julian, *High Art Lite*, London and New York, 1999.

Sussman, Elisabeth, with Thelma Golden, John G. Hanhardt and Lisa Phillips, *1993 Biennial Exhibition* (exh. cat.), Whitney Museum of American Art, New York, 1993.

Chapter 13
New classicism

China Avant-Garde (exh. cat.), Haus der Kulturen der Welt, Berlin, and Museum of Modern Art, Oxford, 1993.

Mussa, Italo, *La pittura colta*, Rome, 1983.

Romani Brizzi, Arnaldo, (ed.), *La pittura ritrovata* (exh. cat.), Museo del Risorgimento, Rome, 1999.

Chronology

1940–49
1940
World War II: Fall of France, British troops evacuated from Dunkirk.
Mondrian leaves London and settles in New York.

1941
German invasion of Russia.
Japanese bomb Pearl Harbor.
Breton, Ernst and Chagall arrive in New York.
Gottlieb begins his *Pictograph* series.
New York: Gottlieb, Motherwell, Pollock and Rothko experiment with automatism.

1942
'First Papers of Surrealism', New York.
Dubuffet resumes painting full time.
Fautrier paints the *Hostages* series.
Battle of Stalingrad.

1943
Gorky paints the *Garden of Sochi* series.
Clyfford Still has his first solo exhibition.
Pollock's first solo exhibition at the Art of This Century Gallery, New York.
Allied troops invade Italy.

1944
The liberation of France.
Breton meets Arshile Gorky.
Dubuffet's first solo exhibition.

1945
Germany surrenders.
Two atomic bombs dropped on Japan.
End of World War II.
Manifesto del Realismo issued by a group of leading Italian artists.
Britain elects reforming Labour government under Attlee.
'Art Concret', Galerie René Drouin, Paris (first post-war major show of abstract art in Europe).

1946
Lucio Fontana issues his *White Manifesto*.
Madí manifesto published in Buenos Aires.

1947
India achieves independence and is partitioned into India and Pakistan.
Pollock begins his 'drip' paintings.
Still exhibits his first colour-field abstractions.
In Britain Paolozzi makes collages with magazine and advertising images.
Abstraction-Création group revived in Paris.

1948
Blockade of Berlin, airlift of supplies.
State of Israel proclaimed.
Gorky commits suicide.

Barnett Newman begins to make colour-field paintings.
The Cobra Group is formed in Paris.
Dau al Set group formed in Barcelona.

1949
Germany divided into German Democratic Republic and the Federal Republic.
Chinese People's Republic proclaimed under Mao Zedong.
Motherwell begins his *Elegies to the Spanish Republic*.
Francis Bacon starts using photographic source material.
Simone de Beauvoir publishes *The Second Sex*.

1950–59
1950
North Korea invades South Korea; start of the Korean War.
Rise of McCarthyism in USA.
Le Corbusier commissioned to build a new capital for the Punjab, Chandigargh.

1951
'Abstract Painting and Sculpture in America', MOMA, New York.
Festival of Britain.
Churchill Prime Minister of Britain.

1952
Eisenhower elected US President.
Publication of *Un Art Autre* by Michel Tapié.
American critic Harold Rosenberg coins the term 'Action Painting'.
Beckett's play *Waiting for Godot*.

1953
Stalin dies.
Kruschev USSR Party Secretary.
Korean War ends.
Arthur Miller's play *The Crucible*.

1954
Beginning of the Algerian War (–1962).
US Supreme Court rules against segregation in public schools.
Foundation of Gutai group, Japan.
Jasper Johns, first *Flag* paintings.
Matisse dies.

1955
First Documenta exhibition at Kassel.
'Man, Machine and Motion', Institute of Contemporary Arts, London.

1956
Suez Canal seized by Egypt; British and French troops invade.
Soviet troops end Hungarian uprising.
'This is Tomorrow', Whitechapel Art Gallery, London.
Pollock dies.

1957
Treaty of Rome; European Economic Community formed.

Macmillan Prime Minister in Britain.
Yves Klein shows monochromes, Milan.

1958
'New American Painting', MOMA, New York.
Group Zero formed in Düsseldorf.

1959
Castro takes over in Cuba.
Groupe de Recherche d'Art Visuel founded in Paris.
'New Images of Man', New York.
Alan Kaprow's '18 Happenings in 6 Parts' at the Reuben Gallery, New York.
Robert Frank publishes his book of photographs *The Americans*.

1960–69
1960
Oldenburg's exhibition 'The Street' at the Judson Gallery, New York.
Warhol makes his first comic strip painting, *Dick Tracy*.
'New Forms, New Media', Martha Jackson Gallery, New York.
César makes his first *Compressions*.
Pierre Restany publishes his New Realist Manifesto.

1961
Berlin Wall constructed.
John F. Kennedy US President.
'The Art of Assemblage', MOMA, New York.
Beuys begins teaching at Düsseldorf Kunstakademie.
Publication of Clement Greenberg's *Art and Culture*.
Independently of Warhol, Lichtenstein paints his first works based on comic strips.
Oldenburg opens his 'Store' on East 2nd Street.
Hockney paints *We Two Boys Together Clinging*.
Nueva Prescencia group (opposed to Mexican Muralism) founded in Mexico.
Wesselmann exhibits his first *Great American Nudes* at the Tanager Gallery, New York.

1962
Warhol paints Marilyn Monroe and Campbell's soup cans; first solo show, Ferus Gallery, Los Angeles.
Ed Ruscha produces his book, *Twenty Six Gasoline Stations*.
'The New Painting of Common Objects', Pasadena Art Museum.
BBC television film 'Pop goes the Easel'.
Pop art covered by *Time*, *Life* and *Newsweek*.

1963
President Kennedy is assassinated.
USA begins its involvement in Vietnam.
'Towards a New Abstraction', Jewish Museum, New York.

'Mixed Media and Pop Art', Albright-Knox Art Gallery, Buffalo.

1964

'Post-Painterly Abstraction', Los Angeles County Museum of Art.

'Amerikanste Pop-Konst', Moderna Museet, Stockholm.

First 'New Generation' exhibition, Whitechapel Art Gallery, London.

Wilson becomes Prime Minister in Britain.

1965

Warhol's first retrospective, Institute of Contemporary Arts, London, and University of Pennsylvania, Philadelphia.

Colombian critic Marta Traba publishes her book *Los cuatro monstruos cardinales* in Mexico City: a further attack on Muralism.

1966

'Primary Structures', Jewish Museum, New York.

'Systematic Abstraction', Guggenheim Museum, New York.

Rauschenberg and Klüver's *Nine Evenings: Theater and Engineering*, New York.

'Art of Latin America since Independence', Yale University Art Gallery.

1967

Six-Day War between Israel and Arab nations.

Che Guevara killed in Bolivia.

'Lumière et Mouvement' exhibition, Paris.

'Light-Motion-Space', Walker Art Center, Minneapolis.

'Arte Povera', Galleria la Bertesca, Genoa.

'Sculpture of the Sixties', Los Angeles County Museum of Art.

'Yves Klein', Jewish Museum, New York.

'Funk', University of California, Berkeley.

The Beatles' album *Sergeant Pepper's Lonely Hearts Club Band*.

1968

Martin Luther King assassinated.

'Les évènements' – rioting in Paris.

Czechoslovakia: liberalization under Dubcek ended by entry of Warsaw Pact troops.

'Minimal Art', Gemeentemuseum, The Hague.

'Earthworks', Dwan Gallery, New York.

'Realism Now', Vassar College Art Museum, Poughkeepsie.

Duchamp dies.

1969

Neil Armstrong the first man on the moon.

'Anti-Illusion: Procedures/Materials', Whitney Museum of American Art, New York.

'When Attitudes Become Form', Kunsthalle, Berne, Museum Haus Lange, Krefeld, and Institute of Contemporary Arts, London.

'Conceptual Art', Städtisches Museum, Leverkusen.

Joseph Kosuth publishes 'Art After Philosophy' in *Studio International.*

First issue of *Art & Language* is published.

Woodstock Music Festival.

1970–79

1970

'Conceptual Art and Conceptual Aspects', New York Cultural Center.

'Conceptual art, arte povera, land art', Galleri Civica de Arte Moderna, Turin.

'Information', MOMA, New York.

Robert Smithson's *Spiral Jetty*, Great Salt Lake, Utah.

Judy Chicago organizes the first feminist art course at the California State College at Fresno.

1971

Fighting in Vietnam spreads to Laos and Cambodia.

'Art and Technology', Los Angeles County Museum of Art.

Linda Nochlin publishes 'Why Have There Been No Great Women Artists?' in *Art News.*

'Contemporary Black Artists in America', Whitney Museum of American Art, New York.

Larry Clark publishes his book of photographs *Tulsa.*

1972

'The New Art', Hayward Gallery, London.

'Sharp-Focus Realism', Sidney Janis Gallery, New York.

'Bloody Sunday', Londonderry, Northern Ireland.

1973

US troops withdrawn from Vietnam.

Allende is overthrown in Chile.

Picasso dies.

'Photo-Realism', Serpentine Gallery, London.

Mary Kelly begins work on *Post Partum Document* (–1979)

1974

Nixon resigns after Watergate.

Joseph Beuys performs *Coyote* in New York.

1975

Last Americans are evacuated from South Vietnam.

'Bodyworks', MOCA, Chicago.

Anthony Caro exhibition, MOMA, New York.

First performance of UK Punk group The Sex Pistols.

1976

'The Human Clay', selected by R. B. Kitaj, Hayward Gallery, London.

'Women Artists: 1550–1950', Los Angeles County Museum of Art.

Carl Andre's *Equivalents I–VIII* bought by Tate Gallery, London.

Christo's *Running Fence*, California.

1977

Opening of the Centre Pompidou, Paris.

'Europe in the Seventies: Aspects of Recent Art', Art Institute of Chicago.

Charles Jencks publishes *The Language of Post-Modern Architecture.*

'Unofficial Art from the Soviet Union', Institute of Contemporary Arts, London.

Cindy Sherman's first *Untitled Film Stills.*

First case of AIDS diagnosed in New York.

1978

'Bad Painting', New Museum of Contemporary Art, New York.

De Chirico dies.

1979

'Moderne Kunst aus Afrika', Staatlichen Kunsthalle, Berlin.

'Joseph Beuys' (retrospective) Guggenheim Museum, New York.

'Un certain art anglais . . . : 1970–1979', ARC/Musée d'Art Moderne de la Ville de Paris.

Judy Chicago's *The Dinner Party*, shown in San Francisco.

Julian Schnabel's first solo exhibition, New York.

Margaret Thatcher becomes British Prime Minister.

1980–89

1980

'Women's Images of Men', Institute of Contemporary Arts, London.

Publication of Bonito Oliva's *La transavanguardia italiana.*

Anselm Kiefer and Georg Baselitz shown at Venice Biennale.

Robert Mapplethorpe exhibits *Black Males*, Galerie Jurka, Amsterdam.

1981

'A New Spirit in Painting', Royal Academy of Arts, London.

'Westkunst', Museen der Stadt, Cologne.

Ronald Reagan becomes US President.

1982

'Transavanguardia', Galleria Civica, Modena.

'Zeitgeist', Martin-Gropius-Bau, Berlin.

'Englische Plastik Heute', Kunstmuseum, Lucerne.

'India, Myth & Reality, Aspects of Modern Indian Art', Museum of Modern Art, Oxford.

Postminimalism', Aldrich Museum of Contemporary Art, Ridgefield, CT.

Documenta VII, Kassel, shows return to painting.

Britain and Argentina at war over the Falklands.

1983
'The New Art', Tate Gallery, London.
Italo Mussa publishes *La pittura colta*.
Mary Kelly publishes *Post Partum Document*.
Miró dies.

1984
'An International Survey of Recent Painting and Sculpture', MOMA, New York.
'Primitivism and 20th Century Art ', MOMA, New York.
'The Hard-Won Image', Tate Gallery, London.
Turner Prize's first winner is Malcolm Morley.
'Content: A Contemporary Focus 1974–1984', Hirshhorn Museum and Sculpture Garden, Washington, DC.

1985
Gorbachev comes to power in Russia – beginning of *perestroika*.
'Kunst in der Bundesrepublik Deutschland 1945–1985', Nationalgalerie, Berlin.
Saatchi Gallery opens in London.

1986
'The Spiritual in Art: Abstract Painting 1890–1985', Los Angeles County Museum of Art.
Beuys dies.
Nuclear accident at Chernobyl, USSR.

1987
'New York Art Now', Saatchi Collection, London.
'Berlin Art 1961–1987', MOMA, New York.
'Art of the Fantastic: Latin America, 1920–1987', Indianapolis Museum of Art.
'Hispanic Art in the United States: Thirty Contemporary Painters and Sculptors', Museum of Fine Arts, Houston.
'Modernidade: art brésilien du 20e siècle', Musée d'Art Moderne de la Ville de Paris.
'Similia/Dissimilia', Städtische Kunsthalle, Düsseldorf.
Warhol dies.
'Black Monday', Stock Market crash.

1988
'Cultural Geometry', Deste Foundation for Contemporary Art, Athens.
'Refigured Painting: The German Image 1960–88', Guggenheim Museum, New York.
'Freeze', Docklands, London.

1989
Berlin Wall comes down.
Tiananmen Square massacre.
George Bush US President.
'The Other Story: Afro-Asian Artists in Post-War Britain', Hayward Gallery, London.

'Black Art: Ancestral Legacy – the African Impulse in African American Art', Dallas Museum of Art.
'L'art conceptuel, un perspective', Musée de l'Art Moderne de la Ville de Paris.
'The New Italian Manner', Mayer Schwarz Gallery, Beverly Hills, CA.
'The Perfect Moment', Mapplethorpe's retrospective on tour in USA.
Linda Nochlin publishes *Women, Art and Power and Other Essays*.
'Magiciens de la terre', Paris.

1990–2000
1990
South Africa: Nelson Mandela released from prison; end of apartheid negotiated.
Margaret Thatcher resigns as British Prime Minister.
Germany is reunited.
Collapse of the Soviet empire.
'The Quest for Self-Expression: painting in Moscow and Leningrad 1965–1990', Columbus Museum of Art, Columbus, OH.
'Contemporary Russian Artists: Artisti Russi Contemporanei', Centro per l'arte contemporanea Luigi Pecci, Prato.
'Artificial Nature', Deste Foundation for Contemporary Art, Athens, Geneva, New York.
'Ilya Kabakov, "He lost his mind, undressed, and ran away naked" ', Ronald Feldman Fine Arts, New York.
'High and Low: Modern Art and Popular Culture', MOMA, New York.
'L'art en France, 1945–1990', Fondation Daniel Templon, Musée temporaire, Fréjus.
'Nuevos momentos del arte mexicano/ New Moments in Mexican Art', Parallel Project, New York.
'Between Spring and Summer: Soviet Conceptual Art in the Era of Late Communism', Institute of Contemporary Arts, Boston, MA.
Lucy R. Lippard publishes *Mixed Blessings: New Art in a Multi-Cultural America*, New York.

1991
Gulf War: UN forces expel Iraq from Kuwait.
Boris Yeltsin becomes President of the Russian Federation.
USSR is dissolved.
'CARA: Chicano Art, Resistance and Affirmation', Wight Art Gallery, Los Angeles.
Damien Hirst's shark piece, *The Impossibility of Death in the Mind of Someone Living*.
'Strange Abstraction', Touko Museum of Contemporary Art, Japan.
'From Art to Archaeology', South Bank Centre, London.

'Arte & Arte', Museo d'Arte Contemporanea, Castello di Rivoli, Turin.
'Mana Tiriti: The Art of Protest and Partnership', Haeta Maori Women's Art Collective, Project Waitangi, Wellington, NZ.
'Headlands: Thinking Through New Zealand Art', Museum of Contemporary Art, Sydney.
'Metropolis', Martin-Gropius-Bau, Berlin.

1992
Ethnic conflicts in former Yugoslavia.
'Post Human', FAE Musée d'Art Contemporain, Pully/Lausanne.
John Cage dies.
Francis Bacon dies.
'Young British Artists', Saatchi Collection.
'Quattro Artisti della Nuova Maniera Italiana', Museum of Modern and Contemporary Art, Città della Pieve.
'Working with Nature: Traditional Thought in Contemporary Art from Korea', Tate Gallery, Liverpool.
Bill Viola's *Nantes Triptych*.

1993
Clinton becomes US President.
'Aratjara: Art of the First Australians', Kunstsammlung Nordrhein-Westfalen, Düsseldorf.
'China Avant-Garde', Haus der Kulturen der Welt, Berlin, and Museum of Modern Art, Oxford.
'Artistas latinoamericanos del siglo XX: Latin American Artists of the Twentieth Century', MOMA, New York.
Biennial Exhibition (the 'politically correct Biennial'), Whitney Museum of American Art, New York.
Louise Bourgeois represents USA at Venice Biennale.
'Abject Art', Whitney Museum, New York.
Timor Novikov founds Novia Akademia in St Petersburg.
Rachel Whiteread's *House*, London.

1994
'Some Went Mad, Some Ran Away . . .', Serpentine Gallery, London.
'Unbound: Possibilities in Painting', Hayward Gallery, London.
'Japanese Art after 1945: Scream Against the Sky', Guggenheim Museum, New York.
Rebellion in Chechnya.
Civil War in Rwanda.
Opening of Channel Tunnel.
Nelson Mandela becomes President of South Africa.
Matthew Barney's *Cremaster 4* video.

1995
Damien Hirst wins Turner Prize.
NATO air attacks on Bosnia- Herzegovina.
'Reconsidering the Object of Art 1965– 1975', Museum of Contemporary Art, Los Angeles.

Oklahoma City terrrorist bombing.
'Rites of Passage: Art for the End of the
    Century', Tate Gallery, London.
Tamil Tigers rebel in Sri Lanka.

1996
'L'informe', Pompidou, Paris.
Hal Foster's *The Return of the Real* is
    published.
Benjamin Netanyahu Prime Minister
    of Israel.
Julian Schnabel's film *Basquiat*.

1997
Hong Kong handed back to China.
New Labour wins UK general election
    after 18 years of Tory government.
Frank Gehry's Guggenheim Museum,
    Bilbao.
De Kooning dies.
Lichtenstein dies.
Cloning of Dolly the sheep.

Death of Princess Diana.
Documenta X at Kassel, globalization and
    politics.
'Sensation!', Royal Academy, London.

1998
Retrospective of Jackson Pollock,
    MOMA, New York; to London 1999.
'Out of Actions: Between Performance
    and the Object 1949-1979', MOCA,
    Los Angeles.
Chris Ofili wins Turner Prize.
Survey and show of Yayoi Kusama,
    MOMA, New York.
Peace agreement in Northern Ireland.
US President Clinton accused of perjury.

1999
T. J. Clark's *Farewell to an Idea: Episodes
    from a History of Modernism* published.
NATO bombs Serbs after massacres of
    ethnic Albanians in Kosovo.
Devolution of power in Scotland and
    Wales.

King Hussein of Jordan dies.
'La Pittura Ritrovata', Museo del
    Risorgimento, Rome.
Environmentalists protest against
    World Trade Organization in
    Battle of Seattle.
Norman Foster completes Reichstag
    Building, Berlin.

2000
Opening of Tate Modern, Bankside,
    London.
Global warming leads to accelerating
    worldwide climate change.
Boris Yeltsin resigns as President of
    Russia.
Disputed presidential election in
    the USA, finally pronounced won
    by George W. Bush.
'Between Heaven and Earth', Museum of
    Modern Art, Ostend.
'Apocalypse', Royal Academy, London.

List of Illustrations

Measurements are in centimetres, followed by inches, height before width before depth

1 Chris Cunningham, *flex*, 2000. Film still. Courtesy Anthony d'Offay Gallery, London. **2** Tate Modern, interior showing the turbine hall and Louise Bourgeois' work *Maman* 1999. Steel and marble, 920 × 891 × 1023 (362¼ × 350¾ × 402¾). Photo © Tate, London 2001. © Louise Bourgeois/ DACS, London/VAGA, New York 2001. **3** Salvador Dalí, *Christ of St John of the Cross*, 1951. Oil on canvas, 205.1 × 116.2 (80¼ × 45¾). Glasgow Museums: Art Gallery and Museum, Kelvingrove. **4** René Magritte, *Exhibition of Painting*, 1965. Oil on canvas, 80 × 65.1 (31h × 25l). Collection Alexander Iolas, New York, Paris, Milan, Madrid, Rome, Geneva. **5** Roberto Matta, *Being With*, 1945–6. Oil on canvas, 455 × 221.9 (179 × 87). Pierre Matisse Gallery, New York. **6** Arshile Gorky, *The Betrothal II*, 1947. Oil on canvas, 128.9 × 96.5 (50 × 38). Collection of Whitney Museum of American Art, New York. **7** Yves Tanguy, *The Rapidity of Sleep*, 1945. Oil on canvas, 127 × 101.6 (50 × 40). The Art Institute of Chicago. The Joseph Winterbotham Collection. **8** André Masson, *Landscape with Precipices*, 1948. Oil on canvas, 205.7 × 254 (81 × 100). Galerie Louise Leiris, Paris. **9** Jackson Pollock at work, 1949. Photo Hans Namuth, New York. **10** Jackson Pollock, *Number 2*, 1949. Oil, Duco and aluminium paint on canvas, 97.8 × 481.3 (38 × 189). Munson-Williams-Proctor Institute, Utica, New York. **11** Robert Motherwell, *Elegy to the Spanish Republic No. LV*, 1955–60. Oil on canvas, 177.8 × 193.3 (70 × 76⅛). Contemporary Collection of the Cleveland Museum of Art. **12** Hans Hofmann, *Rising Moon*, 1964. Oil on canvas, 213.4 × 198.1 (84 × 78). André Emmerich Gallery, New York. **13** William Baziotes, *Congo*, 1954. Oil on canvas, 181 × 151.8 (71¼ × 59¾). Los Angeles County Museum of Art. Gift of Mrs Leonard Sperry. **14** Mark Rothko, *Orange Yellow Orange*, 1969. Oil on paper mounted on linen, 123.2 × 102.9 (48½ × 40½). Collection of the Marlborough-Gerson Gallery, New York. **15** Adolph Gottlieb, *The Frozen Sounds Number 1*, 1951. Oil on canvas, 91.4 × 121.9 (36 × 48). Collection of Whitney Museum of American Art, New York. Gift of Mr and Mrs Samuel Kootz. **16** Franz Kline, *Chief*, 1950. Oil on canvas, 148.3 × 186.7 (58⅜ × 186.7 × 73½). The Museum of Modern Art, New York. Gift of Mr and Mrs David M. Solinger. **17** Philip Guston, *The Clock*, 1956–7. Oil on canvas, 193 × 162.9 (76 × 64⅛). The Museum of Modern Art, New York. Gift of Miss Bliss Parkinson. **18** Mark Tobey, *Edge of August*, 1953. Casein on composition board, 121.9 × 71.1 (48 × 28). The Museum of Modern Art, New York. **19** Willem de Kooning, *Woman and Bicycle*, 1952–3. Oil on canvas, 194.3 × 124.5 (76½ × 49). Collection of Whitney Museum of American Art, New York. **20** Clyfford Still, *1957–D No. 1*, 1957. Oil on canvas, 287 × 403.9 (113 × 159). Albright-Knox Art Gallery, Buffalo, New York. Gift of Seymour H. Knox. **21** Sam Francis, *Blue on a Point*, 1958. Oil on canvas, 182.9 × 243.8 (72 × 96). Private collection. **22** Patrick Heron, *Manganese in Deep Violet: January 1967*. Oil on canvas, 101.6 × 153.4 (40 × 60). Collection J. Walter Thompson Company, London. **23** Pablo Picasso, *Massacre in Korea*, 1951. Oil on canvas, 109.9 × 169.5 (43½ × 66¾). Musée Picasso, Paris. **24** Fernand Léger, *The Constructors*, 1950. Oil on canvas, 302.3 × 215.9 (119 × 85). Musée Fernand Léger, Biot. **25** Georges Braque, *Studio IX*, 1952–6. Oil on canvas, 145.4 × 146 (57½ × 57½). Galerie Maeght, Paris. **26** Henri Matisse, *Zulma*, 1950. Gouache cut-out, 238 × 133 (93¾ × 52⅜). Statens Museum for Kunst, Copenhagen. **27** Graham Sutherland, *Somerset Maugham*, 1949. Oil on canvas, 137.2 × 63.5 (54 × 25). Tate Gallery, London. **28** David Bomberg, *Monastery of Ay Chrisostomos, Cyprus*, 1948. Oil on canvas, 91.4 × 91.4 (36 × 36). Courtesy Marlborough Fine Art Ltd, London. **29** Henri Matisse, *The Snail*, 1953. Gouache cut-out, 726.4 × 983 (286 × 387). Tate Gallery, London. **30** Max Ernst, *Cry of the Seagull*, 1953. Oil on canvas, 94.6 × 130.3 (37¼ × 51¼). Collection François de Menil, Houston, Texas. **31** Joan Miró, *Blue II*, 1961. Oil on canvas, 269.2 × 355.6 (106 × 140). Pierre Matisse Gallery, New York. **32** Frank Auerbach, *Head of Helen Gillespie III*, 1962–4. Oil on board, 74.9 × 61 (29½ × 24). Courtesy Marlborough Fine Art Ltd, London. **33** Leon Kossoff, *Profile of Rachel*, 1965. Oil on board, 86.4 × 61 (34 × 24). Courtesy Marlborough Fine Art Ltd, London. **34** Edward Middleditch, *Dead Chicken in a Stream*, 1955. Oil on board, 136.5 × 109.2 (53¾ × 43). Tate Gallery, London. **35** John Bratby, *Window, Self-Portrait, Jean and Hands*, 1957. Oil on board, 121.9 × 365.8 (48 × 144). Tate Gallery, London. **36** Renato Guttuso, *The Discussion*, 1959–60. Tempera, oil and collage on canvas, 220 × 248 (86⅝ × 97⅝). Tate Gallery, London. **37** Francis Bacon, *Study after Velázquez: Pope Innocent X*, 1953. Oil on canvas, 152.5 × 118.1 (60⅛ × 46½). Collection Carter Burden, New York. **38** Edouard Pignon, *The Miner*, 1949. Oil on canvas, 92.1 × 73 (36¼ × 28¾). Tate Gallery, London. **39** Maurice Estève, *Composition 166*, 1957. Oil on wood, 50.5 × 63.8 (19⅞ × 25⅛). Tate Gallery, London. **40** Jean Bazaine, *Shadows on the Hill*, 1961. Oil on canvas. Galerie Maeght, Paris. **41** Balthus, *The Bedroom*, 1954. Oil on canvas, 270 × 330 (106¼ × 129⅞). Private collection. **42** Francis Bacon, *One of Three Studies for a Crucifixion*, 1962. Oil on canvas (centre panel), 198.1 × 144.8 (78 × 57). Courtesy Marlborough Fine Art Ltd, London. **43** Hans Hartung, *Painting T 54–16*, 1954. Oil on canvas, 129.9 × 96.8 (51⅛ × 38⅛). Musée National d'Art Moderne, Centre Georges Pompidou, Paris. **44** Jean Fautrier, *Hostage*, 1945. Oil on canvas, 27.3 × 21.6 (10¾ × 8½). Private collection, London. **45** Wols, *The Blue Pomegranate*, 1946. Oil on canvas, 46 × 33 (18⅛ × 13). Collection Michel Couturier, Paris. **46** Henri Michaux, *Painting in India Ink*, 1960–7. 74.9 × 105.1 (29½ × 41⅜). Galerie Le Point Cardinal, Paris. **47** Manolo Millares, *No. 165*, 1961. Plastic paint on canvas, 81.3 × 100.3 (32 × 39½). Courtesy Marlborough Fine Art Ltd, London. **48** Alberto Burri, *Sacco 4*, 1954. Burlap, cotton, rinavil glue, silk and paint on cotton canvas, 114.3 × 76.2 (45 × 30). Collection Anthony Denney, London. **49** Antoni Tàpies, *Black with Two Lozenges*, 1963. Oil on canvas, 411.5 × 330.2 (162 × 130). Private collection, Buenos Aires. **50** Jean-Paul Riopelle, *Encounter*, 1956. Oil on canvas, 99.7 × 81.3 (39¼ × 32). Wallraf-Richartz Museum, Cologne. **51** Pierre Soulages, *Painting*, 1956. Oil on canvas, 150.5 × 194.9 (59¼ × 76¾). The Museum of Modern Art, New York. Gift of Mr and Mrs Samuel M. Kootz. **52** Georges Mathieu, *Battle of Bouvines*, 1954. Oil on canvas, 250.2 × 600.1 (98½ × 236¼). Collection the artist. **53** Pierre Alechinsky, *The Green Being Born*, 1960. Oil on canvas, 184.1 × 205.1 (72½ × 80¾). Museés Royaux d'Art et d'Histoire, Brussels. **54** Corneille, *Souvenir of Amsterdam*, 1956. Oil on canvas, 120 × 120 (47¼ × 47¼). Private collection, Paris. **55** Asger Jorn, *You Never Know*, 1966. Oil on canvas, 64.8 × 81.3 (25½ × 32). Arthur Tooth & Sons Ltd, London. **56** Alan Davie, *The Martyrdom of St Catherine*, 1956. Oil on canvas, 182.9 × 243.9 (72 × 96). Collection Mrs Alan Davie. **57** Karel Appel, *Women and Birds*, 1958. Oil on canvas, 174.6 × 130.2 (63¾ × 51¼). Private collection. **58** Bernard Buffet, *Self-portrait*, 1954. Oil on canvas, 146.4 × 114 (57⅝ × 44⅞). Tate Gallery, London. **59** Fritz Hundertwasser, *The Hokkaido Steamer*, 1961. Watercolour on rice-paper with a chalk ground, 47.9 × 66 (18⅞ × 26). Collection S. and G. Poppe, Hamburg. **60** Nicolas de Staël, *Agrigente*, 1954. Oil on canvas, 63.3 × 81 (25⅝ × 31⅞). Private collection, Paris. **61** Jean Dubuffet, *Corps de Dame*, 1950. Watercolour, 31.1 × 23.5 (12¼ × 9¼). Collection Peter Cochrane, London. **62** Max Bill, *Concentration to Brightness*, 1964. Oil on canvas, 105.4 × 105.4 (41½ × 41½). **63** Josef Albers, *Homage to the Square 'Curious'*, 1963. Oil on canvas, 76.2 × 76.2 (30 × 30). Collection R. Alistair McAlpine, London. **64** Richard Lohse, *Fifteen Systematic Colour Scales Merging Vertically*, 1950–67. Oil on canvas, 120.6 × 120.6 (47¼ × 47¼). Kunsthaus, Zurich. **65** Al Held, *Echo*, 1966. Acrylic on canvas, 213.4 × 182.9 (84 × 72). André

Emmerich Gallery, New York. **66** Ellsworth Kelly, *White – Dark Blue*, 1962. Oil on canvas, 147.9 × 83.8 ($58\frac{1}{4}$ × 33). Arthur Tooth & Sons Ltd, London. **67** Jack Youngerman, *Totem Black*, 1967. Oil on canvas, 312.4 × 205.7 (123 × 81). Betty Parsons Gallery, New York. **68** Jack Tworkov, *North American*, 1966. Oil on canvas, 203.2 × 162.6 (80 × 64). Collection the artist. **69** Barnett Newman, *Tundra*, 1950. Oil on canvas, 182.9 × 226.1 (72 × 89). Collection Mr and Mrs Robert A. Rowan. **70** Ad Reinhardt, *Red Painting*, 1952. Oil on canvas, 365.8 × 193 (144 × 76). The Metropolitan Museum of Art, New York. Arthur H. Hearn Fund, 1968. **71** Kenneth Noland, *Cantabile*, 1962. Plastic paint on canvas, 168.9 × 163.2 ($66\frac{1}{2}$ × $64\frac{1}{4}$). Collection Walker Art Center, Minneapolis. **72** Helen Frankenthaler, *Mountains and Sea*, 1952. Oil on canvas, 219.4 × 297.8 ($86\frac{3}{8}$ × $117\frac{1}{4}$). Collection the artist. **73** Morris Louis, *Untitled*, 1959. Magna acrylic on canvas, 264.2 × 193 (104 × 76). Photo Kasmin Gallery, London. **74** Morris Louis, *Omicron*, 1961. Synthetic polymer paint on canvas, 262.3 × 412 ($103\frac{1}{4}$ × $162\frac{1}{4}$). Waddington Gallery, London. **75** Kenneth Noland, *Grave Light*, 1965. Plastic paint on canvas, 259.1 × 228.6 (102 × 90). Collection Mr and Mrs Robert A. Rowan. **76** Frank Stella, *Untitled*, 1968. Acrylic on cotton duck, 243.8 × 487.7 (96 × 192). Collection Lord Dufferin. Photo Kasmin Gallery, London. **77** Larry Poons, *Night Journey*, 1968. Acrylic on canvas, 274.3 × 315 (108 × 124). Collection Carter Burden, New York. **78** Jules Olitski, *Feast*, 1965. Magna acrylic on canvas, 236.2 × 66 (93 × 26). Collection Catherine Zimmerman, Brookline, Massachusetts. **79** Frank Stella, *New Madrid*, 1961. Liquitex on canvas, 193 × 193 (76 × 76). Kasmin Gallery, London. **80** Edward Avedisian, *At Seven Brothers*, 1964. Liquitex on canvas, 91.4 × 91.4 (36 × 36). Kasmin Gallery, London. **81** John Walker, *Touch – Yellow*, 1967. Acrylic and chalk on canvas, 266.7 × 518.2 (105 × 204). Collection the artist. **82** Tess Jaray, *Garden of Allah*, 1966. Oil on canvas, 198.1 × 243.8 (72 × 96). Collection the artist. **83** Robyn Denny, *Growing*, 1967. Oil on canvas, 243.8 × 198.1 (96 × 78). Collection the Peter Stuyvesant Foundation. **84** Jeremy Moon, *Blue Rose*, 1967. Oil on canvas, 218.4 × 251.5 (86 × 99). Tate Gallery, London. **85** John Hoyland, *28.5.66*, 1966. Acrylic on canvas, 198.1 × 365.8 (78 × 144). Tate Gallery, London. **86** Marcel Duchamp, *Fountain*, 1917 (replica 1951). Collection Galleria Schwarz Milan. © Succession Marcel Duchamp/ADAGP, Paris and DACS, London, 2001. **87** Joseph Cornell, *Eclipse Series*, *c.* 1962. Construction, 304.8 × 487.7 × 152.4 (120 × 192 × 60). Collection of Allan Stone, New York. **88** Jasper Johns, *Numbers in Colour*, 1959. Encaustic and collage on canvas, 168.9 × 125.7 ($66\frac{1}{2}$ × $49\frac{1}{2}$). Albright-Knox Art Gallery, Buffalo, New York. Gift of Seymour H. Knox. **89** Enrico Baj, *Lady Fabricia Trolopp*, 1964. Collage, 100 × 81 ($39\frac{3}{8}$ × $31\frac{7}{8}$). Galleria Schwarz, Milan. **90** Robert Rauschenberg, *Barge*, 1962. Oil on canvas, 203.2 × 988.1 (80 × 389). Leo Castelli Gallery, New York. **91** Robert Rauschenberg, *Bed*, 1955. Combine painting, 188 × 7.6 (74 × 3). Collection Mr and Mrs Leo Castelli. **92** Edward Kienholz, *Roxy's*, 1961. Mixed media, 240 × 540.7 × 669.9 ($94\frac{1}{2}$ × $212\frac{7}{8}$ × $263\frac{3}{4}$). Collection the artist. Photo Dwan Gallery, New York. **93** Bruce Conner, *Couch*, 1963. Assemblage, 80 × 671 × 1,831 ($31\frac{1}{2}$ × 264 × 721). Pasadena Art Museum, California. **94** Arman, *Clic-Clac Rate*, 1960–6. Accumulation of photographic apparatus, 60 × 100 ($23\frac{5}{8}$ × $39\frac{3}{8}$). Galleria Schwarz, Milan. **95** Paul Thek, *Death of a Hippie*, 1967. Pink painted hardboard, wax body, 259.1 × 320 × 320 (102 × 126 × 126). Stable Gallery, New York. **96** Christo, *Packaged Public Building*, 1961. Photomontage, 33 × 91.1 (13 × $35\frac{7}{8}$). Collection the artist. **97** Yves Klein, *Feu F 45*, 1961. Oil on paper, 79.4 × 102.9 ($31\frac{1}{4}$ × $40\frac{1}{2}$). Private collection, Paris. **98** Lucio Fontana, *Spatial Concept*, 1960. Oil on canvas, 97.1 × 59.7 ($38\frac{1}{4}$ × $23\frac{1}{2}$). McRoberts and Tunnard Gallery, London. **99** Piero Manzoni, *Line 20 Metres Long*, 1959. Ink on paper. Collection Edward Lucie-Smith, London. **100** Yves Klein, *Anthropometries of the Blue Period*, 1960. Photo Shunk-Kender, Paris. **101** Michelangelo Pistoletto, *Seated Figure*, 1962. Collage on polished steel, 125.1 × 125.1 ($49\frac{1}{2}$ × $49\frac{1}{2}$). Kaiser-Wilhelm-Museum, Krefeld. **102** Martial Raysse, *Tableau simple et doux*, 1965. Assemblage with neon light, 194.9 × 130.2 ($76\frac{3}{4}$ × $51\frac{1}{4}$). Collection André Mourgues, Paris. **103** Tomio Miki, *Ears* (detail), 1968. Plated aluminium, 17.1 × 15.9 × 7 ($6\frac{3}{4}$ × $6\frac{1}{4}$ × $2\frac{3}{4}$). Tate Gallery, London. **104** Richard Hamilton, *Just What is it that Makes Today's Homes so Different, so Appealing?*, 1956. Collage, 26 × 24.8 ($10\frac{1}{4}$ × $9\frac{3}{4}$). Collection E. Janss, Los Angeles. **105** Peter Blake, *Doktor K. Tortur*, 1965. Cryla, collage on hardboard, 61 × 25.4 (24 × 10). Robert Fraser Gallery, London. **106** Richard Smith, *Soft Pack*, 1963. Oil on canvas, 213.4 × 175.3 (84 × 69). Joseph H. Hirshhorn Collection, New York. **107** Peter Phillips, *For Men Only Starring MM and BB*, 1961. Oil on canvas, 274.3 × 152.4 (108 × 60). The Calouste Gulbenkian Foundation, London. **108** Derek Boshier, *England's Glory*, 1961. Oil on canvas, 101.6 × 127.6 (40 × $50\frac{1}{4}$). Grabowski Gallery, London. **109** David Hockney, *Rubber Ring Floating in a Swimming Pool*, 1971. Acrylic on canvas, 90.8 × 121.9 ($35\frac{3}{4}$ × 48). Private collection, Japan. **110** Richard Smith, *Tailspan*, 1965. Acrylic on wood, 119.9 × 212.7 × 90.2 ($47\frac{1}{4}$ × $83\frac{3}{4}$ × $35\frac{1}{2}$). Tate Gallery, London. **111** David Hockney, *Picture Emphasizing Stillness*, 1962–3. Oil on canvas, 182.9 × 152.4 (72 × 60). Collection Mark Glazebrook, London. **112** David Hockney, *A Neat Lawn*, 1967. Acrylic on canvas, 243.8 × 243.8 (96 × 96). Kasmin Gallery, London. **113** R. B. Kitaj, *Synchromy with F.B. – General of Hot Desire* (diptych), 1968–9. Oil on canvas, 152.4 × 91.4 (60 × 36) each panel. Courtesy Marlborough Fine Art Ltd, London. **114** Allen Jones, *Hermaphrodite*, 1963. Oil on canvas, 182.9 × 61 (72 × 24). Board of Trustees of the National Museums and Galleries on Merseyside (Walker Art Gallery, Liverpool). **115** Patrick Caulfield, *Still-life with Red and White Pot*, 1966. Oil on board, 160 × 213.4 (63 × 84). Harry N. Abrams Family Collection, New York. **116** Anthony Donaldson, *Take Away No. 2*, 1963. Oil on canvas, 152.4 × 152.4 (60 × 60). Collection Alistair R. McAlpine, London. **117** Sidney Nolan, *Glenrowan*, 1956–7. Ripolin on hardboard, 91.4 × 121.9 (36 × 48). Tate Gallery, London. **118** Jim Dine, *Double Red Self-portrait (The Green Lines)*, 1964. Oil and collage on canvas, 304.8 × 213.4 (120 × 84). Courtesy Sidney Janis Gallery, New York. **119** Claes Oldenburg, *Study for Giant Chocolate*, 1966. Enamel and plaster, 26.7 × 11.4 × 11.4 ($10\frac{1}{2}$ × $4\frac{1}{4}$ × $4\frac{1}{4}$). Robert Fraser Gallery, London. **120** Roy Lichtenstein, *Hopeless*, 1963. Oil on canvas, 111.8 × 111.8 (44 × 44). Collection Mrs and Mrs Michael Sonnabend, Paris-New York. **121** Roy Lichtenstein, *Whaam!*, 1963. Acrylic on canvas, 172.7 × 40.6 (68 × 160). Tate Gallery, London. **122** Roy Lichtenstein, *Yellow and Red Brushstrokes*, 1966. Oil on canvas 205.1 × 174 ($80\frac{3}{4}$ × $68\frac{1}{2}$). Collection Philippe Durand-Ruel. **123** James Rosenquist, *Silver Skies*, 1962. Oil on canvas, 198.1 × 41.9 (78 × $16\frac{1}{2}$). Collection Mr and Mrs Robert C. Scull. **124** Tom Wesselmann, *Still-life No. 34*, 1963. Oil on canvas, 121.9 (48) tondo. Collection Mr and Mrs Jack Gelman, Kansas City. **125** Larry Rivers, *Parts of the Face*, 1961. Oil on canvas, 74.9 × 74.9 ($29\frac{1}{2}$ × $29\frac{1}{2}$). Tate Gallery, London. **126** Tom Wesselmann, *Great American Nude No. 44*, 1963. Assemblage painting, 265.7 × 243.8 × 25.4 (81 × 96 × 10). Collection Mr and Mrs Robert C. Scull. **127** Andy Warhol, *Race Riot*, 1964. Acrylic and silk-screen enamel on canvas, 76.2 × 83.8 (30 × 33). Leo Castelli Gallery, New York. **128** Jim Dine, *The Car Crash*, 1960. Happening, Photo Robert McElroy, New York. **129** Andy Warhol, *Green Coca-Cola Bottles*, 1962. Oil on canvas, 209.6 × 144.8 ($82\frac{1}{2}$ × 57). Collection Whitney Museum of American Art, New York. Gift of the Friends of the Whitney Museum. **130** Stuart Brisley, *And For Today – Nothing*, 1972. Action, Gallery House, London. **131** Rudolf Schwarzkogler, *Action*, May 1965, Vienna. **132** Gilbert and George, *Singing Sculpture*, November 1970. Photo courtesy of Nigel Greenwood Inc.. **133** Yayoi Kusama, *Endless Love Room*, 1965–6. Environment. **134** Claes Oldenburg, *Store Days*, 1965. Action, New York. **135** David Smith, *Cubi XVII*, 1964. Stainless steel, 294 ($115\frac{3}{4}$).

Courtesy Marlborough-Gerson Gallery, New York. **136** Anthony Caro, *Sun-feast*, 1969–70. Painted steel, 181.6 × 416.6 × 18.4 (71½ × 164 × 86). Private collection. **137** Victor Vasarely, *Metagalaxy*, 1959. Oil on canvas, 159 × 147 (62⅝ × 57⅞). Galerie Enise René, Paris. **138** Carlos Cruz-Diez, *Physichromie No. 1*, 1959. Plastic and wood, 49.8 × 49.8 (19⅝ × 19⅝). Collection the artist. **139** Bridget Riley, *Crest*, 1964. Emulsion on board, 166.4 × 166.4 (65½ × 65½). Rowan Gallery, London. **140** Jésus Rafael Soto, *Petite Double Face*, 1967. Wood and metal, 60 × 38.1 (23⅝ × 15). Collection Mr and Mrs Serge Sacknoff, Washington. Photo courtesy Marlborough-Gerson Gallery, New York. **141** Richard Serra, *Tilted Arc*, Federal Plaza, New York, 1981. Cor-ten steel, 30.5 × 304.8 × 6.4 (12 × 120 × 2½). © ARS, NY and DACS, London 2001. **142** Tony Smith, *Playground*, 1962. Wood mock-up to be made in steel, 162.6 × 162.6 (64 × 64). Fischbach Gallery, New York. **143** John McCracken, *There's No Reason Not To*, 1967. Wood, fibreglass, 412.1 × 45.7 × 8.9 (120 × 18 × 3 ½). Nicholas Wilder Gallery, Los Angeles . **144** Carl Andre, *Plain*, 1969. Thirty-six pieces of steel and zinc, each 182.9 × 182.9 × 1 (72 × 72 × ⅜). John Weber Gallery, New York. Photo E. Marks and P. Katz. © Carl Andre/VAGA, New York/DACS, London 2001. **145** Robert Morris, *Untitled (circular light piece)*, 1966. Plexiglass, 61 × 243.9 (24 × 96) diameter. Dwan Gallery, New York. **146** Donald Judd, *Untitled*, 1965. Galvanized iron and aluminium, 88.8 × 358.1 × 76.2 (33 × 141 × 30). Leo Castelli Gallery, New York. **147** Sol LeWitt, *49 Three-part Variations*, 1967–70. Baked enamel on steel, each part, 20.3 × 20.3 × 58.4 (8 × 8 × 23). Installation at John Weber Gallery, New York 1972. Photo Walter Russell. © ARS, NY and DACS, London 2001. **148** Daniel Buren, *On Two Levels with Two Colours*, 1976. Installation, Lisson Gallery, London. **149** Dan Flavin, *Untitled (to the 'Innovator' Wheeling Beachblow)*, 1968. Fluorescent light (pink, gold and 'daylight'), 243.9 × 243.9 (96 × 96). Dwan Gallery, New York. **150** Larry Bell, *Untitled*, 1971. Coated glass, nine units. Each unit, 182.9 × 152.4 × 0.6 (72 × 60 × ½). Tate Gallery, London. **151** Eric Orr, *Prime Matter*, 1990. 2 bronze columns, water and fire, 1219.2 (480). Xenon light ascends 1 mile into the sky. Downtown Los Angeles, California. Courtesy the artist. **152** James Turrell, *Roden Crater*, work in progress, conceived 1974 . **153** Robert Smithson, *Spiral Jetty*, 1970. Great Salt Lake, Utah. **154** Richard Long, *A Line in Ireland*, 1974. Courtesy the artist. **155** Andy Goldsworthy, *Tree Cairn*, June 1994. Laumeier Sculpture Park, Missouri. Courtesy the artist. **156** Dennis Oppenheim, *Reading Position for Second Degree Burn*, 1970. Stage I and Stage II. Book, skin, solar energy. Exposure time: 5 hours. Jones Beach, New York. Photo courtesy the artist. **157** Jenny Holzer, *The Survival Series: Protect Me From What I Want*, 1985–6. Spectacolour board. Times Square, New York. Courtesy Barbara Gladstone Gallery, New York. **158** Joseph Kosuth, *One and Three Chairs*, 1965. Mixed media. The Museum of Modern Art, New York. Larry Aldrich Foundation Fund. **159** Barbara Hepworth, *Two Figures*, 1947–8. Elm, painted white, 121.9 (48). Collection of the University Gallery, University of Minnesota. **160** Henry Moore, *(Lambert) Locking-piece*, 1963–4. Bronze, 292.1 (115). Collection Banque Lambert, Brussels. **161** Joseph Beuys, *Action in 7 Exhibitions*, 1972. Tate Gallery, London. Photo Edward Lucie-Smith. **162** Joseph Beuys, *Dernier espace avec introspecteur*, 1982. Mixed media. Installation, Anthony d'Offay Gallery, London. **163** Bruce Nauman, *Life Death/Knows Doesn't Know*, 1983. Neon tubing with clear glass suspension frames. Lettering 8.3 (3¼), *Life Death*: 203.2 (80) diameter. *Knows Doesn't Know*: 273 × 271.8 (107¼ × 107) diameter. Private collection. **164** Giuseppe Penone, *Breath I*, 1978. Terracotta, H 160, diameter 100 (63 × 39⅜). Courtesy Galerie Rudolf Zwirner, Cologne. **165** Luciano Fabro, *Golden Italy (Italia d'Oro)*, 1971. Gilded bronze 75 × 45 × 3 (29½ × 17¾ × 1¼). Collection the artist. **166** Alighiero e Boetti, *Bringing the World into the World*, 1973–9. Ball point pen on paper mounted on linen: 2 panels, 134.6 × 179.7 (53 × 70¾), 133.9 × 200.7 (52¾ × 79). Courtesy Salvatore Ala Gallery, New York. **167** Mario Merz, *610 Function of 15*, 1971–89. Newspapers, glass, neon, 50.8 × 86.4 × 692.8 (20 × 34 × 272¾). Courtesy of Margo Leavin Gallery, Los Angeles. Photo Douglas M. Parker Studio, Los Angeles. **168** Giulio Paolini, *Apotheosis of Homer*, 1970–1. Tape recorded sound and 32 photographs. Studio Marconi, Milan. **169** Jannis Kounellis, *Work Incorporating Classical Fragments* (cast of 2nd-century BC head of Athena). Collection of the artist. **170** Anish Kapoor, *Passage*, 1993. Sandstone and pigment, 169 × 172 × 134 (66½ × 67¾ × 52¾). Lisson Gallery, London. Photo Stephen White, London. **171** Richard Wentworth, *Jetsam*, 1984. Steel, galvanized and enamelled, cable, 196.9 × 80 × 80 (77½ × 31½ × 31½). Private collection. **172** Richard Deacon, *Two Can Play*, 1983. Galvanized steel, 183 × 365.8 × 183 (72 × 144.1 × 72). Private collection. **173** Tony Cragg, *African Culture Myth*, 1984. Plastics, 280 × 50, 255 × 47, 270 × 65 (110¼ × 19⅝, 100⅜ × 18½, 106¼ × 25⅝). Courtesy Galerie Crousel-Robelin-Bama, Paris. **174** David Mach, *Thinking of England*, 1983. 2160 HP sauce bottles with liquid dyes, area 183 × 246 (72 × 96). Tate Gallery, London. **175** Bill Woodrow, *Self-Portrait in the Nuclear Age*, 1986. Shelving unit, wall map, wooden box, coat, acrylic paint and globe, 201.9 × 250.2 × 184.2 (79½ × 98½ × 72½). Saatchi Collection, London. **176** Lucian Freud, *Double Portrait*, 1985–6. Oil on canvas, 78.8 × 88.9 (31 × 35). Private collection. **177** Jean Rustin, *The Twins*, 1987. Acrylic on canvas, 162 × 130 (63¾ × 51⅛). Courtesy the Jean Rustin Foundation. **178** A. R. Penck, *T3 (R)*, 1982. Acrylic on canvas, 299.7 × 198.8 (118 × 78¼). Galerie Michael Werner, Cologne. **179** Georg Baselitz, *Die Mädchen von Olmo*, 1981. Oil on canvas, 250 × 248 (98½ × 97½). Private collection. **180** Jörg Immendorf, *Eigenlob stinkt nicht*, 1983. Oil on canvas, 150 × 200 (59 × 78¾). Courtesy Michael Werner Gallery, New York and Cologne. **181** Anselm Kiefer, *Untitled*, 1978. Oil, emulsion, woodcut, shellac, latex and straw in canvas, 260.3 × 189.9 (102½ × 74¾). Anthony d'Offay Gallery, London. Photo Prudence Cuming Associates. **182** Rainer Fetting, *Dancers III*, 1982. Powder paint on cotton, 224.8 × 280.7 (88½ × 110½). Anthony d'Offay Gallery, London. **183** Gerhard Richter, *Three Candles*, 1982. Oil on canvas, 125 × 150 (49 × 59). Private collection, Chicago. **184** Sigmar Polke, *Liebespaar II*, 1965. Oil and enamel on canvas, 190 × 150 (75 × 59). Courtesy Gagosian Gallery, New York. Photo John Webb. **185** Philip Guston, *The Rug*, 1979. Oil on canvas, 193 × 162.9 (76 × 64⅛). The Museum of Modern Art, New York. Gift of Miss Bliss Parkinson. **186** Leon Golub, *Mercenaries V*, 1984. Acrylic on linen, 305 × 437 (120 × 172). Private collection. **187** Julian Schnabel, *Humanity Asleep*, 1982. Painted ceramic relief on wood, 275 × 365.8 (108¼ × 144). Tate Gallery, London. **188** Terry Winters, *Caps, Stems, Gills*, 1982. Oil on linen, 152.4 × 213.4 (60 × 84). Private collection. **189** Susan Rothenberg, *Beggar*, 1982. Oil on canvas, 100.3 × 128.3 (39½ × 50½). Willard Gallery, New York. Photo Roy M. Elkind. **190** Sandro Chia, *Crocodile Tears*, 1982. Oil on canvas, 287 × 234 (113 × 92). Anthony d'Offay Gallery, London. **191** Francesco Clemente, *Toothache*, 1981. Pastel on paper, 61 × 45.7 (24 × 18). Anthony d'Offay Gallery, London. Photo Prudence Cuming Associates. **192** Mimmo Paladino, *It's Always Evening*, 1982. Mixed media on canvas (centre panel of triptych), 219.7 × 480.1 (86½ × 189). Private collection. Photo Prudence Cuming Associates. **193** Enzo Cucchi, *A Painting of Precious Fires*, 1983. Oil on canvas with neon, 298 × 390 (117 × 153). The Gerald S. Elliott Collection of Contemporary Art, Chicago. **194** Keith Haring, *Ignorance = Fear*, 1989. Sumi ink on paper, 61 × 109.5 (24 × 43⅛). Collection The Estate of Keith Haring. **195** Jean-Michel Basquiat and Andy Warhol, *Collaboration*, 1984. Acrylic on canvas, 193 × 249 (76 × 98). Courtesy Mayor/Mayor Rowan Gallery, London. **196** Jeff Koons, *Michael Jackson and Bubbles*, 1988. Porcelain, edition of 3, 106.7 × 179 × 81.3 (42 × 70 ½ × 32). Sonnabend Gallery, New York. **197** Peter Halley, *Yellow and*

Black Cells with Conduit, 1985. Day-glo acrylic and roll-a-tex on canvas, 121.9 × 182.9 (48 × 72). Saatchi Collection, London. **198** Haim Steinbach, *Related and Different*, 1985. Mixed media construction, 91.4 × 52.1 × 50.8 (36 × 20½ × 20). Private collection. **199** Philip Taaffe, *Four Quad Cinema*, 1986. Acrylic, enamel and linoprint collage on canvas, 220 × 221.9 (86⅝ × 87⅜). Private collection. **200** Robert Gober, *Untitled*, 1991. Wood, wax, leather, cotton, human hair, steel, 25.4 × 90.2 × 69.8 (10 × 35½ × 27½). Courtesy Paula Cooper Gallery, New York. Photo Andrew Moore.

201 Judy Chicago, *The Dinner Party*, 1979. Mixed media, length of each side, 119.4 (47). Photo Michael Alexander, courtesy Through the Flower Corporation.

202 Barbara Kruger, *Untitled (Your Gaze Hits the Side of my Face)*, 1981. Photograph 139.7 × 104.1 (55 × 41). Mary Boone Gallery, New York. **203** Cindy Sherman, *Untitled Film Still #7*, 1978. Black and white photograph, 20.3 × 25.4 (8 × 10). Courtesy of Metro Pictures, New York.

204 Robert Mapplethorpe, *Thomas*, 1986. Photograph. Copyright 1986 The Estate of Robert Mapplethorpe. **205** George Dureau, *Wilbert Hines*, 1972. Photograph. Courtesy the artist. **206** Roy de Forest, *Untitled*, 1990. Acrylic on canvas, 185.4 × 215.9 (73 × 85). Courtesy John Natsoulas Gallery, California. **207** William T. Wiley, *Was It Ever Any Different From Now*, 1987. Watercolour on canvas, 57.2 × 77.5 (22½ × 30½). Photo courtesy L. A. Louver Gallery, Venice, California. **208** Roger Brown, *Randie's Donuts with Hollywood Junipers and Ranchhouses*, 1991. Oil on canvas, 122 × 152.4 (48 × 60). Courtesy Phyllis Kind Gallery, New York. **209** David Bates, *Sheepshead*, 1985. Oil on canvas, 167.6 × 213.4 (66 × 84). Arthur Roger Gallery, New Orleans. **210** David Gilhooly, *An Excessive Dagwood Sandwich*, 1987. Clay, 40.6 × 33 × 71.1 (16 × 13 × 28). Sherry Frumkin Gallery, Santa Monica.

211 Robert Arneson, *Californian Artist*, 1982. Glazed ceramic, 198 × 71 × 53 (78 × 28 × 21). Allan Frumkin Gallery, New York. **212** Viola Frey, *Artist/Mind/Studio/World Series I*, 1993. Ceramic, 205.7 × 188 × 89 (81 × 74 × 35). Courtesy of Nancy Hoffman Gallery, New York, Photo Christopher Watson. **213** Peter Saul, *Jeffrey Dahmer*, 1993. Acrylic alkyd on canvas, 182.9 × 167.6 (72 × 66). Frumkin/Adams Gallery, New York. Photo Ken Showell. **214** Ed Paschke, *Minnie*, 1974. Oil on canvas, 128.9 × 96.5 (50⅜ × 38). The Art Institute of Chicago. **215** Sam Gilliam, *Horizontal Extension*, 1969. Acrylic on canvas, 304.8 × 2286 (120 × 900). Installed at the Corcoran Gallery of Art, Washington, D.C. Photo courtesy Annie Gawlak. **216** Martin Puryear, *Noblesse O.*, 1987. Red cedar and aluminium paint, 246.4 × 147.3 × 116.8 (97 × 58 × 46). Dallas Museum of Art, Central Acquisitions Fund and a gift of The 500, Inc.. **217** Romare Bearden, *The Family*, 1948. Watercolour and gouache on paper, 64.8 × 49.5 (25½ × 19½). Evans-Tibbs Collection, Washington, D.C.. **218** Jacob Lawrence, *One of the Largest Race Riots Occurred in East St Louis* from the series *The Migration of the Negro*, 1940–1. Tempera on gesso on composition board, 30.5 × 45.7 (12 × 18). The Museum of Modern Art, New York. Gift of Mr and Mrs David Levy. **219** Hew Locke, *Ark*, 1992–4. Mixed media, 457.2 × 335.2 × 1573 (180 × 132 × 619⅜). Courtesy the artist. **220** Betye Saar, *The Liberation of Aunt Jemima*, 1972. Mixed media, 29.8 × 20.2 × 6.8 (11¾ × 8 × 2¾). University Art Museum, University of California, Berkeley. Purchased with the aid of funds from the National Endowment for the arts (selected by The Committee for the Acquisition of Afro-American art).

221 Keith Piper, *The Nanny of the Nation Gathers her Flock*, 1987. Acryl unstretched canvas. Courtesy the artist. **222** Faith Ringgold, *The Wedding: Lover's Quilt No. 1*, 1986. Acrylic on canvas, tie-dyed, painted, pieced fabric, 196.5 × 147.5 (77½ × 58). Collection Marilyn Lanfear. Photo Bernice Steinbaum Gallery, New York. **223** Mary Kelly, *Post Partum Document, Documentation VI*, 1978–9. Slate and resin, 18 units 35.6 × 27.9 (14 × 11). Arts Council Collection, London. **224** Derek Jarman, *Blood*, 1992. Oil on photocopy on canvas, 251.5 × 179 (99 × 70½). Courtesy Richard Salmon Ltd, London. **225** David Wojnarowicz, *Bad Moon Rising*, 1989. Acrylic, photo and collage on wood, 94 × 92.7 (37 × 36½). Courtesy of P.P.O.W, New York. **226** Ross Bleckner, *8,122+ as of January 1986*, 1986. Oil on linen, 122 × 101.6 (48 × 40). Private collection. **227** Nancy Fried, *The Hand Mirror*, 1987. Terracotta, 25.4 × 24.1 × 20.3 (10 × 9½ × 8). Courtesy the artist.

228 Karen Finley, *The Vacant Chair*, 1993. Chair, flowers, moss and foliage, 165.1 × 91.4 × 106.7 (65 × 36 × 42). Courtesy the artist. **229** Jacobo Borges, *The Betrothed*, 1975. Acrylic on canvas, 120 × 120 (47¼ × 47¼). Photo courtesy the CDS Gallery, New York. **230** Fernando Botero, *The House of the Arias Sisters*, 1973. Oil on canvas, 227 X 187 (89⅜ × 73⅝). Photo courtesy Marlborough Gallery Inc, New York. **231** Frida Kahlo, *Self-portrait*, 1940. Oil on canvas, 62 × 47.5 (24½ × 18¾). Iconography Collection, Harry Ransom Humanities Research Center, The University of Texas at Austin. **232** Víctor Grippo, *Analogía I*, 1971. Paper, electric circuits, measuring instruments, text, wood, 48.5 × 155 × 11 (19 × 61 × 4¾). Courtesy Ruth Benzacar Galeria de Arte, Buenos Aires. **233** Guillermo Kuitca, *Triptych of Mattresses*, 1989. Acrylic on 3 matresses. Courtesy Thomas Cohn, Arte Contemporanea, Rio de Janeiro. **234** Lygia Clark, *Rubber Grub*, 1964 (remade by artist 1986). Rubber, 142 × 43 (55⅞ × 16⅞). Museu de Arte Moderna do Rio de Janeiro. Donated by the artist. **235** Tunga, *Lizart 5*, 1989. Installation. Copper, steel, iron and magnets. Museum of Contemporary Art, Chicago. **236** Arturo Duclos, *Black Mirror*, 1993. Acrylic, oil and enamel on canvas 141.5 × 135 (55¾ × 53⅛). Courtesy the artist and Luz Maria Williamson, Cuerpos Puntados, Chile. **237** Juan Davíla, *The Liberator Simon Bolivar*, 1994. Oil on canvas on metal, 126 × 107 (49⅝ × 42⅛). Courtesy the artist and Luz Maria Williamson, Cuerpos Puntados, Chile. **238** Gonzalo Díaz, *The Founding Father*, 1994. Installation 4000 × 800 × 400 (1574⅞ × 315 × 157½). Courtesy the artist and Luz Maria Williamson, Cuerpos Puntados, Chile.

239 Eugenio Dittborn, *The Car of the Dead Spy*, 1994. Offset on couche paper, 22 × 16.5 (8⅝ × 6½). Courtesy the artist and Luz Maria Williamson, Cuerpos Puntados, Chile. **240** Ilya Kabakov, *My Mother's Life II*, detail from the installation *He Lost His Mind, Undressed, Ran Away Naked*, 1989. 70 framed pages of black and white photos with texts mounted on decorative paper, 78.7 × 58.4 (31 × 23). Courtesy Ronald Feldman Fine Arts, New York. Photo D. James Dee. **241** Eric Bulatov, *Perestroika*, 1989. Oil on canvas, 274.3 × 269.2 (108 × 106). Courtesy Phyllis Kind Gallery, New York. **242** Jiro Yoshihara, *Untitled*, 1971. Oil on canvas, 162 × 131 (63¾ × 51⅝). Tokyo Gallery, Tokyo. **243** Yukinori Yanagi, *Union Jack Ant Farm*, 1994. Coloured sand, plexiglass, plastic, tubes, 206 × 381 (81 × 150). Anthony d'Offay Gallery, London. **244** John Muafangejo, *Lonely Man, Man of Man*, 1974. Linocut print, 47.9 × 45.4 (18⅞ × 17⅞). **245** Chéri Samba, *Pourquoi un Contrat?* 1990. Acrylic on canvas, 130 × 180 (51⅛ × 70⅞). Courtesy Annina Nosei Gallery, New York.

246 Peter Blacksmith, *Japanangka Snake Dreaming*, 1986. Acrylic and house paint on composition board, 110.5 × 210.4 (43½ × 82⅞). National Gallery of Victoria, Melbourne. Purchased through the Art Foundation of Victoria from funds provided by CRA Limited, 1989.

247 Ha, Chong-Hyun, *Conjunction 94–07*, 1994. Oil pushed through back of hemp cloth, 100 × 45 (39⅜ × 17¾). Courtesy the artist. **248** Yu Youhan, *Mao Voting*, 1993. Acrylic on canvas, 118 × 166 (46½ × 65⅜). Courtesy Hanart TZ Gallery, Hong Kong. **249** Ralph Hotere, *The Black over the Gold*, 1993. Wood, glass, paint, gold leaf. Photo Edward Lucie-Smith. **250** Ed Emshwiller, *Thermogenesis*, 1972, video still, 11.55 minutes, colour, with sound. Courtesy Electronic Arts Intermix, New York.

251 Nam June Paik, view of installation at the Solomon R. Guggenheim Museum, New York, 2000. Photograph by Ellen Labenski. © The Solomon R. Guggenheim Foundation, New York. **252** Gary Hill, *Suspension of Disbelief (for Marine)*, 1991–92. Four-channel video installation at Le Creux de l'Enfer, Thiers, France. Courtesy Donald Young Gallery, Chicago. Photo Jean-Paul Judon. **253** Bill Viola, *The*

Sleep of Reason, 1988. Video installation: 3 video projectors, 1 monitor, 1-inch videotape, 2 channels, sound, colour, and black and white, 429.2 × 584.2 × 670.5 (169 × 230 × 264). Collection of the artist. Assistance from Sony Corporation, JBL Professional Products Inc. and Dargate Galleries. **254** Studio Azzurro, *Chorus*, 1995, interactive videoambient in 2 parts (First ambient: carpet and introductive songs; second ambient: interactive carpet and chorus). 9 video projectors, 18 audiospeakers, 9 videodiscs, 1 computer, 370 × 850 (145⅝ × 334⅝). Project by: Leonardo Sangiorgi, Paolo Rosa, Fabio Cirifino, Stefano Roveda. Photo courtesy Studio Azzurro. **255** Tony Oursler, *Mansheshe*, 1997. Ceramic, glass, video player, videocassette, CPJ-200 video projector, sound. Approx. 27.9 × 17.8 × 20.3 (11 × 7 × 8) each. Courtesy the artist and Metro Pictures, New York. **256** Chuck Close, *Untitled Torso Diptych*, 2000. Two daguerreotypes, each image 21.6 × 16.5 (8½ × 6½). © Chuck Close. Courtesy Pace/MacGill Gallery, New York. **257** Per Wizén, *Untitled* (from the series *Reworkings*), 1998. Cibachrome mounted on aluminium, 100 × 173 (39⅜ × 68⅛). Courtesy Zinc Gallery, Stockholm. **258** Olga Tobreluts, *Hercules in the Garden of the Hesperides*, from the series *The Feats of Hercules*, 1996. Cibachrome with videotape. © Art Kiosk, Belgium. **259** Yinka Shonibare, *Diary of a Victorian Dandy: 14.00 hours*, 1998. C-type print, 183 × 228.6 (72 × 90). © Stephen Friedman Gallery. **260** Elisabeth Ohlson, *Last Supper*, from the *Ecce Homo* series, 1998. Colour photograph, 220 × 150 (86⅝ × 59), Stockholm. © Photograph Elisabeth Ohlson. **261** Alexander de Cadenet, *Skull Portrait*, 1999. Unique cibacrome print mounted on aluminium, 250 × 148 (98⅜ × 58¼). Courtesy the artist. **262** Alexander, *Car Crash*, 1989. Film hologram with sound, 111.8 × 111.8 (44 × 44). Photo courtesy the artist. **263** Nan Goldin, *Relapse/Detox*, 1998. 9 mounted cibachrome prints, 106 × 157 (47½ × 62⅛). © Nan Goldin. **264** Ma Liuming, *Fen-Ma Liuming Walks the Great Wall*, 1998. Photo courtesy the artist and Hanart TZ, Hong Kong. **265** Yasumasa Morimura, *Playing with the Gods, No. 1 Twilight*, 1991. Colour photograph, 360 × 250.2 (141¾ × 98½). Courtesy Luhring Augustine Gallery, New York. **266** Andres Serrano, *Piss Christ*, 1987. Cibachrome, silicone, plexiglass, wood frame, 152.4 × 101.6 (60 × 40). Courtesy Paula Cooper Gallery, New York. **267** Joel-Peter Witkin, *Portrait as a Vanité*, New Mexico, 1994. Gelatin silver print, 94.6 × 78.7 (37¼ × 31). © Joel-Peter Witkin. Courtesy Pace/MacGill Gallery, New York. **268** Hai Bo, *They - 3*, 1999. Photograph © Hai Bo. Courtesy Hanart TZ, Hong Kong. **269** Mike Kelley, *Center and Peripheries #5*, 1990. Acrylic on panels, 223.5 × 298.5 (88 × 117½). Courtesy the artist and Rosamund Felsen Gallery, Los Angeles. Photo Douglas M. Parker. **270** Karen Kilimnik, *Cloudy*, 1997. Watersoluble oil colour on canvas, 45.7 × 35.6 (18 × 14). Courtesy Emilt Tsingou Gallery, London. **271** Oleg Kulik, *Deep into Russia*, 1993. Silverprint, 30 × 40 (11 6/8 × 15 6/8). © Olga Kulik. Courtesy Art Kiosk, Belgium. **272** Inez van Lamsweerde, *Final Fantasy, Ursula*, 1993. Fujiflex, perspex, 97 × 150 (38 × 59). Courtesy Matthew Marks Gallery, New York. **273** Damien Hirst, *Away from the Flock*, 1994. Steel, glass, formaldehyde solution and lamb, 96 × 149 × 51 (37¾ × 58⅝ × 20⅛). Courtesy Jay Jopling (London). **274** Jake and Dinos Chapman, *Zygotic*, 1996. Fibreglass, resin and paint, 170 × 210 × 100 (16⅞ × 82⅝ × 39⅜). Courtesy the artists and White Cube. **275** Roee Rosen, *Live and Die as Eva Braun #34*, 1994–97. Acrylic on paper, 55 × 55 (21⅝ × 21⅝). Collection of the artist. Courtesy Rosenfeld Gallery, Tel-Aviv. **276** Mariko Mori, *Nirvana*, 1997. Video still from 3-D video. Courtesy Deitch Projects, NY and Gallery Koyanagi, Tokyo. **277** Sun Yuan and Pen Yu, *Soul Killing*, 2000. Installation. Courtesy the artist and Hanart TZ, Hong Kong. **278** David Ligare, *Areta (Black Figure on White Horse)*, 2000. Oil on canvas, 244 × 295 (96 × 116). Courtesy Koplin Gallery, Los Angeles. **279** Michael Leonard, *Nectarine Man*, 1997. Alkyd-oil on masonite, 39 × 31 (15¾ × 15⅜). © Michael Leonard. **280** Delmas Howe, *Stations, the Triumphs*, 1999. Oil on canvas, 198.1 × 152.4 (78 × 60). Collection of the artist. Photo Judd Bradley. **281** John Currin, *The Old Fence*, 1999. Oil on canvas, 193 × 101.6 (76 × 40). Photo Fred Scruton. Courtesy Andrea Rosen Gallery, New York. **282** Carlo Maria Mariani, *Monument to Poetry*, 1994–95. Oil on canvas, 180 × 180 (71 × 71). © Carlo Maria Mariani/VAGA, New York /DACS, London 2001. **283** Carlo Bertocci, *The Origin of Painting*, 2000. Oil on canvas, 80 × 120 (31½ × 47 2/8). Photo courtesy the artist and Il Polittico Gallery, Rome. **284** Ricardo Cinalli, *Homenaje Humanista Para el Nuevo Milenio* (detail), 1999–2000. Oil on plaster, whole surface, 3000 × 900 (1181⅛ × 354⅜). Cultural Project, Cinalli-Peruchena, Cruz del Sur, Punta del Este, Uruguay. Courtesy the artist and Barbican Consultants Ltd. **285** Roberto Marquez, *La otra primavera*, 2000. Oil on canvas, 182.9 × 152.4 (72 × 60). Private Collection, Reno, Nevada. Courtesy Riva Yares Gallery, Scottsdale and Santa Fe. **286** Timor Novikov, *Oscar Wilde and Locket* (detail), 1993. Textile with mixed media, 156 × 112 (61⅜ × 44⅛). © Art Kiosk, Belgium. **287** Oleg Maslov/Viktor Kuznetsov, *After the Shipwreck*, 1997. Oil on canvas, 90 × 121 (35⅜ × 47⅝). © Art Kiosk, Belgium. **288** Wang Xing-Wei, *Arcadia*, 1996. Oil on canvas, 170 × 240 (66⅞ × 94½). Courtesy Hanart TZ Gallery, Hong Kong.

Index

Italic numerals refer to plate numbers

Abate, Alberto 278–80
Aboriginal art 216, 229–30, *246*
Abstract Expressionism 15–39, 44, 54,
  56–64, 66, 74, 80, 89, 93, 94, 97, 98,
  101, 121–2, 125, 137, 176, 184, 201
Abstraction-Création group 75
Absurd, the idea of the 70
Acconci, Vito 237
'Actions' *see* Happenings
Adler, Jules 8
advertising, influence on art 14, 229,
  238–9, 249
Africa, art in 226–9
African-American art 191, 207–9
'Africanism' 228
Afro-Caribbean art 209
AIDS 192, 195, 199, 212–13, 215–16
Albers, Josef 16, 75–6, 80, 94, 100, *63*
Alechinsky, Pierre 66, *53*
Alexander 252, *262*
Alighiero e Boetti *see* Boetti
Alloway, Lawrence 108
Amaya, Mario 108
American Regionalists 21, 196
Amis, Kingsley 49
Andre, Carl 147, *144*
Anselmo, Giovanni 169, 171, 172
'Apocalypse' exhibition 239–40
Appel, Karel 66, *57*
Arbus, Diane 198, 200, 254–7
Argentinian avant-garde 220
Arman (Fernandez, Armand) 102–4, *94*
Arneson, Robert 204, *211*
Arp, Hans 163
Art Deco 40
Arte Concreto-Invención group 217–20
Arte Povera 168–73, 188, 221, 226, 259,
  277
art informel 54, 65–74, 97
art market 10
Art Nouveau 67
Art of this Century Gallery (New York)
  16, 21, 27, 28
Arts and Crafts Movement 201–4
assemblage 38, 97–102, 222, 241
Auerbach, Frank 48, *32*
avant-gardism, in New York 16
Avedisian, Edward 93, *80*

Bacon, Francis 50–2, 74, 176, *37, 42*
Bada, Carlos Forns 280
Baj, Enrico 98, *88*
Baldaccini, César *see* César
Baldung Grien, Hans 275
Balthus 50, 52, 74, 176, *41*
Banham, Peter Reyner 108
Bardon, Geoffrey 230
Barney, Matthew 240
Baroque art 267
Bartolini, Ubaldo 278
Barzun, Jacques 80
Baselitz, Georg 179, 185–6, 229, *179*
Basquiat, Jean-Michel 190–1, *195*
Bates, David 205, *209*

Bauhaus 56, 75, 140
Bay Area Figuration 201
Bazaine, Jean 53, 54, *40*
Baziotes, William 27, *13*
Bearden, Romare 207, *217*
Beat poets 201
Beauty, ideas about 14
Beckett, Samuel 245
belle peinture 64, 74
Bell, Larry 152–3, *150*
Bengston, Billy Al 204
Benton, Thomas Hart 21, 196
Berlin, centre for art 12
Bertocci, Carlo 278, *283*
Beuys, Joseph 10, 132, 163–5, 167, 171,
  173, 174, *161, 162*
Beverloo, Cornelis van (Corneille) 66, *54*
Billingham, Richard 13, 253
Bill, Max 75–6, *62*
Bischoff, Elmer 201
Blake, Peter 110, *105*
Bleckner, Ross 212, *226*
Body art 159, *158*
Boetti, Alighiero, self-styled Alighiero e
  [and] Boetti 169, *166*
Boltanski, Christian 268
Bomberg, David 45–8, *28*
Bonito Oliva, Achille 187
Booth, Chris 234
Borges, Jacobo 217, *229*
Bortnyik, Alexander 140
Bosch, Hieronymus 267
Boshier, Derek 110, 112, 114, *108*
Botero, Fernando 217, *230*
Bourgeois, Louise 173–4, *2*
Brancusi, Constantin 16, 163, 207
Braque, Georges 24, 42–3, 44, *25*
Bratby, John 48–9, *35*
Bredikhina, Mila 261
Breton, André 15, 18, 23
Brill, Paul 278
Brisley, Stuart 133, 159, *130*
Bronzino, Agnolo 280
Brown, Earle 38
Brown, Roger 205, *108*
Bruegel, Pieter the Elder 267
Brüs, Gunter 134
Buchholz Gallery (New York) 137
Buckle, Richard 108
Buffet, Bernard 71, *58*
Bulatov, Eric 222–5, *241*
Buren, Daniel 150–2, *148*
Burri, Alberto 60, 61, *48*
Burrup, Eddie 230

Cadenet, Alexander de 249–50, *261*
Cage, John 100–1, 163, 281
Calder, Alexander 142
Callot, Jacques 267
Camuccini, Vincenzo 277
Camus, Albert 105
Caravaggio, Michelangelo Merisi da
  49, *31*
Caro, Anthony 138–40, 147, *136*
Carpaccio, Vittore 249
Carracci family 49
Carroll, Lewis 221
Celan, Paul 179
Celant, Germano 168–9

César 140
Cézanne, Paul 17, 24, 232
Chandra, Avinash 235
Chapman, Dinos 267–8, *274*
Chapman, Jake 267–8, *274*
Charlton, Alan 96, 176
Chef, Genia 283
Chia, Sandro 187, 188, *190*
Chicago Imagists 205
Chicago, Judy 195–8, 201, 209
Chilean avant-garde 221–2
China: classicism parodied 283–5;
  fusion of modern and culture
  based art 10–12, 231, 232–4;
  video art 238
Chirico, Giorgio de 14, 188, 276–7, 278, 280
Christo (Javacheff, Christo), 104, *96*
Church, Frederick Edwin 121
Cinalli, Ricardo 280, *284*
cinema, Neo-Realism 45
Civil Rights Movement 207
Clark, Larry 252–3
Clark, Lygia 221, *234*
classical themes and values 13–14,
  273–5, 277–285
Claude 171
Clemente, Francesco 187, 188, *191*
Close, Chuck 248, 250, *256*
Cobra Group 66–7
collage 38, 97, 108–9, 115, *104*
Company School painters 235
computer animation 239,
  see also digitized images
Conceptual art 14, 141, 147, 157–60,
  162, 167, 176, 182, 184, 191, 194,
  217–21, 226, 277
'Concrete art' 76, 217–20
Conner, Bruce 102, 201, *93*
Constructivism 89, 140, 142–4, 145,
  198, 224, 232
Cooper, Emmanuel 215
Corneille *see* Beverloo, Cornelis van
Cornell, Joseph 98, 205, *87*
Courbet, Gustave 8, 52
Cragg, Tony 171, *173*
Cranach, Lucas the Elder 248, 275, 276
Crumb, Robert 184
Cruz-Diez, Carlos 142–3, *138*
Cubism 17, 28, 43, 54, 84, 97
Cucchi, Enzo 187, 188, *193*
Cunningham, Chris 239–40, 276, *1*
Cunningham, Merce, dance company 102
Currin, John 275–6, 285, *281*

Dada 15, 16, 27, 65, 97, 106, 163
Dalí, Salvador 15, 17, 24, 250, *3*
dance 101
Dasburg, Andrew
Davie, Alan 67, *56*
Dávila, Juan 221, *237*
Deacon, Richard 171, *172*
De Forest, Roy 201, *206*
Delacroix, Eugène 41
Delaunay, Robert 116
de Meuron, and Herzog, Tate Modern 7
de Meyer, Adolph 200
Denny, Robyn 94–6, *83*
depressive art 177
Diaghilev Ballet 108
Diaghilev, Serge 281

Díaz, Gonzalo 221, *238*
Diebenkorn, Richard 201
digitized images 9, 13, 14, 249, 254–7, 263,
    see also computer animation
Dijkstra, Rineke 258
Dine, Jim 122, 123, 132, 163, *118*, *128*
Dittborn, Eugenio 221, *239*
Documenta (Kassel) 12, 227
Donaldson, Anthony 119, *116*
Douglas, Aaron 207
Dreamtime paintings 230, *246*
Dubuffet, Jean 36, 44, 67–71, 185–6, *61*
Duchamp, Marcel 16, 97, 141, 142, 168,
    192, 215, *86*
Duclos, Arturo 221, 222, *236*
Duncan, Robert 28
Durack, Elizabeth 230
Dureau, George 200, *205*
Dürer, Albrecht 248

Earth art 154, 156, *152*, *153*,
    see also Land art
East India Company (British)
    see Company School painters
EAT (Experiments in Art and Technology)
    236
Ecole de Paris 53, 70
Eggleston, William 252–3
electronic arts 9
Elsheimer, Adam 278
Emin, Tracey 13, 267
Emshwiller, Ed 239, *250*
entertainment arts 9
environmental art 9, 98, 108, 132, 172,
    208, 209, 221, 226, 232, 235, 238,
    247, 277, 283
ephemeral art 9, 237, 260
Ernst, Max 15, 44, *30*
Estève, Maurice 53, 54, *39*
Euston Road School 110
exhibitions, globalization of art and
    216–17
Existentialism 61, 71
Expressionism 28, 33–6, 41–2, 54, 67,
    145, 179, 188, 205, 228

Fabro, Luciano 169, *165*
Fautrier, Jean 53–4, 56, 60, 61–4, 66, *44*
Fauves 44, 54, 116
Federal Art Project (WPA) 16
Feltus, Alan 273, 276
Feminist art 160, 195–9, 208, 209–12,
    217, 235, *see also* women
Fernandez, Armand *see* Arman
Fetting, Rainer 182, *182*
Fibonacci (Leonardo of Pisa) 169
figurative art 176–9, 184, 201;
    Modernism and 50–2, 71; Pop art and
    110, 121–2, 125–6; in sculpture 138
Fildes, Luke 8
film 237–8, 240
Finlay, Ian Hamilton 277
Finley, Karen 215–16, 228
Flash Art 187
Flavin, Daniel 147, 152, *149*
Fluxus Group 162–3, 241
folk-painting 205, 232, 283
Fontana, Lucio 100, 106, 171, *98*
Forge, Andrew, interview with Anthony
    Caro 138

Formalism 123
Francis, Sam 36, *21*
Frank, Robert 252
Frankenthaler, Helen 36, 36–7, 84, *72*
Freud, Lucian 176–7, *176*
Freud, Sigmund 29
Frey, Viola 204, *212*
Fried, Michael 84–5, 88
Fried, Nancy 215, 227
Fritscher, Jack 200
Fulton, Hamish 156
Funk art 102, 201, 204

Gabo, Naum 142
Gabor, Dennis 250
Galerie Drouin 53, 56
Galleria l'Attico (Rome) 169
Gandolfi, Paola 278, 280
Gaudí, Antoni 185
Gauguin, Paul 234
gay art 195, 212–13,
    see also homosexual art; lesbian art
Gehry, Frank 7
Gentileschi, Artemisia 210
Géricault, Théodore 182
Germany, Weimar Republic 12
Gernsheim, Helmut and Alison 247
Getty Museum 247
Giacometti, Alberto 163, 164
Gilbert and George 134, 262, *132*
Gilhooly, David 204, *210*
Gilliam, Sam 207, 234, *215*
Ginsberg, Allen 28
globalization of art 216–35
Gloeden, Wilhelm von 282
Gober, Robert 194–5, *200*
Goldin, Nan 13, 253, 263
Goldsworthy, Andy 156–7, 171, *155*
Golub, Leon 185, *186*
Gonzáles, Julio 56, 137
Gordon, Douglas 240
Gorky, Arshile 16–21, 56, 137, *6*
Gottlieb, Adolph 29, *15*
Goya, Francisco de 41, 267
graffiti 213
Graffiti movement 179, 190–2
Green, Samuel Adams 127–9
Greenberg, Clement 81, 84
Greuze, Jean-Baptiste 9
Grien, Hans Baldung 275
Grippo, Víctor 217, *232*
Gris, Juan 24
grunge culture 13
Gu, Wenda 232,
Guggenheim Museum (Bilbao) 7
Guggenheim, Peggy 15–16, 21, 64
Gumilyov, Nicolai 281
Gursky, Andreas 249
Guryanov, Georgii 282–3
Guston, Philip 29, 184–5, *17*, *185*
Gutai Group 226
Guttuso, Renato 49, *36*

Ha, Chong Hyun 231–2, *247*
Hai Bo 258, 284, *268*
Halley, Peter *197*
Hamilton, Ann 174
Hamilton, Richard 108–9, *104*
Happenings 65, 98, 105–6, 130–4, 159,
    163, 237

'hard edge' abstraction 75–9, 119
Haring, Keith 179, 190–2, *194*
Harlem Renaissance 207
Harris, Ann Sutherland 210
Hartung, Hans 56, 66, *43*
Harvey, Marcus 262, 263
Hatoum, Mona 235, 238
Hausmann, Raoul 163
Havana Biennale 217
Hayden, Palmer 207
Hayward Gallery (London) 154
Held, Al 78–9, *65*
Hepworth, Barbara 163, *159*
Heron, Patrick 37, *22*
Herrera, Hayden 217
Herzog and de Meuron (architects) 7
Herzog, Jacques 7
Hesse, Eva 173, 174
Hill, Gary 241–3, 245–6, *252*
Hirst, Damien 239, 264–5, *273*
Hoberman, Nicky 263
Hockney, David 112, 114–15, 176, 235,
    109, *111*, *112*
Hoet, Jan 227
Hofmann, Hans 16, 24–5, *12*
Hogarth, William 9
Holl, Frank 8
Hollywood 199
Holocaust themes 267–8
holography 250–2
Holzer, Jenny 160, 167, *157*
Homer 191
homosexual art 199–200, 275
    see also gay art; lesbian art
Hopper, Edward 115, 121
Horn, Rebecca 174
Hotere, Ralph 234, *249*
Howe, Delmas 275, *280*
Hoyland, John 94, *85*
Hundertwasser, Fritz 67, *59*
Huxley, Paul 96

Ideal, the 14
Immendorf, Jörg 182, 229, *180*
Independent Group 108, 109
India, fusion of modern and culture
    based art 234–5
installation art 9, 14, 154–6, 165, 167,
    172, 174, 195–8, 208, 215–16, 217, 221,
    224, 232, 243, 259, 267, 269–72, 277
Institute of Contemporary Arts (London)
    107–8
intermedia 38
Internet, art and the 12, 216, 259, 275
Ionesco, Eugène 70
Irwin, Robert 154
Islamic countries, modern art in 235

Jacquet, Alain 107
Japan: fusion of modern and culture
    based art 10–12, 225–6; video art 237
Japanangka, Peter Blacksmith *246*
Jaray, Tess 96, *82*
Jarman, Derek 212–13, *224*
Javacheff, Christo *see* Christo
Jencks, Charles 273
Jodorowski, Alejandro 240
Johns, Jasper 85–8, 98, 101–2, 106, 110,
    122, *89*
Johnson, William Henry 207

Jones, Allen 112, 114, 115–16, *114*
Jorn, Asger 66–7, *55*
Judd, Donald 147–50, 168, 169, 208, *146*

Kabakov, Ilya 222–5, *240*
Kadish, Reuben 185
Kahlo, Frida 210, 217, *231*
Kahukiwa, Robyn 234
Kakhar, Bhupen 235
Kapoor, Anish 171–2, *170*
Keaton, Buster 240
Kelley, Mike 259–60, 262, *269*
Kelly, Ellsworth 79, *66*
Kelly, Mary 212, *223*
Kiefer, Anselm 179–82, 183, 188, *181*
Kienholz, Edward 102, 130, *92*
Kilimnik, Karen 260–1, 262, 272, *270*
Kimmelman, Michael 198
Kineticism 140–2, 152
Kitaj, R. B. 112, 118, *113*
'Kitchen Sink' painters 45–9, 110
Klee, Paul 56
Klein, Yves 100, 102, 104–6, 145, *97*, *100*
Kline, Franz 28, 29–31, 32, 36, 64, 75, *16*
Klüver, Billy 236, 241
Komar, Vitaly 281
Kooning, Willem de 28, 33–6, 66, 137, 176, *19*
Koons, Jeff 192–5, 260, *196*
Korea *see* South Korea
Kossoff, Leon 48, *33*
Kosuth, Joseph 157, 191, *158*
Kotz, Ilse 253
Kounellis, Jannis 169, *169*
Kozloff, Max 80
Kramer, Hilton 196
Krauss, Rosalind 9
Kruger, Barbara 160, 198, 210, *202*
Kuitca, Guillermo 220, *233*
Kulik, Oleg 261–2, *271*
Kusama, Yayoi 130–2, 271, *133*
Kuznetsov, Viktor 282–3, *287*

Lamsweerde, Inez van 263, 272
Land art 171, *see also* Earth art
Larionov, Mikhail 281
Latin America: conceptual art and installation 217–22; Constructivists 142–3; fusion of modern and culture based art 10–12
Law, Bob 96
Lawrence, Jacob 207, *218*
Le Corbusier (*pseudonym* of Charles-Edouard Jeanneret) 273
Lee, Sadie 215
Léger, Fernand 43, 49, *24*
Leonard, Michael 273, *279*
Leonardo da Vinci 191, 215, 248
lesbian art 213–15,
    see also gay art; homosexual art
Levinthal, David 268
LeWitt, Sol 147, 150, 173, *147*
Libera, Zbigniew 268
Lichtenstein, Roy 107, 122, 123–5, 130, 163, 195, *120*, *121*, *122*
Ligare, David 273, 276, *278*
'Light and Space' group 152–5, 204–5
Lissitzky, El 198
Lisson Gallery (London) 152
Livadiotti, Massimo 278

Locke, Hew 209, *219*
Lohse, Richard 75–6, *64*
Long, Richard 156–7, 171, *154*
Louis, Morris 31, 80, 81–9, 94, 97, 207, 73, *74*
Lucas, Sarah 267
Lynes, George Platt 200

McCracken, John 147, *143*
McQueen, Steve 240
Mach, David 171, *174*
Madí group 142–3, 217
Magritte, René 17, *4*
Malevich, Kasimir 143, 145
Ma Liuming 253–4, *264*
Manet, Edouard 126, *125*
Mannerist art 267, 275, 280
Man Ray 16
Manzoni, Piero 106, 145, 262, *99*
Maori art 234
Mapplethorpe, Robert 199–200, 247, *204*
Marden, Brice 96, 176
Mariani, Carlo Maria 14, 277, *282*
Marini, Marino 163
Marquez, Roberto 280, *285*
Martin, Agnes 145
Maslov, Oleg 282–3, *287*
masochism 159
Masson, André 15, 18, 28, *8*
Mataré, Edwin 163
Mathieu, Georges 64–5, 66, *52*
Matisse, Henri 16, 24–5, 43–4, 94, 115–16, *26*, *29*
Matta, Roberto 15, 18, 27, 28, *5*
'matter painters' 60
Melamid, Alexander 281
Mendieta, Ana 238
Meneguzzo, Marco 168, 172
Mengs, Anton Raphael 277
Merz, Mario 169, *167*
Meuron, Pierre de 7
Michaux, Henri 57, *46*
Middleditch, Edward 48–9, *34*
Mies van der Rohe, Ludwig 56, 273
Miki, Tomio 107, *103*
Millares, Manolo 61, *47*
Minimalism 7, 10, 12, 96, 98, 100, 145–57, 162, 167–8, 168–9, 171, 176, 183, 208, 271
Miró, Joan 17, 29, 44, 94, *31*
mixed media 38, 96
mobiles 142
Modernism 8, 10–12, 17, 53, 71, 93, 163, 273, 278; figurative painting and 50–2, 71, 110
Modersohn-Becker, Paula 210
Modigliani, Amedeo 234
Moholy-Nagy, László 56, 140
Molinier, Pierre 257
Mondo Cane (film) 105
Mondrian, Piet 89, 143
Monet, Claude 41
Monroe, Marilyn 36, 107, 129
Moon, Jeremy 96, *84*
Moog Audio Synthesizer 239
Moore, Henry 138, 163, 164, *160*
Mori, Mariko 269–71, 272, *276*
Morimura, Yasumasa 254, *265*
Morris, Robert 147, 150, *145*
Motherwell, Robert 25–8, 29, *11*

Muafangejo, John 228, *244*
Muehl, Otto 134
Mühely Academy (Budapest) 140
Mukhina, Vera 224
Munch, Edvard 66, 187
Murger, Henri 13
murals 185, 217, 280–1
Murger, Henri 13
Museum of Modern Art: New York 32, 92, 97–8, 271
Museum of Modern Art: San Francisco 195–6
museums: growth of 7, 9–10; popular entertainment and 240–1, 246
musicians 38, 100–1, 105

Nadeau, Maurice, on Surrealism 15
naturalism 115
Nauman, Bruce 165–8, *163*
Nebreda, David 257–8
Neo-Classicism 14, 273–85
Neo-Concretists 221
Neo-Dada 27, 98–106, 122, 163
Neo-Expressionism 29, 177–88, 190, 229
Neshat, Shirin 238
Newman, Barnett 27, 80–1, 88, 89, *69*
new media 8–10, 236–46, 249–58
New Realism 102–7
'A New Spirit in Painting' exhibition 176–9
New York: centre for art 12, 15–16, 32, 137, 190; East Village galleries 13, 190, 192
Nilsson, Gladys 205
Nitsch, Hermann 134
Nochlin, Linda 210
Nolan, Sidney 121, *117*
Noland, Kenneth 81, 85–9, 93, 94, 101, 71, *75*
Nolde, Emil 182
Novecento group 188
Novia Akademia (St Petersburg) 14, 282–3, 285
Novikov, Timor 281–2, *286*
La Nuova Maniera Italiana 14
Nutt, Jim 205

Ofili, Chris 262, 263
O'Hara, Frank 24, 130, 137
Ohlson, Elisabeth 248–9, 257, *260*
Oitica, Hélio 221
Oldenburg, Claes 122–3, 132, 163, *119*, *134*
Olitski, Jules 93, *78*
Op art 76, 93, 114, 140–4
Oppenheim, Dennis 157–9, *156*
Oppenheim, Meret 249
optical illusion effects 75, 76, 140
Orozco, José Clemente 185, 217
Orr, Eric 154, *151*
Osborne, John 49
Oursler, Tony 245–6, *255*
'outsider' art 205

Paik, Nam June 232, 241, *251*
painting, death of proclaimed 176
Paladino, Mimmo 187, 188, *192*
Paolini, Giulio 169, 277, *168*
Paolozzi, Eduardo 108, 140
papier découpé technique 44
Papunya Tula Artists' Collective 230

Paris: centre for art 12, 40, 53–6;
    Salons 8
Park, David 201
Parmigianino, Il 275
Paschke, Ed 205, 214
Pasmore, George see Gilbert and George
Penck, A. R. 179, 178
Penone, Giuseppe 169, 171, 172, 164
Pen Yu 271–2, 277
perestroika art 12, 222–5, 232, 281
Performance art 159, 174, 176, 208, 232,
    253–4
Perugino, Pietro 249
Phillips, Peter 110, 112–14, 107
photo-collages 115
photographic media 9, 13, 14, 107, 110,
    115, 156–7, 157–60, 193–4, 198–200,
    204, 247–58, 261, 269, 282, 282–3
photomontage 160
Picabia, Francis 14, 16, 183, 278
Picasso, Pablo 16, 17, 24, 28, 40–2, 64,
    115, 137, 179, 23
Piero della Francesca 52, 249
Pignon, Edouard 53, 54, 38
Piper, Adrian 208
Piper, Keith 209, 221
Pissarro, Camille 8
Pistoletto, Michelangelo 107, 101
Pittura Colta 14
poetry and poets 28, 32, 179, 201, 264
Poirier, Anne and Patrick 277
'political correctness' 193
'Political Pop' 232–4
politics, and art 8, 10, 15, 185, 196, 205,
    209, 237
Polke, Sigmar 183–4, 184
Pollock, Jackson 21–4, 28, 29, 33, 36, 38,
    57, 65, 75, 80, 84, 88, 137, 195, 9, 10
Pontormo, Jacopo 280
Poons, Larry 93, 77
Pop art 29, 36, 93, 94, 97, 98, 101, 106–32,
    140, 163, 167–8, 171, 172, 176, 183,
    204–5, 232, 259
pornography 193–4
Possibilities (magazine) 27
'postal art' 221
Post-Modernism 10–12, 14, 182, 226,
    273, 278
Post-painterly abstraction 75–96, 97
post-perestroika art 261–2
Post-Pop 269–72, 285
Poussin, Nicolas 43, 49, 74, 284
Pre-Raphaelites 110
Proesch, Gilbert see Gilbert and George
Prud'hon, Pierre-Paul 107
psychedelic images 205
Puccini, Giacomo 13
Punk Rock, art and 13, 263–4
Puryear, Martin 207–8, 234, 216

Rauschenberg, Robert 98–102, 106,
    122, 145, 163, 236, 241, 281, 90, 91
Raysse, Martial 107, 102
Realism 44–9, 110
Reinhardt, Ad 78–80, 100, 145, 70
Restany, Pierre 102, 107
Richter, Gerhard 182–3, 184, 183
Riley, Bridget 141–2, 139
Ringgold, Faith 208, 222
Riopelle, Jean-Paul 56–7, 71, 50

Rivera, Diego 21, 217
Rivers, Larry 126, 125
Rodchenko, Aleksandr 140, 142
Rodin, Auguste 16
Romanesque painting 188
Romanticism 13, 108, 262
Rome 14
Rose, Barbara 16, 80
Rosenberg, Harold 17–18, 24, 28, 121
Rosenblum, Robert 193
Rosenquist, James 122, 123, 125–6, 123
Rosen, Roee 268, 275
Rosler, Martha 253
Rossellini, Roberto 45
Rothenberg, Susan 186, 189
Rothko, Mark 27, 28–9, 31, 75, 14
Rousseau, Henri (Le Douanier) 16, 235
Royal Academy of Arts (London) 8, 176
Royal College of Art, London 110, 112, 119
Ruscha, Ed 204
Rustin, Jean 177, 177
Ryman, Robert 145, 176

Saar, Alison 208
Saar, Betye 208, 220
Saatchi, Charles 264
sado-masochism 134
St Petersburg 14
Samba, Chéri 229, 245
Sander, August 258
sand painting, Native American 21
São Paulo Biennales 12, 217
Sartre, Jean-Paul 70, 71
Saul, Peter 205, 213
Schinkel, Karl Friedrich 179
Schmidt, Edward 273
Schnabel, Julian 185–6, 187
School of Baroda 235
Schulze, Alfred Otto Wolfgang see Wols
Schwarzkogler, Rudolf 134, 159, 131
Schwitters, Kurt 101, 172
sculpture: abstract 137–40, 163–5; African-
    American 207–8; African tribal 230;
    Arte Povera 171–4, 176; environment
    277; figurative references 138; kinetic
    art (mobiles) 142; Pop art and 127, 140
Segal, George 127
Seitz, William C. 97–8
Sekula, Allan 253
Self, Colin 102
Serra, Richard 145, 141
Serrano, Andres 257, 266
sexual representations and allusions
    8, 174, 177, 193, 199, 200, 221, 237
shamanistic rituals 164
Sher-Gil, Amrita 234
Sherman, Cindy 198–9, 203
Shonibare, Yinka 248, 257, 259
Shterenberg Brothers 198
Siqueiros, David Alfaro 185, 217
Sironi, Mario 188
Smith, David 137–40, 145, 147, 135
Smith, Jack 48–9
Smith, Richard 110, 114, 106, 110
Smith, Tony 145–7, 150, 142
Smithson, Alison 108
Smithson, Peter 108
Smithson, Robert 156, 173, 153
Snyder, Gary 32
Socialist Realism 8, 222–4, 232, 283, 284

Soto, Jesús Rafael 142–4, 140
SOTS Art 281
Soulages, Pierre 64, 66, 51
South Korea, fusion of modern and
    culture based art 231–2
Souza, Francis Newton 234–5
Speer, Albert 179
Staël, Nicolas de 71–4, 93, 94, 60
Staller, Ilona 193
Stasio, Stephano di 278
Stedelijk Museum (Amsterdam) 155
Steinbach, Haim 194, 198
Stella, Frank 89–93, 168–9, 76, 79
Stieglitz, Alfred 16
Still, Clyfford 36, 88, 20
Stirling, James 7
Strand, Paul 257
Strausova, Julia 283
Structuralism 89, 210
Stuck, Franz von 280
Studio Azzurro 243–6, 247, 254
Stuttgart, New State Gallery 7
Sui Jianguo 284–5
Sun Yuan 271–2, 277
Super Realism 194
Suprematism 145
Surrealism 15–17, 21, 23, 27, 44–5,
    56, 65, 97, 172, 174, 205
Sutherland, Graham 44–5, 27
Sylvester, David, interview with
    Francis Bacon 50
Symbolism 14, 280
Szarkowski, John 252

Taaffe, Philip 194, 199
Tanguy, Yves 17, 24, 7
Tapié, Michel 54–6
Tàpies, Antoni 60–1, 49
Tate Modern 7, 2
technologies, new, art and 8–9, 13,
    236–46
television, reportage on art 12
Thek, Paul 102, 95
Tobey, Mark 31–3, 78, 18
Tobreluts, Olga 249, 283, 258
Top Value Television (TTV) 237
Trans-Avantgarde 187–8, 276
Tunga (Antonio José de Mello Mourão)
    221, 235
Turner Prize 267
Turrell, James 154–6, 205, 152
Twombly, Cy 176
Tworkov, Jack 80, 68

Uccello, Paolo 244
underground magazines 184

Vasarely, Victor 140–1, 143, 137
Velázquez, Diego 41, 52, 37
Venice Biennales 12, 155, 160, 174,
    217, 226
Versace 282
video art 9, 12, 167, 174, 176, 235,
    236–46, 261, 269–71, 276
Vienna Group 134
Villata, Guillermo Perez 280
Viola, Bill 243, 245–6, 247, 253

Wagstaff, Sam 200, 247
Walker, John 96, 81

Wall, Jeff 249
Wang Xingwei 284, *288*
Warhol, Andy 31, 36, 106, 107, 122,
  127–30, 163, 167–8, 176, 195, 260,
  127, *129*, *195*
Weiner, Lawrence 160
Wenda Gu 232
Wentworth, Richard 171, *171*
Wesselmann, Tom 126, *124*, *126*
Westermann, H. C. 205
Whitechapel Art Gallery (London) 108
Whiteread, Rachel 264–5
Wiley, William T. 201, *207*

Wilford, Michael 7
Willard Gallery (New York) 137
Winckelmann, Johann Joachim 277
Winters, Terry 186, *188*
Witkin, Joel-Peter 257, 267
Wizén, Per 249, 257
Wojnarowicz, David 212–13, *225*
Wols (Alfred Otto Wolfgang Schulze)
  56, 61–4, 66, *45*
women: African-American 208;
  Arte Povera and 173–4,
  see also Feminist art
woodcarvings 194, 234

Woodrow, Bill 171, *175*
WPA *see* Federal Art Project
Wright, Frank Lloyd 145

Yanagi, Yukinori 226, *243*
YBAs *see* Young British Artists
Yoakum, Dwight 205
Yoshihara, Jiro 226, *242*
Young British Artists (YBAs) 13, 265–8
Young Contemporaries exhibition 110–14
Youngerman, Jack 79, 67
Yu Youhan 232, *248*